DIHUM

Quality of Life and Disability

of related interest

Inclusive Research with People with Learning Disabilities
Past, Present and Futures
Jan Walmsley and Kelley Johnson
ISBN 1 84310 061 4

Working with People with Learning Disabilities
Theory and Practice
David Thomas and Honor Woods
ISBN 1 85302 973 4

Women with Intellectual Disabilities
Finding a Place in the World
Edited by Rannveig Traustadottir and Kelley Johnson
ISBN 1 85302 846 0

Sexuality and Women with Learning Disabilities
Michelle McCarthy
ISBN 1 85302 730 8

Advocacy and Learning Disability
Edited by Barry Gray and Robin Jackson
ISBN 1 85302 942 4

Helping People with a Learning Disability Explore Choice
Eve and Neil Jackson, illustrated by Tim Baker
ISBN 1 85302 694 8

Helping People with a Learning Disability Explore Relationships
Eve and Neil Jackson, illustrated by Tim Baker
ISBN 1 85302 688 3

User Involvement and Participation in Social Care
Research Informing Practice
Edited by Hazel Kemshall and Rosemary Littlechild
ISBN 1 85302 777 4

Quality of Life and Disability

An Approach for Community Practitioners

Ivan Brown and Roy I. Brown

Foreword by Ann and Rud Turnbull

Jessica Kingsley Publishers
London and New York

First published in the United Kingdom in 2003
by Jessica Kingsley Publishers Ltd
116 Pentonville Road
London N1 9JB, England
and
29 West 35th Street, 10th fl.
New York, NY 10001-2299, USA

www.jkp.com

Copyright © Ivan Brown and Roy I. Brown 2003

Library of Congress Cataloging in Publication Data
A CIP catalog record for this book is available from the Library of Congress

British Library Cataloguing in Publication Data
A CIP catalogue record for this book is available from the British Library

ISBN 1 84310 005 3

Printed and Bound in Great Britain by
Athenaeum Press, Gateshead, Tyne and Wear

*To our parents, from whom we first learned
about personal and family quality of life*

Contents

List of Figures

List of Tables

Foreword

After reading and reflecting on *Quality of Life and Disability* by Ivan Brown and Roy Brown, we especially appreciate its incorporation of universal design. What is 'universal design'? Originating as a concept in architecture, universal design was first used as an approach to ensure that buildings were accessible to all people, especially those who experienced mobility impairments. This involved a major effort to reconceptualize how buildings could be constructed from the outset to meet the needs of all users so that they would not need to be retrofitted later. Although universal design for buildings started before 1990, it is only in the last couple of years that the concept of universal design for learning has been applied to books and other curricular material. Drawing from its successful application to architecture, universal design for learning is a process which 1. considers the needs of a broad array of learners from the beginning of the planning stage and 2. designs curriculum and instruction with sufficient flexibility so that each student can benefit.

Ivan Brown and Roy Brown are the masters in applying universal design to the theory, research and best practice related to quality of life for individuals with disabilities and their families. Similar to so many other topics that too often remain esoteric, theory and research on quality of life has been written in a way that academicians find stimulating but practitioners and families find obtuse and even irrelevant because of how it is 'packaged'. By this we do not mean that quality of life itself is irrelevant, but that the way that it is presented restricts its applicability to people who do not enjoy reading dense conceptual material. Ivan and Roy break free of these constraints and provide us all with an incredibly helpful resource in the 'least restrictive environment' of everyday language. They take complicated and complex concepts and present them with such straightforward elegance that readers are eager for more rather than turned off and overwhelmed. Ivan and Roy provide comprehensive coverage of a broad range of quality of life topics:

- past, present and future perspectives
- identification of needs and the provision of supports/services
- individual and family perspectives
- policy and management.

Throughout all of these topics, they interweave real-life stories, reflective questions, and resources (readings and websites). Their presentation of content represents the clear paradigm shift in the field from a deficit-oriented, medical model to a preference-oriented, quality of life model. They not only suggest *what* practitioners, families and advocates might do to enhance quality of life but they also address the nuts and bolts of *how* to accomplish their suggestions.

We encourage you to read this book not only to enhance the quality of life of individuals with disabilities to whom you are committed but also to enhance your own quality of life and those of all people you hold dear. The principles of this book apply across the board to people with and without disabilities alike, but because people with disabilities and their families are often at greater risk of experiencing challenges related to quality of life, this book is especially for them.

Ann and Rud Turnbull
Beach Center on Disability, The University of Kansas

Preface

We are very pleased to bring to you this book on quality of life. Throughout the planning and writing process, we have tried to keep in mind that, above all, we wanted to produce a book that would bring quality of life ideas closest to those who are in the best position to apply them – the practitioners. We envision it to be useful in the field of disability in its broadest sense. We also intend it to be of interest and use to people who are not practitioners, and to people in fields other than disability. We wanted it to be particularly useful to field practitioners, including care staff who work in the community, private homes of people with disabilities, group homes, vocational settings, schools, hospitals, nursing homes, and many others. We also wanted it to be useful to professionals whose work supports people with and without disabilities, such as occupational therapists, social workers, counsellors, teachers, psychologists, people in the legal field, family physicians and nurses, hospital workers, and psychiatrists.

In addition, we had in mind that there are many practitioners in the field of disability who do not have formal training, and we wanted this book to help provide some knowledge that might be useful to them in their work. There are also a great many people who do very valuable volunteer work with people who have disabilities, and we hope the information in this book will help them to carry out their work more easily. We have not particularly addressed the book towards researchers, but the material arises from our broad knowledge of quality of life research and our contribution to it over the last two decades. Thus, we expect that there is considerable indirect application to research between these covers. In presenting the book, we hope we have achieved what we set out to do. Essentially, what we had in mind was a book written in a sufficiently straightforward way that, upon finishing the book, readers would say, 'So *that* is what quality of life is all about!'

To help achieve this, we have written the book in fairly plain language, and we hope this makes it accessible to readers, especially to those who are reading about quality of life for the first time. In keeping with this style, we have purposely used only a few references in the text, although we have included a selected bibliography for most chapters. Our aim, in providing this bibliography, is to alert practitioners to major material in the area, rather than to justify material based on published research. Consulting the material we have provided in the bibliography should enable readers to follow up on any key issues in which they are particularly interested.

Readers will note that we have used some terms interchangeably. We very often use the word *practitioner*, for example, but sometimes we use *professional* or a more specific term related to a specific job, such as *teacher* or *nurse*. Work with people who have disabilities is called different things, and we have tried to capture some of this diversity by using rehabilitation, disability services, special education and other terms to represent the broad range of 'fields' that support people with disabilities. This was done on purpose to try to be inclusive. Another reason is that this book is meant to be for an international audience, and terms are used somewhat differently in different countries. Thus, a variety of terms may be helpful to a broad spectrum of readers.

How did the book emerge?

This book developed out of a concern over the life experiences of people with disabilities. Both of us have carried out a considerable amount of work in the area of quality of life with people who have a wide range of disabilities and lifestyles. We, like many, have written about the theory, models and research into this area. We have also worked at the face-to-face level with people with disabilities.

While making such contributions, though, we have become aware that much of the work on quality of life is spoken about, but not practised – or at least not practised in a way that we believe is essential if life experience for those with disabilities is to be greatly improved. Words abound about quality services and quality experiences, but, at a day-to-day level, many individuals appear to be frustrated, sometimes neglected, and frequently at the mercy of rules and regulations that thwart their ability to practise and experience a life of quality.

In this book, we have suggested ways of answering some of these concerns. We believe that many of the answers are generic – that is, they apply across disabilities and are intrinsic to the life experiences of the individuals concerned. We anticipate that as people read to the end of this book they will comment, as many have done to us after we have given presentations, 'Really you are talking about everyone.' And that is indeed the fact of the matter.

But perhaps this is also the reason why many quality of life issues do not get addressed. Quality of life is made up of extraordinary events at times but, more frequently, the ordinary and everyday events are critical. It is these that tend to be pushed to one side when rehabilitation is required, due to the more urgent needs that are typically met by medical, health, social work, educational and social services practitioners. Traditionally, the condition is still treated, and rehabilitation structures tend to be addressed separately from what are seen as the ordinary needs of the person. The individual may get services such as rehabilitation, special education, or formal counselling, and these structures are important. Too often, though, such interventions override many of the issues that contribute to the individual's quality of life. Further, they tend not to take place in the home and community environment where so much of life's quality occurs. These everyday needs, wishes and requirements need to be blended into the overall rehabilitation picture. Formal rehabilitation needs to bend to these requirements and, at best, include them in a seamless structure. We seek a way of integrating the whole. We have attempted to do so by giving examples and posing questions to make the reader think, consider and question. It is our hope that the book will be of assistance to those working and living in the disability field, but we know it is only effective when these ideas are integrated into practice.

Use of real-life stories

One of the challenges in writing a text is to help the reader consider new values and attitudes. We recognize that this is difficult. For this reason, we have introduced real-life examples and questions for thought and discussion. We ask that all readers, but students in particular, consider them seriously. When doing so, we ask readers to give detailed thought to their existing value systems and attitudes, and to consider how they might make desirable changes to develop more effective professional practice.

We have not answered all the questions we have posed. Some are under active consideration at various levels of policy and professional practice, as well as at the public level. This is the case, for example, with sterilization and rights. What is seen as effective and acceptable practice today may be illegal or seem undesirable tomorrow, and vice versa. We have attempted to raise issues that we see as important, ones where quality of life principles may be useful in resolving dilemmas and conflicts.

Throughout the book, we have made use of real-life stories and presented them as vignettes. Some of these seem extraordinary to us, since some of the experiences are ones we hoped might never have arisen. Others we hope represent the everyday application of supportive, caring, quality of life principles. We have collected our vignettes from our own practical experiences and have recorded with permission others from our students and colleagues. Where possible, we have acknowledged these people, but, as always occurs, some may have been overlooked, and we thank them also for their interest and commentary.

It is our hope that the vignettes function to bring specific points to life. We realize, in writing them the way we have, that they are only part descriptions of people's whole lives, and that there are many other aspects to the real people's lives we describe.

Other valuable sources

In finalizing the content of the book, we have attempted to get input from a variety of colleagues from both academic and applied fields. Several people have reviewed our materials, and we thank each one for the time spent and the helpful comments that we have received. There are a few we wish to acknowledge and thank more specifically: Mary Brown, for her detailed editing comments, questions and suggestions; Roy Ferguson, School of Child and Youth, University of Victoria, for his comments on the chapters on intervention, and ethics and professional practice; Ann and Rud Turnbull, for their help in preparing the chapter on family quality of life and for their encouraging words and enthusiasm in agreeing to write the foreword. We are grateful to Barbara Matthews and Richard Gates for their sensitive account of rehabilitation and grief, and, in addition, to Barbara for her helpful comments as a practitioner on intervention.

We also recognize the contribution of numerous people from the 'quality of life family' that spans many countries. We have had an opportunity to meet and work with many of these people, especially within the field of intellectual disabilities where a great deal of valuable work has been carried out – work that is applicable to all populations. Quality of life has been a dynamic area of thought and study for about the past 15 years, and those who have developed quality of life ideas have demonstrated a remarkable spirit of cooperation and collegiality. This sense of working together has resulted in a certain degree of blending of ideas. Thus, although we take responsibility for the words written in this book, many of the central ideas emerge from a broader body of work in quality of life – one in which we have both played an active role along with many others.

We would like to thank our publisher Jessica Kingsley and, in particular, Amy Lankester-Owen for her encouragement and support, as well as Leonie Sloman. The guidance and support we have received has been helpful to us in shaping the content of this book.

Ivan's personal notes. Besides the many people from several countries who have helped shape my ideas in quality of life, I wish to thank a variety of colleagues at the University of Toronto for many helpful discussions on quality of life over the past several years. In particular, I am indebted to Rebecca Renwick and Dennis Raphael, with whom I developed quality of life work throughout the 1990s at the Centre for Health Promotion, Department of Public Health Sciences. We would not have been able to accomplish this without the support of many service organizations, the Ontario government, and the dedicated work of dozens of people, both paid and volunteer. Ted Myerscough, who has been with us since nearly the beginning, has been particularly valuable to our work. I also thank the Centre for Health Promotion and the Faculty of Social Work for providing a supportive milieu in which to complete this book. Numerous people from a number of countries and family members and friends here in Canada were generous enough to share specific examples of quality of life from their own lives. I have incorporated some of these into the text, including all of the examples used in Chapter 4. Such participation gives the material a 'real-life' feel, precisely because the examples used are from their real lives. Finally, I thank members of my household for creating a quiet environment every Sunday for months on end while I completed my part of the writing.

Roy's personal notes. I wish to thank Lynn Miller and Jo Shearer for suggestions to the intervention chapter and examples from our joint work on evaluating 'Options' for people with disabilities in South Australia. In this context, I recognize the interest and comments of Dr David Caudrey, Director of Disability Services of the Government of South Australia. I wish to recognize the numerous students, many of whom were practising professionals across Canada and Australia, plus students and professionals in Singapore and Japan, who, in discussion and presentation, have provided examples and concerns relating to the development and practice of the quality of life approach. I am grateful to students attending my courses at the University of Calgary, Flinders University of South Australia and the University of Prince Edward Island. I am indebted to Dr Vianne Timmons for one particular example of assessment from her doctoral thesis. I am also grateful for the field examples of practice and disability that occurred through practice at the Vocational and Rehabilitation Research Institute during my time as Director. A special note of thanks goes to Christine MacFarlane, who as research assistant to our original Rehabilitation Programmes Study drew my attention early on to the relevance of quality of life articles relating to the general population and their possible application to the disabilities field. I also acknowledge the many discussions I have had with Trevor Parmentor, who as a friend and colleage has stimulated my thinking.

This book emerges from the expressions of interest and excitement about quality of life from so many practitioners over the past several years who have spoken to us about their wish to implement quality of life ideas into their work. It is our wish that this book will help them do that for the benefit of those they support and serve. The final responsibility is ours – the content, views and errors must stand at our door. Our major hope is for the content to be considered and to cause discussion that will, in turn, create better knowledge, policies and field practice.

I.B. & R.I.B.
October, 2002

CHAPTER 1

Introducing Quality of Life

Getting started: An orientation

What is this book about?

This book is about the conceptualization of quality of life and how to use it in practical ways. It does this through examples, models and principles that have been developed over the past 15 years or so. It is about how to understand what quality of life means to people in general, what it means to each individual person, and how individuals can be helped to improve their quality of life. It focuses particularly on people with disabilities, since we want to highlight disability, but the reader will soon see that the concepts contained within quality of life and the strategies for improving quality of life apply to all people. Thus, this book is especially about quality of life for people with disabilities and their families, but, significantly, it is also about quality of life for everyone.

Who is this book for?

This book is for practitioners and student practitioners – in a variety of fields – who are charged with helping others to improve their quality of life. Who do we have in mind? The list is quite long, but definitely includes people in the areas of social services, health and education. It includes frontline workers of all types, occupational therapists, nurses, rehabilitation practitioners, and counsellors. It is relevant to social workers, health and social policy makers, teachers and educational authorities. Quality of life should be taken into account by medical practitioners who work in such areas as paediatrics, family medicine and mental health. It is also relevant to the work of psychologists. In addition, people whose work sometimes touches the lives of people with disabilities – such as those who work in the legal system, government, urban planning, public services, and both public and private business – could usefully apply the principles described in this book. Quality of life is especially important, though, for practitioners who work in communities, those who frequently advise individual persons with disabilities and their families, and those who provide intervention, support and care in a variety of settings that relate to individual and family well-being.

This is not just a book for professionals, however. Many people with disabilities who do not have an academic background may find descriptions within these covers that will enable them to take greater action for improving their own lives. Family members, and friends too, will be able to understand and apply the quality of life ideas to help improve life for their family member or friend with a disability, for themselves and for their families. This book is about using a quality of life approach in everyday living and in day-to-day professional work. For this reason, it is intentionally written in language that is commonly used in everyday life.

Quality of life until now

Quality of life is a term that has been used for several decades, but it has come into its own in the last 15 years. A great deal has been written about it, and a considerable amount of research has been carried out concerning aspects of people's lives and their environments that are associated with quality of life. Two books that cover a wide range of issues related to quality of life are by Renwick, Brown and Nagler (1996) and Romney, Brown and Fry (1994).

Quality of life has been studied and written about in a variety of fields, such as sociology, psychology and medicine. For people with disabilities, more specific work has been carried out in rehabilitation, nursing and medical care, health promotion and, to a lesser degree, education. Much of what we know today about quality of life for individuals with disabilities, however, has been developed within the field of intellectual disability. This work has yielded very rich information that is highly applicable to people with other disabilities, and indeed to all people with or without disabilities. In fact, we believe that the work in quality of life – no matter where it came from – is relevant to all people right across the disability field and in the wider society. Further, we argue that the use of quality of life reduces the need to label because it is concerned with the particular things individuals do as they live their own lives in their homes and communities. Thus, quality of life is relevant to everyone, everywhere.

Where do we find this information? Quality of life is the topic of numerous books that have been specifically written to help us understand this term better, and a large and growing number of articles are scattered throughout journals in a variety of academic areas. When this literature is looked at as a whole, it can seem confusing. Certainly, it clearly demonstrates the twists and turns that are characteristic of a new and evolving idea. There has been considerable effort recently, however, to bring together the fundamental principles and ideas that have been agreed upon within the quality of life literature, a process that has been given impetus by some helpful critical appraisals. There are also a growing number of websites that provide information about a wide variety of quality of life projects, and these can be very helpful to practitioners who are looking for how others attempt to help improve quality of life. A search of 'quality of life' and 'quality of life and disability' on the Internet brings up a vast array of relevant materials.

Still, many of the concepts and strategies contained within quality of life work are not as simple and easy to understand as practitioners might like. For this reason, it is our aim in this book to explain them in such a way that practitioners can understand them readily, and be in a better position to make sense of the quality of life literature that is available. Having said this, it must be recognized that some researchers and practitioners in the field of disabilities have raised concerns about the concept (for examples of concerns expressed, see Hatton 1998; Taylor 1994; Wolfensberger 1994).

Understanding what we mean by quality of life

Quality of life is a term that is recognized and used today in a variety of ways. When we talk about positive quality of life, we are talking about having a life that is very meaningful to individuals and that provides them with resources. Many people, when first thinking about it quickly, assume this means living in a certain house, driving a car that suits their image, and travelling to exotic corners of the world. But, on second thought, they realize it means much more than this. It can mean having an interesting and enjoyable job to go to, feeling safe, confident and happy with yourself, feeling close to those people who share your life, having fun, and living life according to the beliefs and values that are important. It also means having the freedom to choose to do the things you wish, and having a richness of opportunities to choose from. These are things that are important to almost all people everywhere in the world. For this reason, they provide an effective way of describing the quality of life of groups of people in general. Thus, it is possible to think of quality of life in general terms for all people by focusing on those aspects of human life that almost all people share.

When you think of your own life, though, you will quickly realize that it is different from that of other people and that there are many things you do not share with others. The things that are the most meaningful to you and that add the most richness to your life are often a little different from the things that are meaningful and add richness to the life of your best friend. For many people in the world, having food and water, basic shelter or family support may be the most important things. For others, spiritual needs may be especially important. For you, it may be something different again. To make this more complicated still, what is important to each individual changes over time. This complexity among individuals, though troublesome for some scientists and practitioners, is one of the fascinating things about quality of life: the unique features that make us interesting as individuals result in quality of life taking different forms. Indeed, it would be a very dull world if people were all the same, or if quality of life meant precisely the same thing to each one of us. Moreover, such uniqueness also provides each of us with a means to develop a positive and unique self-image. When we recognize and value our uniqueness, we become empowered to develop the self-image that is most suited to our own characteristics, environment and values. This is essential to positive, individual quality of life.

This is a particularly important point for practitioners to understand, for when they work to help other people improve their lives, it can never be assumed that what is important to the practitioner has the same importance for other people. People have their own ideas about what is most meaningful for them, what fits their self-images best, and what adds richness to their lives. Assisting people to exercise choices that reflect these ideas empowers them to improve their own lives and to develop positive self-images that reflect their own needs, wishes and values.

To help make the point more clearly it may be worth trying this short exercise. You will probably find it interesting, and perhaps a little surprising!

Meaningful and rich aspects of my life

Take a few minutes to think of five things that are particularly meaningful to you and add richness to your life. Ask a family member or friend to do the same thing, thinking of things in relation to his or her life. Then share your lists.

1.

2.

3.

4.

5.

Understanding three types of quality of life

Now that you have an idea of what we mean by quality of life, let us go back briefly to look at how other people have used the term, because it is important to understand that it has been used by different people to describe different things. Some different 'types' of quality of life have been developed and used, not one of which is either right or wrong. Nor is one necessarily better than the others. Rather, each type has its own purposes and its own perspective on people's lives. We will briefly describe three of the most commonly used types: quality of life of large populations; health-related quality of life; and quality of life in improving individuals' whole lives. It is the third type that we will focus on for the remainder of the book, since we consider it to be very relevant, on a day-to-day basis, to the quality of life of people with disabilities.

Quality of life of large populations

The quality of life of large populations is described by attributes that are considered to be important to almost everyone and to society as a whole. These attributes are often called social indicators. Some commonly used social indicators are national security, housing, access to health care and social services, social equity, and levels of income, employment and education. This type of quality of life is very useful for describing and comparing two or more large populations on broad aspects that are thought to be important or valued by most people in various countries. It is also useful for describing a group of people over time, such as comparing a city's population today with its population 20 years ago. The information on which it is based is usually considered to be reliable, and it is almost always available from public sources.

Some have argued that subjective measures of social indicators, such as how happy or satisfied people feel about their lives and their environments, should be considered separately from objective measures. The rationale for this is that the value of objective measures is not always reflected in subjective measures, since human beings tend to 'make the best of things' in many situations where they find themselves. In addition, getting what we want does not necessarily result in increased happiness or satisfaction. On the contrary, it can sometimes lead to increased dissatisfaction as people begin to realize what else might be possible.

An example of quality of life of large populations seen in the popular media is the quality of life of countries. Sometimes this is simply described in newspapers as 'the best country to live in' or the 'best aspects of life' in the country in which you live. Examples of social indicators are shown in Table 1.1, where unemployment rates and number of years of formal education are contrasted for ten countries. The assumption is that life is better in countries that have lower unemployment rates and in countries that have higher levels of education.

This is the way quality of life is very often reported to the public, but its limitations need to be clearly understood. First, this type of data may not be comparable across countries. For example, ten years of formal education in Mexico may not correspond to ten years of formal education in Germany, nor may it be equally valued in the two countries. Second, these data do not take into account any number of possible related factors. For example, the relatively similar unemployment rates for Korea and Sweden may be misleading

Table 1.1 Unemployment rates and years of education as social indicators

	Unemployment [1] *% seeking employment*	*Education* [1] *Number of years of formal schooling*
Australia	6.6	16.6
Belgium	7.0	15.8
Canada	7.2	14.8
Colombia	14.7	10.0
Germany	7.9	15.3
Korea, Republic of	4.1	14.6
Mexico	1.7	11.5
Sweden	4.7	16.5
United Kingdom	5.5	16.4
United States of America	4.8	15.2

1. Figures are for single years, varying among countries from 1995–2001.

Adapted with permission from United Nations Statistics Division
http://unstates.un.org/demographic/social/unempl.htm and
http://unstats.un.org/demographic/social/education.htm (2003)

because of the many cultural and lifestyle differences between the two countries. Third, quality of life from a social indicators perspective does not
attempt to look at what individuals do, nor does it usually take into account
what individuals like and dislike or how happy they are. Thus, although the
indicators selected are assumed to be of value to the large groups of people
described and thus to measure their quality of life, they are not necessarily the
indicators that are most meaningful to individuals who live within those large
groups or add the greatest richness to their personal lives.

Moreover, quality of life as a social indicator in an industrial country may
have different parameters for people in less well-developed countries. Where

there is greater poverty, nutrition becomes not just an issue of quality or choice, but falls into the area of necessity. Thus, to a degree, quality of life relates to a hierarchy of primary and secondary needs and drives, as in Maslow's well-known model. It may be helpful to bear this in mind as we move to a discussion of the nuances of quality of life.

Health-related quality of life

A great deal of valuable work done in recent years stresses the importance of considering the quality of life of individuals in health and medical treatment. This is a welcome trend, for it shifts medical practice away from viewing the treatment and eradication of disease as its sole focus, and towards including it with intervention and treatment that takes into account what individual patients want, what results in the least discomfort for them, what is best for their lifestyles, and what impact treatments have on their environments and future lives. Health-related quality of life has focused on the overall approach to health and medical treatment, and also on specific diseases and conditions (e.g. arthritis, HIV infection, diabetes) and treatments (e.g. chemotherapy, mammograms, cardiovascular surgery).

Health-related quality of life has also highlighted important issues associated with managing pain, and the sometimes opposing choices of lessening pain and shortening lifespan. Pain management is an example of how critical it is to consider ethical issues. A society may reject euthanasia as an option for dealing with terminal pain, but, if so, we then have to look at the issues confronting the individual who experiences pain. Sometimes society does not have sufficient medical resources to benefit an individual's quality of life in this context. The situation becomes ethically complex, intertwining social, medical, spiritual and personal issues.

The box on pages 26 – 27 shows an adaptation of a general health-related quality of life measure, the HRQOL-14 from the United States Centres for Disease Control and Prevention, Health Care and Aging Studies Branch. This measure contains four items and ten supplementary items. Such scales are generally considered to be practical because they address some of the general health issues that are common to most patients and because they can be used quickly and efficiently even in busy medical settings. You will notice that the HRQOL-14 is designed to address only aspects of life directly related to health, and omits other aspects of a person's life. This is typical of health-related quality of life measures, as their purpose is not to describe the quality of life of the whole person, but rather to describe some of the impacts of a disease, a condition or a treatment on the person concerned. Numerous other measures, many related to more specific diseases and conditions, are available (for one list, see the Quality of Life Instrument Database of the MAPI Research Institute, http://195.101.204.50:8081).

Quality of life in improving individuals' whole lives

A third type of quality of life is the one that is the focus of this book, because we believe it is most relevant to each person with a disability (i.e. it is specific to individuals rather than general to groups of people, and it relates to their whole lives). Here, quality of life is a term that is used to describe an individual's whole life. It looks at all aspects of life together, on the assumption that all are interconnected and also affected by and connected to all parts of the environment in which the person lives. It also looks at the processes – such as exercising individual choice – that act as the means of achieving quality in life.

This is the most personal and comprehensive type of quality of life. For this reason, it is the most complex to understand and explain, but it also has strong potential for being meaningful at the personal level and for being highly relevant and applicable to individual people's lives.

Improving your whole life: The basics

Quality of life is about having a life that is rich and meaningful to each individual. In fact, the main reason for focusing on, and using, a quality of life approach is to encourage improvement in people's lives so that they become enriched and more meaningful. In this section, we will describe the basics of quality of life that you will need to understand. A life is a complex process, and, because quality of life deals with all aspects of a person's life, it too is necessarily complex. A quality of life approach takes the complexity of life and simplifies it somewhat so that we can understand and use it more easily. There are dangers in simplifying a complex attribute, because this can give rise to shortcuts, assumptions, erroneous decisions and other errors. In practical terms, we recognize that we are not presenting a perfect or complete approach, but rather one that helps people discover how to function more effectively and enable them to grow. It also helps others support these processes. One analogy that might be helpful here is to compare quality of life

Adapted questions from the HRQOL-14

A health-related quality of life measure from the US Centres for Disease Control and Prevention, Health Care and Aging Studies Branch.

Section 1: Health status

1. Would you say that in general your health is: Excellent, Very good, Good, Fair, or Poor?

2. Now thinking about your physical health, which includes physical illness and injury, for how many days during the past 30 days was your physical health not good?

3. Now thinking about your mental health, which includes stress, depression, and problems with emotions, for how many days during the past 30 days was your mental health not good?

4. During the past 30 days, for about how many days did poor physical or mental health keep you from doing your usual activities, such as self-care, work, or recreation?

Supplemental quality of life module

1. Are you LIMITED in any way in any activities because of any impairment or health problem? Yes or No (go to Q. 6)

2. What is the MAJOR impairment or health problem that limits your activities? Arthritis/rheumatism; Back or neck problem; Fractures, bone/joint injury; Walking problem; Lung/breathing problem; Hearing problem; Eye/vision problem; Heart problem; Stroke problem; Hypertension/high blood pressure; Diabetes; Cancer; Depression/anxiety/emotional problem; Other impairment/problem

4. Because of any impairment or health problem, do you need the help of other persons with your PERSONAL CARE needs, such as eating, bathing, dressing, or getting around the house? Yes or No

5. Because of any impairment or health problem, do you need the help of other persons in handling your ROUTINE needs, such as everyday household chores, doing necessary business, shopping, or getting around for other purposes? Yes or No

6. During the past 30 days, for about how many days did PAIN make it hard for you to do your usual activities, such as self-care, work, or recreation?

7. During the past 30 days, for about how many days have you felt SAD, BLUE, or DEPRESSED?

8. During the past 30 days, for about how many days have you felt WORRIED, TENSE, or ANXIOUS?

9. During the past 30 days, for about how many days have you felt you did NOT get ENOUGH REST or SLEEP?

10. During the past 30 days, for about how many days have you felt VERY HEALTHY AND FULL OF ENERGY?

Reprinted with permission from the Centers for Disease Control and Prevention http://www.cdc.gov/nccdphp/hrqol/pdfs/hrqolm2000.pdf (2003) with the London Underground map. This map is far from perfect and cartographers could legitimately criticize it on several grounds (e.g. the distances between stations are not accurate, the indicators of direction are not precise). But the map helps people to move around effectively and enables others to help people get to their destinations.

Some of the terms and ideas we use will be familiar to you, because quality of life work has borrowed them from other fields, then drawn them together and clustered them in new ways. Other terms and ideas will be new to you.

Guiding principle

The guiding principle of effective quality of life is that all humans are entitled to enjoy quality lives. When applying a quality of life approach, this principle ensures we focus on ways to help people enjoy their lives to the fullest possible extent.

Starting off: A three-level framework for a quality of life approach

A quality of life approach for individuals' whole lives needs some place to start. We start by providing a simple three-level framework into which aspects of life of all individuals everywhere can be placed:

Level 1: Attaining the basic necessities of life.

Level 2: Experiencing satisfaction with aspects of life that are important to the person.

Level 3: Achieving high levels of personal enjoyment and fulfilment.

Quality of life can be improved by working on any one of these levels, or all three at once. But the reason this three-level framework is helpful is that it is sometimes important to focus more on Level 1 before moving to Levels 2 and 3, or more on Level 2 before moving to Level 3. Here are two real-life examples:

Example 1

In a country in Eastern Europe, where many people are currently struggling to make ends meet, state funding for children with disabilities is very low. One state-run hospital, where hundreds of children with disabilities are housed, is so understaffed and has so few supplies that the children spend most of their days tied into their beds that are placed in long rows. They have little interaction with other people and only very intermittent personal hygiene care. Food and water are of poor quality and scarce, and they do not have enough clothes.

Where do we begin to improve quality of life for these children? Obviously, we need to focus almost all our efforts on Level 1, providing the basic necessities for an adequate life. They need better physical care, higher quality food and water, sufficient clothing, freedom and encouragement to move about and exercise, closer involvement with people, and stimulating activities to occupy their time. Their satisfaction with life and personal fulfilment are important, but, at the present time, not nearly as important as the basic necessities of life.

Example 2

Joyce is a 36-year-old woman with an intellectual disability who was helped by a community agency to obtain paid work in a store and her own rent-subsidized apartment. From the point of view of her agency, she is well set up to lead an independent life and requires few outside supports. This life is not the life Joyce wishes to lead, however. She does not value work, and, as a consequence, her motivation to do a good job and to get along with her co-workers is low. She would prefer to receive a disability pension, for which she is eligible. She also does not value living on her own, and would prefer to share with others so she would have more people around. Some day, she would like to have a close, intimate relationship with someone, but not in the immediate future.

Where does Joyce begin, and how do we support her? Her life is set up so that the basic necessities of life are already provided. Even if she stops working in the future, she will be able to receive a disability pension. However, two aspects of her life, her work and her housing, are not things she values and as a result she is not satisfied with them. In the future, higher levels of personal satisfaction may be sought, but, for now, it is most important to help her arrange her life so that it contains those things that are of value to her and that she is reasonably satisfied with them.

These two examples show that the three-level framework helps us think about where to start helping people improve their lives. They also show that it is often necessary to focus on a lower level before proceeding to a higher level. You do not always have to focus on just one level, though, when you are using a quality of life approach. Sometimes improving the necessities of life and increasing satisfaction with life go hand in hand, and sometimes becoming more satisfied with life and achieving higher levels of fulfilment also go hand in hand.

Five essential ideas in a quality of life approach

Five ideas are central to a quality of life approach and need to be kept clearly in mind throughout any discussion. It is a good idea to refer back to these peridically when you are using a quality of life approach to check that you are on the right track.

1. *Quality of life addresses similar aspects, attributes and processes of life for all people.* In general, quality of life addresses things that are important to all human beings. Thus, issues such as nutrition, health, social connections, housing and leisure are important to all people who have or do not have disabilities, who live in all countries, and who live in various periods of history.

2. *Quality of life is personal.* Although quality of life addresses similar processes for all people, these similarities diverge when individuals make choices or respond to their unique needs. Thus, quality of life also has a personal meaning. As we have said before, quality of life means something a little different to each individual, and we need to look for that personal difference. To a large extent, it is the unique interaction between a person and the attributes of their environments that determine quality of life. Understanding this uniqueness and providing effective intervention is key to helping improve quality of life. Second, quality of life is ultimately best viewed from the individual's own perspective. We can help others improve their lives, but it is really the person concerned who needs to have the final say on his or her own quality of life. This variability among individuals is fundamental to the concept of quality of life.

3. *Individuals can judge specific aspects of their own lives.* A quality of life approach allows us to look at specific aspects of our lives and assess how effective they are for us. Some of the specific aspects of life that should be considered are: possessions, finances, social connections, beliefs, growth and learning, leisure, physical health, mental health, self-determination, social inclusion, and rights. You may think of others. In choosing what to focus on first, it is usually a good idea to choose the aspect of life that seems most important to the individual at the time. No matter which way you

do it, it is easier to focus on one or just a few aspects of life at one time, rather than on all of them at once.

For practitioners, it is essential to understand that individuals need to judge aspects of their own lives, and that they are almost always in the best position to know what adds to or detracts from the quality of their lives. Their choices, priorities and preferred sequence of action may seem surprising – or even ill-advised – to the professional, but quality of life requires a certain degree of trust that people know what is best for their own quality of life. On the other hand, if there is reason to think that individuals' judgements about their own lives will lead to harm, the practitioner has a responsibility to try to effect a more positive choice. In doing so, practitioners must understand that their own personal dispositions and biases probably differ from those of individuals, and thus great care must be taken in these situations to act in the best interests of such individuals.

4. *All parts of your life are interconnected.* It is essential to remember this interconnectedness. For example, finances affect our leisure activities, and both affect our social connections. In addition, all parts of our lives are influenced by the environments in which we live, and, in turn, have an influence on those environments. This interconnection sometimes seems to make aspects of quality of life complicated, but at other times it helps people make important overall judgements about their lives.

5. *Quality of life is ever-changing.* Quality of life can change from year to year, and even from day to day. Any number of planned and unplanned events can occur to change the quality of a person's life. In addition, as we move through life, we have different priorities and value different things. Thus, the things that contribute to an individual's quality of life at one stage may be quite different from those that contribute to it later on. In other words, there is also variability within each individual over time.

What does a quality of life approach achieve?

When we use a quality of life approach, we focus specifically on six key application principles to build upon the five essential ideas described above. The quality of life approach:

1. Focuses attention on the processes that are most *important* to the person at the present time; this includes those things that the person shares with other humans and those things that are more individually valued by the person and relevant to his or her life.

2. Works to ensure that the person is *satisfied* with those aspects of life that are important, and not dissatisfied with other aspects of his or her life; human beings are never fully satisfied with all aspects of their lives, and this characteristic keeps us striving for improvement; in taking a quality of life approach, we strive for feeling quite well satisfied overall, and for feeling much more satisfaction than dissatisfaction in our lives.

3. Stresses that *opportunities* to improve must be within the person's grasp.

4. Insists that *personal choice* should be exercised, wherever possible, in selecting opportunities.

5. Improves the person's *self-image.*

6. Increases levels of personal *empowerment.*

Final words

In this chapter, we have introduced you to a quality of life approach. We have learned what quality of life means, who can use this approach, and the basic ideas needed for helping people improve their lives.

For thought and discussion

1. Are all people entitled to lives of quality?

2. Look back at the three-level framework again. Think of a time in your life when each of the levels was particularly important to you.

3. Select a country in another part of the world. Think of a person of about your age and the same sex as you. Give that person a name. Now consider these two questions: What things would improve quality of life for both of you? In what ways is quality of life a personal thing for each of you?

4. Think of one thing that came into your life after you took action that now adds quality to your life. Now relate that to the six things that a quality of life approach achieves by asking: How important is it to you? How satisfied are you with it? What opportunities were available to you from which you could choose? Did you exercise personal choice? Has it changed your self-image? Has it empowered you?

Selected bibliography

Note to readers. At the end of most chapters, we provide some readings that will expand or further explain the text. We have listed book and chapter readings and a few journal references that we believe may be particularly helpful. Readers will find many additional articles, books and websites by following standard procedures for literature searches.

Albrecht, G.L., Seelman, K.D. and Bury, M. (eds) (2001) *Handbook of Disability Studies.* Thousand Oaks, CA: Sage.

Barton, L., Ballard, K. and Folcher, G. (1991) *Disability and the Necessity for a Socio-political Perspective.* Monograph 51. Durham, NH: University of New Hampshire.

Brown, I. (1999) 'Embracing quality of life in times of spending restraint.' *Journal of Intellectual and Developmental Disability 24*, 4, 299–308.

Brown, I. (2003) 'Abuse and neglect of disabled and non-disabled children: establishing a place in quality of life study.' In M.J. Sirgy, D. Rahtz and A.C. Samli (eds) *Advances in Quality-of-Life Theory and Research, volume 4.* Dordrecht, The Netherlands: Kluwer Academic.

Brown, R.I. (ed) (1997) *Quality of Life for People with Disabilities: Models, Research and Practice, 2nd edition.* Cheltenham, UK: Stanley Thornes.

Brown, R.I., Bayer, M.B. and Brown, P.M. (1992) *Empowerment and Developmental Handicaps: Choices and Quality of Life.* London: Chapman & Hall.

Campbell, A. (1981) *The Sense of Well-being in America.* New York: McGraw-Hill.

Campbell, A., Converse, P. and Rodgers, W.L. (1976) *The Quality of American life: Perceptions, Evaluations, and Satisfactions.* New York: Russell Sage Foundation.

Clarke, A.M. and Clarke, A.D.B. (2000) *Early Experience in the Life Path*. London: Jessica Kingsley Publishers.

Evans, D.R. (1994) Enhancing quality of life in the population at large. *Social Indicators Research 33*, 47–88.

Goode, D. (ed) (1994) *Quality of Life for Persons with Disabilities: International Perspectives and Issues*. Cambridge, MA: Brookline Books.

Hatton, C. (1998) Whose quality of life is it anyway? Some problems with the emerging quality of life consensus. *Mental Retardation 36*, 104–115.

Journal on Developmental Disabilities (1994) Special issue on quality of life, vol. 3, part 2. www.oadd.org

Journal on Developmental Disabilities (1997) Special issue on quality of life, vol. 5, part 2. www.oadd.org

Keith, K.D. and Schalock, R.L. (eds) (2000) *Cross-cultural Perspectives on Quality of Life*. Washington, DC: American Association on Mental Retardation.

Lord, J. and Hutchison, P. (1993) The process of empowerment: Implications for theory and practice. *Canadian Journal of Community Mental Health 12*, 1, 5–22.

Myers, D.G. (1992) *The Pursuit of Happiness: Who is Happy and Why*. New York: William Morrow.

Quality of Life Instrument Database, MAPI Research Institute, http://195.101.204.50:8081

Renwick, R., Brown, I. and Nagler, M. (eds) (1996) *Quality of Life in Health Promotion and Rehabilitation: Conceptualizations, Issues and Applications*. Thousand Oaks, CA: Sage.

Romney, D.M., Brown, R.I. and Fry, P.S. (eds) (1994) *Improving the Quality of Life: Recommendations for People With and Without Disabilities*. Dordrecht, The Netherlands: Kluwer Academic.

Schalock, R.L. (ed) (1990) *Quality of Life: Perspectives and Issues*. Washington, DC: American Association on Mental Retardation.

Schalock, R.L. (ed) (1996) *Quality of Life, volume I: Conceptualization and Measurement*. Washington, DC: American Association on Mental Retardation.

Schalock, R.L. (ed) (1997) *Quality of Life, volume II: Application to Persons with Disabilities*. Washington, DC: American Association on Mental Retardation.

Taylor, S.J. (1994) In support of research on quality of life, but against QOL. In D. Goode (ed) *Quality of Life for Persons with Disabilities: International Perspectives and Issues*. Cambridge, MA: Brookline.

Wolfensberger, W. (1994) Let's hang up "quality of life" as a hopeless term. In D. Goode (ed) *Quality of Life for Persons with Disabilities: International Perspectives and Issues*. Cambridge, MA: Brookline.

CHAPTER 2

Four People with Disabilities
A Glance at their Lives

In the first chapter, we began to learn about quality of life. We began to think about our own quality of life. Now, we present briefly the lives of four people who have disabilities. It will quickly be understood what things are sources of quality in their lives and what things detract from quality. After each person, we provide some questions and issues to think about and discuss. All of these questions and issues are addressed later on in the book, but it is relevant to discuss your initial reactions now. It will also be interesting to come back and discuss them again after you have read and studied the whole book.

Three important things should be kept in mind as you read about the people we highlight. First, each of the four people portrayed below has a disability or several disabilities that are described in some detail. Our descriptions may seem to overemphasize disability or to depict it in blunt and clinical terms. Our intention, however, is to explain disability as clearly as possible so that readers will be able to understand its place in each person's life. Further, the descriptions are those used by the individuals themselves. Second, we ask you to adopt the view that disability is neither good nor bad, but rather a part of the individual and group life of all human beings. Disability is magnified as a problem – or sometimes it is only seen as a 'disability' – if groups of people have not learned how to adapt to it and treat it as part of the everyday human experience. Third, please keep in mind that the four people highlighted in this chapter are real people who have taken a risk by giving us permission to share details of their private lives. All four did so because they consider the topic of this book to be important, and because they want to make personal contributions to the quality of life of people with disabilities. It is important during discussions to be respectful of the fact that we are discussing details of real people's lives.

Sam

A snapshot of Sam's life

Sam describes himself as happy-go-lucky, someone who just likes to enjoy life. He is 37, and has his own apartment in a highrise building. He receives a disability pension, which provides him with enough money to pay for only the very basic necessities of life, and occasionally he works at part-time or temporary jobs to supplement his income. This is not particularly difficult for Sam, since he is highly sociable and talks to both friends and strangers with equal ease. He simply goes into shops and other potential workplaces, begins to chat, and asks if there is any work he can do. He has some material possessions, but does not place high value on them. For example, he shuns getting a mobile telephone and even a VCR, claiming that he doesn't need them.

One of the reasons Sam takes on part-time work is that he very much enjoys travelling. When he has saved up enough money, he plans a trip to a city he has heard about but has never visited before. He knows how to make his available money stretch when he is travelling by seeking out bargains and cheaper ways of doing things. By doing so, he is able to see more things and have more experiences than most travellers.

Sam has numerous hobbies, but music is probably the one that is most important to him. He has considerable natural musical ability, and although he has never had any formal training, he can 'make do' on a number of instruments. This is a source of considerable pleasure to him when he is alone, and an activity that he shares with friends and acquaintances who are amateur musicians. He has been offered more formal training on numerous occasions, but each time he has begun he has quickly grown tired of the required discipline. Sam also enjoys playing cards, writing letters to pen pals, taking part in groups that make various crafts, and being a football fan.

Sam has many acquaintances, and prides himself on having good social and leadership skills. He also has a number of long-term friends who have come to understand him and enjoy his company over the years. However, many of the friends he makes, mostly through his leisure activities, do not last very long. These people unknowingly make the mistake of doing something or saying something that displeases Sam. It is not his way to give relatively new friends a second chance. He simply makes other new friends.

Think about Sam's quality of life...

You have read a brief summary of Sam's life, and next you will read about his disabilities. Before you go on, though, spend some time thinking about his quality of life. Think about the two questions below, and discuss them with others.

1.   What things add quality to Sam's life?

2.   What things detract from the quality of Sam's life?

Sam's disabilities

Sam has been blind in one eye and moderately deaf since birth. His blindness went undetected until he was a teenager, mostly because he had adapted so well to using his sighted eye and because he had hearing and behaviour problems that were the focus of other people's attention.

Sam's deafness was not diagnosed until after he started school, so as a result he had difficulty learning language in his preschool years. In fact, he communicated primarily in non-verbal ways when he began school, in spite of an apparent ability to convey his meaning clearly. Once fitted with hearing aids for both ears, Sam was able to hear most things, as long as other people spoke louder than usual and there were not competing sources of sound. He quickly learned to speak both English and French, French being the language that his parents spoke in their home.

A number of factors within Sam's family and social environment appear to have contributed to the development of difficult behaviour in his childhood, but his inability to hear clearly was probably the most significant. Whatever the causes, Sam's parents had difficulty shaping his developing behaviour in ways that were socially acceptable, and were continuously frustrated in their attempts to cope with his behaviour. When he was 14, he moved from his family home and lived until age 21 with foster parents who were skilled in dealing with and positively shaping difficult behaviour.

Sam's identity as a man with disabilities

VISION

Although Sam clearly understood from early childhood that people typically see out of two eyes, incredibly he had never mentioned to anyone – including his parents and teachers – that he could see out of only one eye. In fact, his blindness in one eye was detected only by accident when he was a teenager by a teacher during a physical education exercise. Sam claimed at the time – and still claims today – that he didn't want people to know about his blindness because they would think he was 'weird'.

As Sam has got older and after a considerable amount of counselling in his adulthood, he has gradually developed some comfort in discussing his blindness with people he knows very well. For example, when walking with close friends, he will ask to walk on the right-hand side so he can see them more easily. However, he rarely explains that he can only see out of his left eye.

As often happens with people who do not have vision in one eye, Sam sometimes bumps into people on his right side. When this occurs, he reacts with anger, blaming the other people for not watching where they were going. When questioned closely on how other people can be expected to know that he cannot see out of his right eye, his response has always been emphatically that 'they should know if a person has a disability'. Yet, he has almost no facility for telling or showing others that this is the case. For the most part, Sam simply lives his adult life, as he did his childhood, not letting on to other people that he is blind in one eye.

HEARING

Sam rarely mentions his hearing disability to anyone, including close friends. Unlike his blindness, though, Sam cannot hide his hearing disability because he wears hearing aids in both ears. This visual message to others is often helpful, because it lets them know that when he does not hear what they say, they need to speak more loudly or more clearly. At the same time, the presence of the hearing aids sometimes results in two other problems. First, some people – especially those who are not accustomed to living or working with disabilities – simply do not notice that he is wearing hearing aids, and thus have no idea that he cannot always hear what they are saying. For his part, Sam is self-conscious of his hearing aids, and in spite of many attempts to help him understand, it is simply incomprehensible to him that others are not fully aware that he has difficulty hearing. The view that he expresses strongly and consistently is that other people should know to speak loudly 'because they can easily see my hearing aids'.

A second problem that arises is that most other people, unless they have been specifically told or have had experience with hearing disabilities, do not speak more loudly or more clearly to people who wear hearing aids. Nor does it usually occur to them to ask if the person with hearing aids can hear what they are saying. Because Sam will not say anything about this himself, he misses a great deal of what others say.

Sam's reaction to both these problems is to dismiss those people he can't hear. He wants to understand what others are saying, but if they do not speak to him so that he can hear, he typically ends the conversation quickly and, from the point of view of the others, very rudely. He claims that people should know how to talk to him, but refuses to take any part in helping them to learn how to do so.

BEHAVIOUR

Today, Sam is friendly, cooperative, and polite most of the time, but he can also occasionally be abrupt and disrespectful to others. Generally, he is displeased with other people either because he cannot hear or see sufficiently, or because they are doing things or talking about things in which he has little interest. When he is displeased, he typically makes a quick comment that is not to the liking of the others, whirls around, and walks away. This behaviour, which other people invariably view as rude and unpleasant, is always justified in Sam's mind because others are 'stupid' or 'ignorant'. The difficulty – and the irony – is that, although he fully expects others to understand his disabilities and to know precisely how to react to them, Sam himself is not really very tolerant of difference in other people.

Sam's plans and dreams for the future

Sam is very much aware of the changes that occur in all of us as we pass through the years. He has noticed that he has put on some weight in the past few years, that his energy level is a little different from what it used to be, and that some of his interests have changed. Although he is still almost three years away from being 40, he wonders aloud what his life will be like when he is in his 40s. He can articulate no clear vision about this, even after a prolonged conversation, but he is beginning to question and wonder.

At times, Sam has toyed with the idea of marriage, or at least a serious ongoing relationship. To date, all his relationships with women have been quite casual and short-lived. He has seen male friends become involved in long-term and stable relationships, and has often expressed the wish that he could 'meet a woman like that'. When pressed even a little on this point, though, he is always quick to remark that 'a wife would be too much trouble'. Thus, although he seems to wish for an intimate relationship, he does not see this as a realistic part of his future.

For the immediate future, Sam has no shortage of ideas of things he wants to do. He has numerous trips planned, numerous events he wants to attend, and numerous people he wants to visit. Plans and dreams emerge abundantly, although he has no expectation that more than a few of them will actually become a reality. For Sam, though, they are more likely to become a reality if they are in the not-too-distant future. The long term just doesn't bear thinking about.

Thinking again about Sam's quality of life

Now that you have read more about Sam's life, think about and discuss these two questions:

1. How do Sam's disabilities affect his quality of life?

2. To what degree are other people responsible for Sam's quality of life?

In addition, think about these two questions again:

3. What things add quality to Sam's life?

4. What things detract from the quality of Sam's life?

Cynthia

A snapshot of Cynthia's life

Cynthia has spent the last six years trying to be a good mother to her daughter Claire. As a single mother, still only 26, she has found this difficult at times, but tries very hard to make it work. She is estranged from Claire's father, and has not seen him for the past four years. Cynthia and Claire live in a small geared-to-income apartment building that is close to her aunt's home, which they visit often. It is sometimes hard to make ends meet, since the money Cynthia makes from working in a local bakery is their only source of income. For the past three years, Claire attended a daycare centre in their neighbourhood, but, now that she is in school, she stays with a neighbour for a few hours until Cynthia gets home from work in the late afternoon.

Cynthia takes Claire to visit her parents and her sister's family about once a month. Cynthia's parents, especially, always seem to have something special for Claire when she arrives. In fact, Cynthia usually has to take Claire with her wherever she goes, although her aunt sometimes offers to babysit, especially if groceries are needed. These outings provide a good way for Cynthia and Claire to have fun and enjoy each other's company, but it is sometimes hard for Claire to be interested when they have to go out for shopping, laundry or errands. Cynthia thinks of herself as an 'ordinary' person who enjoys the ordinary things of life. In the evenings, she likes to relax and watch her favourite television programmes or chat on the telephone with her two close friends or a member of her family.

Thinking about Cynthia's quality of life...

Now that you have read the brief snapshot about Cynthia's life, think about her quality of life. It will be easier this time.

1. What things add quality to Cynthia's life?

2. What things detract from the quality of Cynthia's life?

This time think also about:

3. How does Claire add quality to Cynthia's life?

Cynthia's disabilities

Cynthia has mild intellectual disabilities, such that she can read and write only a little. She knows her numbers and uses money well, but can get confused when she has to add things up or when she is getting change back at the store. Still, she enjoyed her years at school and speaks fondly of her teachers and the friends she made there. These disabilities do not noticeably affect her work in the bakery, where she chats and laughs with her co-workers as they carry out their various tasks. She likes to work alongside someone else, and likes to try to help out as much as she can.

One skill that is particularly troublesome for Cynthia is getting around the city. She has a great deal of difficulty even visualizing the streets and buildings in her own neighbourhood. As a result, she cannot describe where things are or how to get to specific places. When she is outside, she has little sense of direction. She does have a very good memory, however, and she uses this well to commit to memory a whole array of 'signposts' that can guide her to wherever she is going. Many of these she does not even remember, but recognizes them along the way. Her family and friends often remark on her uncanny ability to get to places, when logic suggests that she doesn't have any idea how to get there.

Cynthia was diagnosed several years ago with a minor psychiatric problem and takes a mild medication daily to treat it. She visits her psychiatrist once a year to have her medications reviewed. Usually, family, friends and co-workers do not notice any behaviour that they attribute to her psychiatric problem, but periodically she mentions that other people think of her as a prostitute and can take considerable delight in providing details of their conversations. The results of several follow-up sessions with these people strongly suggest that such conversations did not, in fact, occur.

Cynthia's identity as a woman with disabilities

Cynthia has little to say about disabilities. She understands well that there are some things in life that she cannot do as well as other people, and that she needs help doing certain things. But, in her opinion, everyone needs help doing some things. She simply doesn't think of herself as a person with disabilities. Rather, she thinks of herself as an ordinary person, trying to lead an ordinary life. To her, nothing she does or says is out of the ordinary. Disability is in no way troublesome to her, because she doesn't see it as being part of her life.

The views of Cynthia's family and friends

Unlike Cynthia, her parents, sister and aunt are very much concerned with what they perceive to be her disabilities. They look out for Claire as much as they can, even contributing financially when cash is low. They are concerned that she might not have sufficient parenting skills, that she will not have enough money for herself and Claire, and that other people may take advantage of her. They let Cynthia lead her own life, but are ready to jump in if needed. They are never far away.

By contrast, Cynthia's two best friends see her as very much like themselves. Both have children of their own, although both receive disability pensions and do not work outside the home. The three friends swap stories about their children, and sometimes pick up tips on how to do things better. Her work friends think of her as less skilled than themselves, but not as someone who leads a life that is out of the ordinary because of disability.

Cynthia's plans and dreams for the future

Cynthia thinks about her future life and talks about it with other people. She wants to continue her job at the bakery as long as she can, because she finds it an interesting and 'good' place to work. She imagines herself and Claire continuing to live in their current apartment for many years, because they know the neighbourhood and the rent is low. She has some plans for Claire as well. She wants her to go to camp and to join some clubs at school or at their nearby community centre. In the longer term, she would like Claire to finish high school and get a good job so that she will have enough money to support herself.

Thinking again about Cynthia's quality of life

Now that you have read more about Cynthia, let's think again about these two questions:

1.   What things add quality to Cynthia's life?

2.   What things detract from the quality of Cynthia's life?

Here are two new questions to think about:

3.   Do members of Cynthia's family help or hinder her quality of life?

4.   Is Cynthia an ordinary person leading an ordinary life?

Cody

A snapshot of Cody's life

Cody is seven years old and he has Down syndrome. He is the second child in a family of four children, with one older brother, one younger brother and one younger sister. His parents both work, his mother as a factory worker, and his father as a mechanic. In addition, he is very close to his grandmother, who frequently invites him for overnight visits and takes considerable delight in baking his favourite cookies. Cody speaks very fondly of his grandmother, and appears to be very close to her.

Cody's family unit is close-knit, one that does a great many things together and one in which all family members help and support one another. The activities they do together have given him a great deal of life experience which he remembers and refers to at times. He has gone everywhere in his community that his brothers and sister go to – the library, the park, the shopping malls, and the corner shops. He has participated in games and sports with his brothers and sister, and goes on all the family outings and vacations. He has been to swimming pools, amusement parks, museums, movies, children's theatre, and many other places that constitute children's culture. He has taken a train ride, and periodically travels to Toronto by bus, an activity that he particularly enjoys. These experiences all contribute to making his life seem quite full and eventful for a boy his age.

Think about Cody's quality of life...

You have read a very brief snapshot of Cody's life. It is time to put together your initial thoughts about his quality of life.

1. How does Cody's family add to his quality of life?

2. In Chapter 1, you learned that having opportunities to explore and enjoy is one essential aspect of good quality of life. Choosing from these options is another. What role do opportunities and choice appear to play in Cody's life?

Cody's disabilities

One of Cody's main problems is communicating with other people. He has trouble pronouncing his words so that they come out clearly, and he has not yet learned to insert all the little words into his sentences (e.g. instead of saying 'My brother has a blue coat', he says 'Brother blue coat'). In addition, he seems to forget events that occurred even in the recent past, such as what he did on the weekend. Perhaps for these reasons, he often leaves out details when he is relating a short story, so others have to listen very carefully to pick up his meaning. Most people have at least some difficulty understanding what he is trying to say, and this makes him very frustrated. His reaction is to become very annoyed, flatly refusing to repeat himself.

Compared with other children his age, Cody has difficulty performing tasks that require fine motor control, such as printing, using scissors, doing up buttons, tying his shoelaces, using a computer mouse, and other activities that young children are learning to do with their fingers. He also has problems with gross motor activities, such as running, catching a ball, skating, or cycling. He can be perceived by other people to be stubborn and negative, especially initially, but if a power struggle can be avoided, he will usually go

along with almost everything. He shows fear of situations where there is considerable noise or a great many people, such as activities in the school gym.
Going to places that are closed in or dark, such as concerts, public meetings or
a dark bedroom, are problematic because Cody frequently feels he is locked
in. He is afraid of being with many animals, especially dogs. He needs to get
used to these kinds of situation very gradually before he feels comfortable
with them. Cody eats well, but tires easily and seems to catch more than his
share of colds and other respiratory illnesses.

Cody expresses very definite likes and dislikes. Unfortunately, he shows
more dislikes than likes when relating to other children his own age. If he
dislikes you, he lets you know in no uncertain terms: 'Go away!' or 'I don't like
you!' Sometimes he will just ignore you and simply walk away. He has not yet
learned very well to play cooperatively with other children, preferring instead
to play in parallel, such as creating action with his own imaginary friends or
imitating the actions of people he knows (e.g. pretending he is fixing a truck
like his dad). In general, Cody needs strong and constant reminders and modelling to be able to interact with other children in socially constructive ways.

Strengths

Cody is very sociable, and very much enjoys relating to adults. To those few
children he likes, he shows tenderness, loyalty and affection. He seems to
enjoy his sense of touch, and is ready to show his affection to others by giving
hugs and kisses. For many of the people in his life, he has also learned what
makes them laugh and he is frequently ready to play on this. With his mother,
for example, he likes to pretend to forget when his bedtime is, but then unex-
pectedly he will come over to her and whisper the almost-correct information
into her ear, knowing to change it just enough to make her laugh. At home,
Cody plays particularly well with his younger brother and loves to sleep
downstairs with his older brother on weekends. He hugs his younger sister,
picks her up, and calls her his baby. He has been taught good manners by his
parents, and applies these in the various situations of his life. For example, he
always remembers to say 'please' and 'thank you', and will remember to ask
'Are you okay?' after a slight mishap.

Cody enjoys routine, and is easily encouraged to do things that follow his
usual routine. He can also be motivated to cooperate with his parents, teacher
or sitter through many hours with the promise of some seemingly simple

reward, such as playing with a toy, playing a game together or having an ice-cream cone. This works especially well if it is part of a routine that he has followed previously.

He loves any kind of food, and loves playing outside. He also loves to clean and sort. He vacuums, dusts and sweeps the floor at home, and he organizes his desk and the teacher's shelves at school. He loves to help his Mom fold clothes and put them away. In the mornings, he helps get everyone's clothes out and ready for the day.

Cody's parents encourage him to wear clothes that are currently in fashion for children, and he responds to this readily, imitating his older brother to a considerable degree. He has also learned that dressing fashionably brings praise and additional interaction from other people. A comment like 'Wow, nice jeans!' makes his face beam with pride. Similarly, he has learned that other people, especially adults, find it amusing when he repeats words or phrases that seem to be just a little too streetwise for a seven-year-old boy with Down syndrome. When he says things like 'Cool, man' or 'Okay, honey', even the most restrained adults find it difficult not to smile or comment. These things encourage Cody to be like other children, although his parents and teacher try to ensure that he does not over-rely on such strategies. Cody's mother described the way she and Cody's father treat him at home: 'It is very important not to treat Cody, or anyone with disabilities, differently from anyone else. We have always tried to treat Cody the same as our other children, because we believe that makes him feel accepted, loved, and more respected.'

At school

Cody goes to his neighbourhood school, and spends his full day in a classroom with his peers. All school programmes need to be adapted to his learning needs, however, and he requires a great deal of individual attention from the classroom special needs assistant and the classroom teacher. He has begun to read from a book especially designed for children with Down syndrome that uses familiar life words and integrates some spelling and phonics skills. He also works with one-digit numbers in a concrete way, and can count to 20. After considerable familiarization, he remembers words and concepts, although it is sometimes difficult to assess the degree to which he actually understands. Cody's teachers consider that he will need special instruction all through his school life.

Cody's classmates are very accepting of him on the whole. They appear to be fascinated by how he learns and by how the teacher and he interact. They often surreptitiously watch this interaction, and, when noticed by the teacher, they smile. They seem to accept that he is different, but do not show in any way that this makes a difference to them. Classmates are shy to approach him, however, and need to be encouraged to ask him questions. On the playground, it is more obvious that he is different from his peers. The other boys play football, but he does not join in. The other children do not usually ask him to play with them, nor do they join in his play. The school uses two strategies to address this: involving him in organized team sports, and assigning one child each week to encourage him to join in. The organized sports work especially well for Cody, as there is usually a teacher or a coach to encourage him, but his peers are not always very good at knowing how to involve him. One factor that is helpful to Cody, but also keeps him from playing with his peers, is that he seems perfectly happy most of the time to play on his own. In fact, he is sometimes irritated when the others try to draw him into cooperative play. He just wants to play in his own way, but most other children his age have difficulty understanding why this is.

Part of Cody's learning programme involves learning how to speak effectively with others, and to express himself as clearly as possible. The special needs assistant uses two main strategies here: she drills him on routine phrases he uses in his life, and she gives him numerous opportunities to create new sentences and even short stories from the words he knows. One focus of teaching in both strategies is to encourage him to pronounce all the words that are customarily used by others. His teacher describes this as learning to use all the small words in life. The overall strategy used in his classroom appears to be effective. Both Cody's parents and the other teachers in the school say that he is really blooming this year.

Cody's mother explained the importance of having him attend his neighbourhood school: 'It is so important to integrate children with disabilities at school. Cody was placed in a regular classroom because he can learn better and faster there. He learns how to act appropriately in a classroom of his peers. He also learns to make friends and share with others. It makes a tremendous difference to his life to be in a place where he feels accepted, loved and respected for being just himself – Cody.'

Hopes and dreams for the future

In the past, Cody wanted to fix cars like his Dad but now he wants to be a teacher. In the meantime, he loves doing his homework and helping his siblings with their projects. His parents have their own hopes and dreams for Cody's future: 'We hope Cody will graduate from secondary school and hopefully go to college. We believe he will get a job, and we hope he will get married and live on his own or in a group home. We have the highest hopes for Cody.'

Thinking more about Cody's quality of life

You have learned more about Cody at school, at home and with his peers. Again, think about these two questions:

1. What things add quality to Cody's life?

2. What things detract from the quality of Cody's life?

In addition, consider these new questions:

3. How do Cody's family and teachers try to help him have a positive self-image?

4. Thinking of Cody's life, what helps him feel empowered to do the things that are important for him?

5. Should Cody be encouraged to play with his peers more?

6. Overall, does Down syndrome increase or decrease the quality of Cody's life?

Margaret

A snapshot of Margaret's life

Margaret, now 78, has been living alone in her family home since the death of her husband ten years ago. She has two daughters who live in the same city and who visit her regularly, helping with shopping, cleaning, taking her to medical appointments, and the many other things that need to be done. At least one of her three grandchildren drops by about once a week, and Margaret always keeps special cookies on hand as a treat for them, even though they are now in their late teens.

Margaret is popular with other people wherever she goes. She acts equally kindly towards friends, acquaintances and strangers. She has quite a number of long-time friends, although some of them can't get out to see her as often as they did in the past. Also, her relationship with some of her friends has changed since her husband died, because they have stopped the activities they formerly did as couples. Still, Margaret makes or receives several telephone calls a day, and very much enjoys chatting with her old friends this way. She also enjoys swapping stories with them about their mutual hobbies – mostly knitting and sewing for their grandchildren or for charities.

Religion has been a strong influence on Margaret's beliefs and values, and both the worship services and social groups she has attended have formed a strong part of her weekly routines for many years. Over the past few years, however, she has had to cut down on these activities, but her feelings, thoughts and actions all continue to be guided strongly by the basic beliefs and values of her religion.

Margaret still has her own car and drives to familiar places. This gives her a sense of independence and she speaks proudly of being able to strike out on her own outings. The unspoken message here, from the perspective of her family at least, is that she has lost independence in many other areas of her life.

Think about Margaret's quality of life…

Once again, after this brief introduction, think about Margaret's quality of life.

1. What things add quality to Margaret's life?

2. What things detract from the quality of Margaret's life?

Also think about:

3. How has growing older affected Margaret's life?

Margaret's disabilities

Margaret began to experience problems with mobility in her knees about 20 years ago. Shortly after her husband's death, she underwent a knee replacement, and four years later had a replacement for her other knee. These operations, and the considerable rehabilitation and adjustment that followed, were sources of stress; but, in time, she began to see the replacements as a real benefit to her. She continues to experience some difficulties with mobility, but is able to take two daily walks for exercise and drive her car short distances.

About three years ago, Margaret began to repeat the same stories to her family and friends, and to ask the same question several times in a short period of time. About the same time, she had a particularly strong interest in the events of her childhood and teen years, and put together a very comprehensive scrapbook of her family life with her parents when she was a girl. More recently, although she does not admit to it, she often forgets people's names when she sees them, even if she clearly recognizes their faces. In conversation with family and long-time friends, she appears to have little or no recollection of many people she formerly knew. To her daughters especially, she appears very restless and unreasonably insistent at some times, but not always. Her family is beginning to worry because she forgets where she puts things, and some of her possessions – including long-cherished treasures – are nowhere to be found. Most worrisome to them, though, is the fact that she appears not to bathe regularly, even though she claims she does.

Margaret has also experienced some physical health problems over the past few years, especially high blood sugar and angina. She visits her family physician regularly, and takes several daily medications. Her daughters are becoming increasingly concerned that she may not be taking the correct medication.

Margaret's adjustment to her lessening abilities

Although Margaret had been realistic throughout her adult life about the disabling effects of growing older, she found it difficult to accept these in herself. Other people grew old, in her mind, but she viewed herself as a healthy, able, robust woman. Her knee problems represented her first major confrontation with lessening physical abilities, and it took her a considerable time to begin to see herself as a woman who could not always get around easily and without pain. Still, her knee problems and other physical health conditions came on rather gradually, and this allowed her time to adjust both mentally and physically. In the end, she seems to have grown accustomed to being an 'older' woman with some problems that are being managed by medical care.

The signs of dementia reflect changes in Margaret's cognition, and some apparent changes in her personality. She occasionally admits to forgetting that she did something or forgetting someone's name, but otherwise flatly denies any other changes or problems. Medical advice to her daughters is that this is not unexpected in people who show early signs of dementia. The question they ponder between themselves from time to time is whether or not she will ever identify herself as a person with lessening cognitive abilities.

Margaret's future

Margaret wants to continue living in her family home. When asked about the possibility of moving to a nursing home or other care facility some time in the future, she simply says she does not need to and, in any case, does not want to move to a 'home'. On the other hand, Margaret's daughters consider that her personal care needs are increasing and that she will probably require more care in the future. They are beginning to explore in their minds the types of care that would be best.

Thinking more about Margaret's quality of life

You have now read about Margaret. As before, think again about these two questions:

1.   What things add quality to Margaret's life?

2.   What things detract from the quality of Margaret's life?

In addition, consider these new questions:

3.   Should lessening abilities related to aging be called disabilities?

4.   How do lessening abilities related to aging affect the quality of life of Margaret's daughters? Her grandchildren? Her friends?

5.   How has Margaret's self-image changed? How can this change be positive for her?

6.   How can Margaret exercise personal choice? How can she remain empowered?

A few last words

In this chapter, you have read something of the lives of four people and you have had an opportunity to think about and discuss their lives in terms of quality of life. As you read the rest of the book and learn about other new ideas, think back to Sam, Cynthia, Cody and Margaret, and think about how these new ideas might work in their lives.

Selected bibliography

Note to readers. There are many accounts of life experiences written by people with a variety of disabilities and their family members. We have listed here a few such books and chapters. Readers are encouraged to seek out other accounts that are widely available in printed form.

Bauby, J.-D. (1997) *The Diving Bell and the Butterfly* [trans. from French by J. Leggatt]. New York: A.A. Knopf (distributed by Random House).

Brown, C. (1990) *Down all the Days*. Portsmouth, NH: Heinemann.

Burke, C. and McDaniel, J.B. (1991) *A Special Kind of Hero*. New York: Doubleday.

Grandin, T. (1995) *Thinking in Pictures and Other Reports from My Life with Autism*. New York: Doubleday.

Kreuger, J. and Brown, R.I. (1989) 'Quality of life: A portrait of six clients.' In R.I. Brown, M.B. Bayer and C. MacFarlane (eds) *Rehabilitation Programmes: Performance and Quality of Living of Adults with Developmental Handicaps*. Toronto: Lugus.

The Magnus Family (1995) *A Family Love Story*. Salt Spring Island, British Columbia: Alea Design and Print/Author.

McPhail, E. (1996) 'A parent's perspective: Quality of life in families with a member with disabilities.' In R. Renwick, I. Brown and M. Nagler (eds) *Quality of Life in Health Promotion and Rehabilitation: Conceptual Approaches, Issues, and Applications*. Thousand Oaks, CA: Sage.

Peter, D. (1997) 'A focus on the individual, theory and reality: Making the connection through the lives of individuals.' In R.I. Brown (ed) *Quality of Life for People with Disabilities: Models, Research and Practice, 2nd edition*. Cheltenham, UK: Stanley Thornes.

Schalock, R.L. (ed) (1990) *Quality of Life: Perspectives and Issues*. Washington, DC: American Association on Mental Retardation.

Sidransky, R. (1990) *In Silence: Growing Up Hearing in a Deaf World*. New York: Ballantine Books.

Velde, B. (1997) 'Quality of life through personally meaningful activity.' In R.I. Brown (ed) *Quality of Life for People with Disabilities: Models, Research and Practice, 2nd edition*. Cheltenham, UK: Stanley Thornes.

Williams, D. (1992) *Nobody Nowhere*. Toronto: Doubleday.

Selected videos and documentaries

If I Can't Do It. Walter Brock Productions. USA. 1998.

When People with Developmental Disabilities Age. New York State Developmental Disabilities Planning Council. Albany, NY, USA. 1990.

Selected websites (at time of writing)

'Portraits of our lives' book series, Roeher Institute
    http://www.roeher.ca/comersus/subject.htm

Disability discussion forum: Finding what we have in common one story at a time
    http://www.tell_us_your_story.com/alldisc.html#ARCHIVES

Brisbane stories
    http://www.brisbane_stories.powerup.com.au/

The Disability Action Hall (The Hall)
    http://disability.activist.ca/

Disability arts and advocacy
    http://www.thalidomide.ca/gwolbring/newpage1.htm

Sunshine dreams for kids
    http://www.sunshine.ca/dreams_real_john.htm

Stories
    http://www.bethesdabc.com/stories.htm

Disability
    http://www.drrecommend.com/Dir/Health/Consumer_support_groups/
    Disability/

Personal stories
    http://www.cdss.ca/excerpt4.html

The disability mural
    http://www.icomm.ca/iarts/home/mural/mural.htm

CHAPTER 3

Understanding the Social and Historical Roots of Disability

Disability and society

In Chapter 2, we recounted something about the lives of four people with various kinds of disabilities, and you began to think about and discuss their quality of life. You will have noticed that when people with disabilities endeavour to improve the quality of their lives, they value the same things in general that non-disabled people do – friendships, family life, meaningful activities, secure and interesting environments, freedom to do what they wish, good health, enjoying oneself – and that there are unique aspects of their lives that bring them personal joy.

But, through all this, the disabilities themselves always have to be taken into account. The reality of disabilities is that there are simply some things that are impossible or difficult to do, even if the person with disabilities would like to do them. Jonathan, who has no sight, can listen to television programmes, but cannot see the pictures even though he wishes he could; Janice, who uses a wheelchair and likes to participate in sports, is a member of three team sports but there are some sports she cannot play because of her disability. Thus, helping people with disabilities improve their quality of life is often more complicated and effortful than it is for people without disabilities.

This chapter addresses something else that complicates the improvement of quality of life for people with disabilities – namely, the views of other individuals and of society in general towards disability. These views range quite widely, but include, among other things, acceptance, pride, admiration, empathy, recognition, tolerance, sympathy, pity, shame, regret, fear and revulsion. Views about disability have changed throughout history, sometimes towards the positive and sometimes towards the negative. These changes are discussed in detail in a number of other interesting books, some of which we have listed in the bibliography.

Why is this essential to know about?

People with disabilities live with their disabilities every moment of their lives. Everything they do in life, large or small, has to accommodate these disabilities. This is something that people without disabilities only think about from time to time, if at all, because they do not live with this experience. For this reason, it is impossible for people who are not disabled to understand *fully* the experience of disability, no matter how close they are to it and no matter how much they learn about it and understand it. It is a personal experience.

Still, it is people who do not have disabilities who make most of the decisions about how societies work. If people with disabilities are to improve or maintain their quality of life, it is imperative that non-disabled people understand, to the fullest extent they can, the experience of disability. Non-disabled people need to see clearly that all the things they think, value, feel and do as societies dramatically affect what happens to people with disabilities. If society were arranged in such a way that disabilities were fully a facet of everyday human life, it would be much easier for people with disabilities to attain the quality of life they seek. Coincidentally, in most instances the changes would make life easier for people without disabilities as well.

This chapter tries to paint an overview of the development of society in relation to disability. However, we recognize that society has developed differently in different parts of the world. This account largely relates to Western society. Even here, events took place at different times and in slightly different ways in different places. It will be necessary for readers to take these differences into account to understand how a quality of life approach can interact with the environments in which they function.

How does a quality of life approach help?

As you read this chapter and other material on the history of disabilities, you will note that many practices have developed over time that help to improve quality of life. Family members, friends, professionals and other caring people have helped many people with disabilities to have better lives by carrying out these practices effectively, and often tirelessly. This has gone on for thousands of years, and continues today. Quality of life provides an approach where these and other new ideas, principles and practices can be bound together as a comprehensive method for supporting people with disabilities to have the best possible lives in today's world.

The concept of care

Care as an aspect of our human heritage

Even in very early human societies, some notion of care and support seems to have occurred. Archaeological studies of early *Homo sapiens* suggest that the earliest primitive societies took care of individuals with arthritis and broken limbs. Traumatic accidents resulting in injuries to all parts of the body, including head injuries that must have resulted in brain injury, have also been noted. The condition of skeletal remains shows that some individuals had been sufficiently impaired that they could not have survived without the help of other members of the community. At death, some of these individuals were buried with care and ritual.

We know that a wide range of disabilities has been present in all societies throughout history, and that, in some of these societies at least, individuals with disabilities survived for many years. For tens of thousands of years humans have helped some of their more vulnerable members of society. Although we do not know how extensive this practice was, the tradition of care and support to our fellow humans has been an ancient and ongoing characteristic of human life.

Care and persecution in early recorded history

Today, we are often concerned about why society supports people with disabilities a great deal, but at the very same time discriminating against them in so many ways. It may be helpful to our current thinking to know that this seeming contradiction is certainly not new. Here are a few examples from well-known cultures. The ancient Hebrews, as recorded in scripture, considered a person with a condition that we would call a disability today to be blemished and thus unfit to 'offer the bread of his God'. At the same time, though, a rich tradition of caring for those who were in need was developing. Both the Bible and the Koran speak to care of people with disabilities. The ancient Greeks believed that when a baby was born with disabilities the Gods were showing their anger, but this same culture developed pensions for soldiers who were disabled in battle. In Roman culture, people made fun of those with disabilities who were trained to entertain in homes, at social gatherings and in circuses. But the Romans also invented and used medical procedures intended to prevent or cure various disabilities.

Care and persecution before the industrial revolution

Thus there are centuries-old traditions throughout the world of care for people whom we would consider today to have disabilities. Even though the concept of disabilities as we know it today did not exist in previous centuries, other concepts that described disabling conditions did exist. In Western cultures, the tradition of care varied somewhat from era to era in response to changing religious and social values, but, in general, it was characterized by the notions of charity and obligation towards those 'less fortunate' than oneself, and an ethic of responsibility for providing for those who were less able to provide for themselves or deemed to be one's dependants.

Prior to the industrial revolution, this care was provided mostly within the homes and villages where people with disabilities lived. Those with minimal disabilities simply blended into the overall life of their villages, and were accepted to the degree that they formed a part of local life. Disability was probably not very well understood or appreciated – indeed, it was often openly ridiculed – and the provision of even adequate care required either personal affection, spiritual values or the strong influence of religious and other leaders. At times, disability was even religiously viewed as sacred, and charity towards people with disabilities was considered a highly moral act. People with disabilities have been viewed with admiration and as highly appropriate recipients of alms. In Europe, various disability groups organized themselves as guilds, sometimes even sharing their resources and helping one another. Fools, who were people with disabilities or people who acted as if they had disabilities, were often valued for their ability to provide public entertainment and candid advice to others.

But fools were also ridiculed, and sometimes they were punished mercilessly and unfairly. In other cases, children or adults with disabilities were expelled from villages, and some committed suicide. It was common practice for many people with disabilities, especially in the cities, to spend the greatest part of their lives as street beggars. In rural villages, the fate of a child or adult with disabilities sometimes depended upon the disposition of a feudal lord or other 'superior' to whom a family was accountable. People with disabilities were, at times, considered to be witches, and were burned and drowned. Still others with abnormal features were singled out and destroyed. On the whole, there were considerable numbers who were hidden away, ignored, ridiculed and persecuted. Life expectancy was much lower than it is today, and this was dramatically the case for people with disabilities. People with severe disabilities often did not survive long, many even dying as newborns or infants. Those who were least able to speak up on their own behalf, thus exercising little power, were very often the first to be treated very unjustly.

Such practices, though becoming rarer, have continued to modern times. The last witch was put to death in Scotland in the 19th century, and even now in the United States people with disabilities wait on Death Row (a matter currently being discussed by the judiciary in the United States), even though there have been major questions raised about whether or not some of them had committed any crime.

In spite of the fact that we might look at some treatment of people with disabilities in pre-industrial Europe with concern or even horror, we sometimes look back today on these times with a degree of satisfaction. This comes from the fact that in many places people with disabilities often lived simply and openly as individuals among their families and friends and experienced the full range of life activities that were available to their non-disabled peers – a goal of community integration today. Certainly, there are many practices from this period that can be adapted for use today, but there were also attitudes that need to be challenged today as well as practices and pitfalls to avoid.

The industrial revolution

With the coming of the industrial revolution, things changed quite dramatically in Europe and North America. The inquiry that had begun to become widespread amongst philosophers, scientists and others as part of a renaissance expanded to identifying and solving problems through exploration, logic and invention of specific tools. This was considered to be the way to progress, and such progress quickly became highly valued as a very good thing indeed, at least by those in positions of power. Science increasingly became regarded as the best way to identify and solve all problems, including social problems. As a result, society itself came to be viewed over time, metaphorically, as a giant machine that was made up of many component parts. In this view, society could be manipulated and improved by inventing and developing new parts of it and fitting them together. The goal was to perfect and produce an ideal and efficiently run society.

Disability was one of the parts of the giant machine called society, and was perceived as one of the less effective parts. In the minds of the social industrialist, people with disabilities needed to be separated, but could be cared for and protected in places of asylum. These could run efficiently and could provide, in their view, the best possible life for those who lived there.

With this in mind, places of care and respite were set up for those who were destitute as children and others with physical and mental illnesses and disabilities, often under the auspices of religious organizations. Farms, workshops and above all healthy air, water and food were often associated with these new institutions, as they came to be called. The intentions of those who built and operated institutions, as well as those who sent their family members with disabilities there, were often honourable for the most part, in keeping with the prevailing philosophy of the times. Many leaders in religion, medical care and education were strong proponents of the institutions, holding out great hope that they were the way of the future. This was an age of considerable hope and innovation. Indeed, many practices emerged during the 19th century that were later widely adapted to full-scale use in the 20th century.

But even if many institutions started out as the benign well-oiled machines they were envisioned to be, they rusted out in time. Little knowledge was available that was consistent with the practices of the industrial era for providing rehabilitation, and so care remained largely at the custodial level. Authorities simply did not know how to handle the many and varied situations they faced. Experiments, demonstrations and clinical opportunism occurred in an effort to find cures and treatments, but, on the whole, there was little adequate progress. There was also great confusion between what constituted mental illness and what constituted disabilities, such as cerebral palsy, epilepsy or, particularly, intellectual disability. It was not until the early 20th century that the term 'mental deficiency' even became conceptually separated from mental illness. Moreover, separated, congregate care made society less familiar with disabilities, and stereotyping was common. By the end of the 19th century, experience and communication around disability was reduced for most of the population. But the fact there were positive attempts to rehabilitate and support, as well as to use restrictive and punitive methods, is well illustrated in a book by Sloan and Stevens, entitled *A Century of Concern: A History of the American Association on Mental Deficiency 1876–1976*.

As medical advances were made, psychopharmacological solutions became more common. Use of drugs enabled some individuals to be released from institutions and locked wards and even promoted their return to communities. For other individuals, though, the opportunity for rehabilitation decreased, because drugs were used as a method of controlling their undesirable behaviour and resulted in them remaining dependent.

Probably the main factor in the ultimate lack of success of institutions was that they were seen as the solution for just too many people in the population. Indeed, in several Western countries there were those who collected children and young men and women and sent them to institutions believing they were contributing to the degeneration of society (see e.g. the video *Stolen Lives*). People with physical disabilities, intellectual disabilities and mental illness were all thought to be ideally placed in institutions, but even those who were simply poor or in debt were sometimes forcibly placed in institutions, such as poorhouses and debtors' prisons. People with serious head injury were often banished to an institution to receive care. People with various disabilities were placed together in wards that became more and more crowded and that became increasingly more poorly maintained and provisioned. The 'machine system' eventually became clogged, so that it was almost impossible for effective rehabilitation to occur and for people to be released from institutions, thus exacerbating the problem of overcrowding.

Not everyone with a disability could be placed in an institution, because there was simply not enough room. Moreover, people from the more wealthy families usually chose not to place family members with disabilities in institutions; rather they had them looked after in their own homes or, later, in private institutions. Such people, often unseen and largely silent, might be looked after but, in keeping with prevailing views, were usually a source of family embarrassment. The literature of the past two hundred years provides many examples of such situations, including those involving royal or powerful families.

People with disabilities from less wealthy homes, though, were often ignored and displaced, especially those from environments of extreme poverty and hardship that were common among the fast-growing industrial working class. Many found themselves in the crowded and dirty cities that sprang up and expanded quickly after the start of the industrial revolution. Crowded conditions, lack of adequate housing, poor nutrition, inadequate supplies of healthy water and mounting crime, which included abuse of children, became rampant. These appalling conditions were ignored by most, but numerous philanthropists of both substantial and modest means emerged to address some of the challenges. Even prior to the industrial revolution, there were philanthropists, such as Captain Thomas Coram of London, England, who developed a charity for the care of needy and orphaned children. There were many others like him in many other Western countries, and philanthropy expanded during the 19th and 20th centuries. However, this example from England is important as it demonstrates how an innovation associated with care and support of children can be linked to a later initiative consistent with these ideas. The Thomas Coram Research Unit at the University of London with which Dr Jack Tizard was closely associated was set up in the second half of the 20th century.

In time, changing views and circumstances forced governments to become involved. In the mid-19th century, for example, the British government led by Benjamin Disraeli and his Home Secretary, Henry Richard Cross, set about dealing with some of these basic necessities by, for example, installing proper sewerage and water supplies. As science developed, knowledge about the causation of disease increased and treatment of disease improved. In these ways, social problems, of which disability was one, began to be identified and addressed outside of institutions as well as inside them.

Eugenics

The theory of evolution that emerged in the middle of the 19th century gave rise to the concept of social evolution. This concept involved viewing society in an analogous way to plants and animals – as something which evolves over time and is selected because it suits a specific environment at a particular time.

Out of the concept of social evolution, the idea emerged that it should be possible to take action purposely to help society change and adapt in the best possible ways. Eugenics was the science and practice of purposely influencing the genetic makeup of a society in ways that seem to improve it. The thinking at that time was that by improving its overall genetic makeup, a society would be in a better position to make what was then regarded as progress, because it would have more able members and would have fewer members who were thought to hamper development.

In the latter part of the 19th and the early part of the 20th centuries, eugenics was popular in the United States, many countries of Europe, and other countries that they influenced, including Canada and Australia. Its primary concern was to curb over-procreation among those of the lower social classes who were thought to be less socially desirable, and to promote higher levels of procreation among those who were considered to be of more worth to future society. To accomplish this, social and medical experts warned the lower classes against the moral and physical dangers of lust, especially the practice of masturbation and sexual relations outside wedlock. Industrial, religuous, legal, academic and social leaders supported the belief in eugenics in the wide variety of ways in which they carried out their functions. Dr John Kellogg, for example, who was an American physician with an interest in nutrition and eugenics, is said to have believed that the new breakfast cereal he created in 1897, corn flakes, had a blandness that would help curb the sexual appetites of the patients in his mental hospital in Battle Creek, Michigan – people for whom such appetites would certainly have been considered undesirable.

The effects of the eugenics movement were felt strongly by all groups of people who were considered to be socially undesirable, but especially by people who were referred to as 'feebleminded'. These were individuals we would think of today as having a variety of mental and intellectual disabilities and some physical disabilities (e.g. epilepsy), those who had fallen on 'hard times' or had been born into poor or abusive families, and also many people from native or aboriginal cultures because they were different. Those who were thought of as 'feebleminded' were made particular targets of prohibition against procreation. Eugenicists believed that feeblemindedness was largely hereditary, and that if they could prevent feebleminded people from having children, they would mostly eradicate this problem from their societies. An infamous example concerned a man called Kallikak, whose offspring resulting from two sexual relationships were used by the legal, political and social establishments of the time to 'demonstrate' how undesirable it was to allow the feebleminded to reproduce. It is now acknowledged that environmental factors, not inheritance alone, played a critical role in the ability levels of his children. This is carefully summarized in the text by Clarke and Clarke (1975): *Mental Deficiency: The Changing Outlook.*

Many ways were found to put eugenics into practice. Isolation from the opposite sex, something that persists to this day in the care of people with disabilities, was widely practised for the purpose of preventing pregnancy. Sterilizations, typically without consent, were also widely practised, and persisted legally in some jurisdictions until well past the middle of the 1900s. In most developed countries, sterilization still occurs through new and less overt forms, such as through requests by family members or guardians as an expression of 'reproductive choice', or on medical recommendation for so-called health or social reasons.

The practice of eugenics escalated markedly in Nazi Germany during the period 1933–1945. Under the leadership of Adolf Hitler, it became public policy to develop a pure and able Aryan race as quickly as possible. At first, this was accomplished primarily by persecuting and removing the personal rights of those thought less socially desirable, but later, under the shadow of the Second World War, great numbers of these people were killed, including millions of Jews, hundreds of thousands of children and adults with disabilities, people who were mentally ill, gypsies, homosexuals, and people from a wide variety of ethnic groups. It is of interest to note that some surgeons and others were sent from Nazi Germany to the United States to learn, since the practices of isolation and sterilization of feebleminded people were so effectively carried out in that country. Following the Second World War, eugenics quickly faded as a social philosophy within developed countries, although we can still see remnants of its influence when we look at our current practices of care for people with disabilities. We have accented eugenics in this section, since it is an issue that is coming to the fore again today in the form of the role of genetics and genetic control. This is emerging as an important professional and ethical issue throughout the field of disabilities.

Modern views on care and disabilities

Over the past 50 years, there has been a growing interest in the scientific understanding of disabilities and in the development of supportive technology. There have also been remarkable advances in our knowledge of the causes and the characteristics of numerous disability-related conditions. We have come to understand and use more effective social, educational and psychological interventions, medical treatments, assistive devices, and many forms of accommodations. These include the removal of curbs for those in wheelchairs; simplified language in brochures for those with language and cognitive difficulties; and the use of 'tilt' buses for those in wheelchairs.

At the same time, our views of how people with disabilities fit into society have advanced substantially, strongly influenced by the human rights and self-advocacy movements. Concepts such as normalization, social role valorization, social deconstruction, community living, and inclusion have been used and adopted to help develop a widespread belief in people with disabilities participating fully in their physical and social environments and in those environments being accessible to all. The rights of people with disabilities are now being addressed, and the concept of discrimination on physical, social or educational grounds is becoming better recognized both in legislation and in legal and quasi-legal procedures.

Quality of life takes these views even farther. It integrates them by maintaining that all people with disabilities are entitled to lives of quality, and that it is the responsibility of society as a whole, and of individual members of society, to try to ensure that satisfactory quality of life is attained.

Characteristics of modern services

Many characteristics are typical of modern services, and seven of the most pertinent are discussed here. They have an important influence on how people with disabilities can enjoy good quality of life.

DIFFERENTIATION

One aspect of the considerable growth in our scientific and social knowledge of disabilities over the past 50 years is that care has differentiated. This means that as we understand more about the specific kinds of disability and their genetic and environmental causes, we can treat each one in a somewhat different way. For example, services to people with disabilities differentiated into mental health and mental deficiency. Many classifications and sub-classifications of disability were developed that were helpful to a clearer and more specific understanding. But this process also caused some problems. Some people were classified inappropriately, treated incorrectly, or were sent to the wrong settings. Others could not be classified at all and 'fell through the cracks'. This still occurs to some degree. Some erroneous notions about what causes disability have arisen, and seem comical now. For example, in the early 1960s, a British scientist, examining his retrospective research data, mistakenly thought there was evidence that Down syndrome was caused by mothers falling during pregnancy. Yet this is how science develops, with ideas being advanced, checked and re-evaluated.

Finally, there is a danger that differentiation may encourage us to see something of a 'pecking order' among the various disabilities themselves, with some considered to be the better disabilities and others to be the not-so-good ones. Despite these difficulties, which are inherent in classification, they do help us to clarify our thinking and therefore our knowledge, provided we allow for continuous questioning and revision.

INFLUENCE OF THE SOCIAL SCIENCES

Another aspect occurring over the past few decades is that those running services for people with disabilities have changed in most developed countries. Formerly, institutions and hospitals for people with disabilities were run by medical practitioners and nurses. By the middle of the 20th century, the social sciences were developing quickly, and services for people with disabilities soon saw the introduction and increase in the number of professionals from these fields, primarily psychologists, social workers and educators. Other professions also developed, such as developmental service workers, physical and occupational therapists, vocational and residential support workers, rehabilitation counsellors, speech therapists, and many others. To illustrate how comparatively recently all this has occurred, one of the present authors, Roy

Brown, did part of his internship in England with the first clinical psychologist to be appointed to the British health service.

The influence of the social sciences on disabilities has, in general, been considered to be positive, because it has supported and encouraged multi-disciplinary care of people with disabilities. In doing so, it helped to dispel the belief that disability was primarily a medical problem. Today, multi-disciplinary teams of professionals are associated with disabilities of all kinds, and the influence of family physicians, psychiatrists and other medical professionals is primarily confined to the important areas of physical care and psychiatric health care. Paradoxically, a challenge that has arisen in several Western countries in recent years is that there is a scarcity of medical and health practitioners who have special skills in mental health and disability.

DEINSTITUTIONALIZATION

Probably the greatest change that has occurred over the past 50 years, as evidence grew of the negative effects of institutions, is deinstitutionalization. This trend, which occurred in almost every developed country, saw children and adults move out of institutions and into community residences. The asylums, hospitals and other institutions fell into disrepute, as housing options for people with disabilities developed, and they began to close. The negative views associated with institutions were strengthened by a whole series of public scandals in several countries, scandals that involved sexual abuse, physical and emotional neglect, and inadequate and inappropriate housing and working conditions. Taken together, they made the case that institutional environments posed a great risk. Institutional living came to be seen as wrong, and integrated community living was considered to be ideal for all people with disabilities. A brave new world was thought to be underway with the rejection of old beliefs that no longer worked.

How has deinstitutionalization affected the way society as a whole views people with disabilities? There has been some resistance to the trend, especially at the beginning, and there has been some opposition to people with disabilities living in specific neighbourhoods. But as community living became more and more a reality, public awareness and acceptance of disability has gradually increased. Supportive public policy, such as making sidewalks, stores and public buildings accessible, has developed markedly over the past 20 years, although there are still many improvements to be made. On the whole, the non-disabled population has become fairly supportive of the idea that people with disabilities have the right to live where they choose. It is interesting to note that the many people who initially objected to having people with disabilities as neighbours often stopped thinking of them as disabled once community integration took place.

NORMALIZATION/SOCIAL ROLE VALORIZATION

The development of normalization, which later became further clarified under the term 'social role valorization', introduced the concept of 'normal' and valued lifestyles for people with disabilities. Although this first occurred in relation to individuals with intellectual disabilities, the concept is now seen to be relevant to people with a wide range of disabilities. Normalization encouraged ascribing to people with disabilities valuable, acceptable and recognized roles within community settings, especially concerning social relationships, residential accommodation and employment. The concept of normalization is an important one in setting the stage for quality of life enquiry, since it would be difficult to focus on quality of life without first accepting normalization and social role valorization as concepts and principles. As we shall see, however, quality of life principles in turn modify some of the ideas set by social role valorization, particularly in the area of perception and choice.

INCLUSION

Inclusion is a widely used concept that has come to mean different things to different people. At the very least, it refers to access to all aspects of society by people with disabilities, although it sometimes is used in the sense that society has an obligation to accept and accommodate every one of its members, including all people with disabilities. Inclusion comprises several other concepts, including acceptance, personal control, equal civil rights, access to opportunities, and equal provision of services and public supports.

Inclusion has been clearly recognized and debated within educational systems. There have been strong movements to include children in regular classes, both with and without additional supports. Today, in many school systems around the world, inclusion has resulted in the development of support personnel who assist children with disabilities in learning activities. The debate about educational inclusion still goes on, though, since some parents do not want their children included but rather wish them to receive education within a special school or class. There are also some contrary views about the need for inclusion and whether or not it suits all children with various disabilities. However, educational inclusion has been an important development and is very relevant to the concept of quality of life. It should perhaps be noted that both advocacy for and opposition to social role valorization and educational inclusion may be seen as social and political statements. Although this could also be true of quality of life, this concept is not all-or-nothing and recognizes the need to look at individual variability.

Inclusion is put into practice in various other ways as well. In vocational support, for example, it often takes the form of closing sheltered workshops and promoting community-based work instead. Sheltered workshops, which were designed to provide locations where people with disabilities could have steady work that they were able to perform, came to be seen as places encouraging segregation and letting society 'off the hook' for including people with disabilities in regular work positions. Many types of community-based vocational programmes have arisen as a result that attempt to help people with disabilities find work with employers in the community. In some countries, legislation requires that companies take a certain percentage of people with disabilities. There are many positive aspects to these programmes, including the development of personal relationships between people with and without disabilities, and the success of individuals with disabilities in the workplace. But there are some drawbacks that limit its effectiveness. Lack of peers, some experiences of poor long-term employment success, lack of understanding of disabilities in workplaces, impatience or unwillingness to accommodate the needs of people with disabilities over the long haul, and the changing interests of employers over time have been major barriers to the success of integration in the workplace. Some believe that legal enforcement requiring companies to take a percentage of people with disabilities means more people being labelled or perceived as disabled.

Similar advantages and barriers to inclusion exist in other aspects of life. During the Second World War, people with disabilities in institutions or sheltered workshops were often given work in factories and other community settings because workers were needed. Many of these people did very well, but, like women, they were less called upon when the war was over. In adult life, access to partnership and marriage, and leisure and recreation are examples of other areas of concern and dissatisfaction for many people with disabilities. Access to a normal adult lifestyle is still often restricted, partly because of the difficulties encountered in forming and maintaining social relationships. For others, though, such difficulties result from legal, procedural and social policy barriers that could be redressed. For example, some people with disabilities are provided with living environments within which there is little opportunity for supportive social relationships to emerge, yet they face financial penalties should they choose to move or to share their accommodation with a chosen partner.

TECHNOLOGY: BANE OR BLESSING?

Technology provides us with the instruments and skills to support both scientific and ideological advances. Certainly, for many people with disabilities, technology has helped a great deal – talking computers, motorized wheelchairs, accessible public transportation, 'chirping' stoplights, and many more. In an era when responsibility for the care of people with disabilities is increasingly being given to less formal supports such as those provided by family members, technological advances can and should provide considerable advantage. However, this is not always the case.

Technology has recently brought us an aeroplane that can fly pilotless from the United States to Australia. This might be seen as the development of many small children's dreams using control systems to send aeroplanes whizzing without pilots through the sky. This is a remarkable achievement, but, at the same time, there are a great many families who have children or other family members with disabilities who need more support. There are very real and still unresolved challenges for a great many families. The box below provides an illustration.

Marie is a mother of Raymond, a child with Prader-Willi syndrome. Raymond is so obese that Marie cannot lift him, let alone manage his outbursts of aggression arising from his never-ending demand for food. So severe are some of his behavioural problems that his day programme sends him home when personnel can no longer cope with them. But Marie has no choice. She has to cope at home.

So, while our society develops its technology and flies unmanned craft across the skies, and while scientists become 'sucked into computer cyberspace', there remain unmanaged basic needs and members of our society desperate for care or support. What is it, in a 'civilized' society, that makes us put so many of our resources into some things, while we ignore the plight of so many people with disabilities? Perhaps our views may be considerably more primitive than we sometimes think them to be!

THE IRRELEVANCE OF THE TERM 'DISABILITY'

Disability could be, or perhaps should be, a term that is irrelevant. There are three reasons for thinking along these lines.

First, we are beginning to recognize that the term 'disability' is losing its distinct meaning because more and more people are being considered as disabled. Indeed, the term often includes people with a wide variety of alternative learning styles, physical and emotional attributes, effects of aging, and specific ability deficits. Sometimes, it even refers to behaviour or characteristics that are easily accommodated. If, in addition, we think of disability as disadvantage and in terms of not being able to do something, we may be approaching the time when we are suggesting that most people have disabilities of one kind or another at some time in their lives.

This considerable broadening of the definition of disability is interesting to think about. Disability, in its literal meaning, refers to 'dis-ability' or the lack of ability to do certain things. Logically, we might include in the disability category all those who are unable to grasp certain concepts or to master certain skills that most able humans might be expected by the culture in which they live to grasp at a similar time in their lives. For example, a teenager or young adult who cannot grasp calculus may be said to have a disability in the same way as does a child who cannot learn to read or a child who cannot learn to walk. Almost all of us, in our own ways, have difficulty with specific life tasks, such as an inability to remember directions, being colour blind, or not being able to sing a tune accurately. Do we all have disabilities? Or do all of us simply have alternative sets of abilities and ways of doing things?

A second argument for the term 'disability' being irrelevant is that, even if we accept a narrower view of disability, our very civilization has created conditions where a great many people are rendered 'disabled' in one way or another. The concept of dyslexia, for example, is not necessary in communities where people do not depend on our invented reading symbols. Computer illiteracy, in our present age, now that a large number of people are taught to use computers, is in danger of being regarded as a disability that may result in tests, assessment and diagnosis. The number of such civilization-induced disabilities is growing rapidly, and it is not always easy to distinguish them from other, more 'intrinsic' disabilities.

Third, a perspective that is strongly held by many people today is that it is the obligation of society to include everyone with disabilities in all aspects of its functioning. If this is thought of in its ideal sense, society would, for example, provide accommodation appropriate for everyone with and without disabilities, and there would be little that any members of society could not access or in which they could not participate. Certainly, everyone faces challenges at some stage, and dealing with these challenges should be a normal process regardless of the degree of difficulty. In this sense, it is not necessary to single out some people as being disabled and others as not disabled. Thus, in the ideal world, disability would be an irrelevant term. In the meantime, disability is relevant to the extent that it explains how far we still are from achieving that ideal.

Social and historical roots of disability at-a-glance

1. Care of people with disabilities has been with us as long as civilization has been in existence.

2. Disabilities have been dealt with by various societies in complex and different ways. Care has been provided alongside punitive measures. People with disabilities have been helped and marginalized at the same time.

3. Most 'advances' have had some positive and some negative outcomes.

4. Services for people with disabilities have differed across history, according to prevailing social and religious values, but almost all have included the notions of care and protection.

5. For at least 2000 years, the major world religions that have influenced Western thought, especially Christianity, Islam and Judaism, have had doctrines of care, and have promoted respect for those with disabilities, though actual practice quite often deviated from this.

6. An understanding of the different kinds of disabilities is relatively recent.

7. The removal of people with disabilities to institutions was promoted for positive reasons, but became a poor service due to overcrowding, and many other problems.

8. Scientific and technological developments are not always consistent with care or inclusion.

9. Society's views on disability and what we think is the 'right' or 'moral' way to approach it are very much a product of the more general philosophies of the eras in which we live.

10. In today's world, the principle of inclusion – where people with disabilities are included in all aspects of life – has been successful to some degree, but there are many clear examples that indicate a less than total commitment to inclusion.

11. Society's views on disability are still not defined primarily with sufficient input from people with disabilities. Indeed, the concept of disability is segregationist and does not recognize the fact that everyone faces serious and debilitating challenges over the lifespan.

12. The increasing complexity of society creates new disabilities (e.g. computer illiteracy). This will increasingly cause challenges for individuals as society becomes more complex. We should not treat these as disabilities in the traditional sense, but we must evolve systems and practices to deal with them in proactive ways that do not damage the self-image of individuals or restrict their desires to be included in activities of choice.

Final words

The ways other people, and society as a whole, view disability has a strong influence on how people with disabilities can enjoy an effective quality of life that they find acceptable. Thus, when our purpose is to help people with disabilities improve the quality of their lives, we need to understand clearly how all of us, and our societies, think about disability. We also need to understand what laws, policies and behaviours help people with disabilities to enjoy those aspects of life they wish to. Essentially, we want to live in a society where our concerns about disability matter much less, and our concerns about individual people matter much more. We want to live in a society where we do not have to fight to have disability recognized, but rather in one where disability is recognized as part of the life we are all trying to enjoy.

For thought and discussion

1. Near the beginning of the chapter, we said others have looked upon people with disabilities with various emotions – acceptance, pride, admiration, empathy, recognition, tolerance, sympathy, pity, shame, regret, fear and revulsion. Think of each of these emotion-related words separately, and remember honestly a time in your life when you felt these ways towards others. Were any of them people with disabilities?

2. You have learned that, throughout history, people with conditions we would consider today as disabilities were both supported and discriminated against. In what ways do we both support and discriminate against people who have disabilities today? What values make us support people with disabilities? What values make us discriminate against people with disabilities? Is it possible for contradictory values to exist within the same person at the same time?

3. As much as we may not wish to admit it today, most of our ancestors – ordinary people like us – who lived in Western nations upheld, at least to some degree, the beliefs of the eugenics movement. Place yourself in the shoes of one of those people, and write some strong arguments why the eugenics point of view ought to be supported. Now, from your vantage point this year,

write some strong arguments why eugenics should not have been supported.

4.   Near the end of this chapter, we suggested the term 'disability' may be becoming irrelevant. Discuss whether this is actually the case, or whether we may be merely changing our understanding of the term 'disability'.

5.   Think of your own assets and deficits. What challenges you? To what extent are these deficits or challenges normal variations in human behaviour, and to what extent should they be regarded as disabilities? Even if you do not see yourself as disabled, would it help you if you could be supported or helped to deal with them?

Selected bibliography

Note to readers. This chapter has provided an overview of the social and historical roots of disability. This is a topic that has been explored in considerable depth by numerous scholars, however, and readers are encouraged to expand their understanding in this important area on an ongoing basis. A useful special journal issue of historical developments and attitudes relating to disability, particularly intellectual disability, is the *Journal on Developmental Disabilities*, 2001, volume 8, issue 2, Timothy Stainton and Patrick McDonaugh guest editors.

Aly, G., Chroust, P. and Pross, C. (eds) (1994) *Cleansing the Fatherland: Nazi Medicine and Racial Hygiene.* Baltimore, MD: Johns Hopkins University Press.

Barnes, C. (1991) *Disabled People in Britain and Discrimination.* London/Calgary, Canada: Hurst and Co./University of Calgary Press.

Braddock, D. (ed) (2002) *Disability at the Dawn of the 21st Century and the State of the States.* Washington, DC: American Association on Mental Retardation.

Clarke, A.M. and Clarke, A.D.B. (1975) *Mental Deficiency: The Changing Outlook.* London: Methuen.

Friedlander, H. (1994) *The Origins of Nazi Genocide: From Euthanasia to the Final Solution.* Chapel Hill, NC: University of North Carolina.

Goode, D. (ed) (1994) *A World Without Words: The Social Construction of Children Born Deaf-Blind.* Philadelphia: Temple University Press.

Goodey, C.F. (2001) 'What is developmental disability? The origin and nature of our conceptual models.' *Journal on Developmental Disabilities* 8, 2, 1–18.

Jackson, M. (2000) *The Borderland of Imbecility: Medicine, Society and the Fabrication of the Feeble Mind in the Late Victorian and Edwardian England.* Manchester, UK: Manchester University Press.

Mithen, S. (1996) *The Prehistory of the Mind.* London: Phoenix.

Neugebauer, R. (1979) 'Medieval and early modern theories of mental illness.' *Archives of General Psychiatry 36*, 477–483.

Oliver, M. (1990) *The Politics of Disablement.* London: Macmillan.

Roeher Institute (1996) *Disability, Community and Society: Exploring the Links.* Toronto: Author.

Sarason, S. and Doris, J. (1979) *Educational Handicap, Public Policy and Social History.* New York: The Free Press.

Schalock, R.L. (1998) 'Three decades of quality of life.' In M. Wehymeyer and J.D. Patton (eds) *Mental Retardation in the 21st Century.* Austin, TX: PRO-ED.

Schalock, R.L., Baker, P.C. and Croser, M.D. (eds) (2002) *Embarking on a New Century: Mental Retardation at the End of the Twentieth Century.* Washington, DC: American Association on Mental Retardation.

Scheerenberger, R.C. (1987) *A History of Mental Retardation: A Quarter Century of Promise.* Baltimore, MD: Paul H. Brookes.

Sloan, W. and Stevens, H.A. (1976) *A Century of Concern: A History of the American Association on Mental Deficiency 1876–1976.* Washington, DC: American Association on Mental Deficiency.

Stainton, T. (1994) *Autonomy and Social Policy: Rights, Mental Handicap and Social Care.* London: Avebury.

Thomson, M. (1998) *The Problem of Mental Deficiency: Eugenics, Democracy, and Social Policy in Britain c.1870–1959.* Oxford, UK: Clarendon Press.

Trent, J. (1992) *Inventing the Feeble Mind: A History of Mental Retardation in the United States.* Berkeley and Los Angeles: University of California.

Wolfensberger, W. (1976) 'The origins and nature of our institutional models.' In R. Kugel and A. Shearer (eds) *Changing Patterns in Residential Services for the Mentally Retarded.* Washington, DC: President's Committee on Mental Retardation.

Wright, D. and Digby, A. (eds) (1996) *From Idiocy to Mental Deficiency.* London: Routledge.

Selected videos and documentaries

The Sterilization of Leilani Muir. National Film Board of Canada, Ottawa, Canada. 1996.

Stolen Lives. Testimony films for Channel Four. London, UK. 1994.

Selected websites (2002)

Beyond affliction: The disability history project
http://www.npr.org/programs/disability/intr_pre.html

Disability social history project
http://www.disabilityhistory.org

CHAPTER 4

Life Gardening
Improving Quality of Everyday Life

We have learned a considerable amount about quality of life in the first three chapters – how the concept developed and what its principal ideas are. We have related some of what we know about quality of life to the individual experience of disability and to the place of disability in society. In Chapter 2, we did this in a focused way by considering the lives of four people with various kinds of disabilities and thinking about their quality of life.

Now, we will begin to look at how enjoying effective quality of life is rooted in the everyday things people do – many of them things that they already do and enjoy. The intention, in doing so, is to build an awareness of the close links between quality of life and the many things that individuals do in the course of carrying out their daily lives, ranging from the very rewarding to the challenging, that make their lives meaningful and worthwhile. For practitioners, thinking first of their own lives should prove beneficial because building awareness of the ties between quality of life and daily living will enable them to help improve their own quality of life as well as that of others. Thus, it is a good idea for practitioners to think about their own lives as they learn about quality of life and everyday experiences, and to apply its principles and ideas to themselves. In this chapter, we want practitioners to examine the quality of their own personal lives; we use the pronoun *you* throughout the chapter as a way to invite the reader to do so.

Disability is still the focus in this application, but the close links between quality of life and the experiences of everyday life are equally valid for people who have disabilities and those who do not. It bears repeating that all the concepts put forward in this book are relevant to all people, and this very fact fades whatever borders we have created to distinguish disability from non-disability. Disability just adds another dimension to quality of life that needs to be emphasized. In this chapter, then, we explore how all people with and without disabilities can use quality of life concepts to maintain and improve positive aspects of their lives, while drawing upon their own positive everyday life experiences to improve their quality of life.

Life as a garden

What is life gardening?

Living in a quality way takes many forms. There are many ways to live effectively, and to have positive life experiences. There are many things to enjoy and a great many ways to enjoy them. There are many ways to do things well, many ways to be productive, and many ways to have a constructive influence on the people and things around you.

In this chapter, we use the metaphor of life as a garden to illustrate how to select, from the many aspects of quality of life, what is best for each individual. Life as a garden provides a concrete image of something that grows for both aesthetic and practical purposes, and that has a constantly evolving life force to produce the colours, shapes and textures of your own liking and your own doing. A garden is not grown just anywhere, but rather within a context of people and places that have a strong influence on how it turns out. A garden is a place where seeds of our own choosing can be planted alongside seeds that blow in with the wind, a place where roots can be dug up and transplanted, a place where weeds sometimes grow along with the flowers, and a place that we can fertilize, water and tend. All gardens require work and activities that are not always enjoyable, even to the most avid gardener. Gardens are not all roses. But, on the whole, a garden is usually a positive, enjoyable place where we like to be, and where we cherish and long to enhance what we have grown.

How large should your garden be?

There are a great many things to enjoy in life, whether by yourself, with family and friends, at work, in your community and even in the world at large. A garden of life can be very large indeed, and can offer numerous possibilities.

All these possibilities can seem a little overwhelming at times, but a quality life should not be overwhelming. Rather, a quality life needs to have a variety of experiences that are positive, meaningful and enjoyable to the individual, and only a few negative experiences. In life gardening, your garden should be large enough to grow a variety of things you want and enjoy, but not so large that the job of tending them becomes onerous or that they become overtaken by weeds.

What do you choose for your garden?

You need to choose what to grow in your own garden. When you look around at your own life, you are able to assess what you enjoy and what you do not enjoy. You will know what things are important to you and interest you, and what things do not. These are the things you need to maintain or develop, or minimize or eliminate. There are also many lessons to be learned from other people, and careful observation and assessment of what others do can provide many ideas and options for things you can do in the future.

When thinking about what to grow in your garden, it is helpful to focus on a general rule: *Maintain and develop things that add quality to your life, and minimize or eliminate things that detract from it.* But there is a modifying aspect to this rule. Making decisions about what to cultivate in a garden often requires us to select from more than one available option. Selecting one thing over others reduces the possibility of those other things adding quality to our lives, so our choices need to be made carefully. People who have clear ideas of what they want and need and who have positive self-images typically make good choices about what to cultivate, but, even here, there are factors in everyone's life that work against choices turning out as successfully as might be hoped. Thus, even with the best decisions, compromises and adaptation to challenges are necessary to find the best balance for an effective quality of life: mostly good consequences, with only a few counterbalancing problems. (See the following box for a brief reminder of the rule.)

Searching through life gardens

A charming characteristic of human beings as individuals is that we are unique in the combination of things we want to enjoy in life. No two of us search through our own gardens – or other people's gardens – in the same way or to the same extent. Nor do we search in quite the same places for things that are

---

Remember this 2-part rule...

- Maintain and develop things that add quality to your life.
- Minimize or eliminate things that detract from quality in your life.

But – recognize that compromises and adaptations are necessary to find the best balance for an effective quality of life.

---

pleasurable and add quality to our lives. Some people always seem to be searching for new things to do and new places to enjoy, while others seem content not to search very much at all.

Marion is a woman who very actively maintains the sources of quality in her life. The 16 sources of quality, which she lists in the following box, show that almost all these sources, present and potential, are close to home – near her family, her home community and familiar surroundings. Yet, items 7 and 9 in particular suggest that she very much enjoys searching for new things in the outermost regions of her garden as well.

A challenge for practitioners that arises from this is how it is possible to support Marion in her search to learn about new and interesting things, and have a new project 'on the go' without taking her too far away from the other things that add so much quality to her life. Marion might extend her search for quality farther afield, but in doing so she might risk losing sight of some of the things close to home that are fulfilling to her. She needs to find the balance: ideally her search for novelty should take her for as much time and distance as is necessary to satisfy her needs comfortably, and only to the degree that she does not lose the important sources of quality she already has. For practitioners who are helping others improve their quality of life, it is essential to understand that all people, like Marion, should search in their gardens to a distance and for the time that is best for them individually.

When considering how extensively to provide such help, many professionals might think that promoting overall quality of life is outside what they typically do in their practice. A quality of life approach forces us to look beyond traditional professional boundaries, however, and to take a more general and holistic approach to well-being within a daily living context.

Marion's 16 sources of quality

1. Carrying out my daily activities.

2. Being close to my family and being in regular contact.

3. Having a home where my stuff is kept.

4. Having work I like to do, and getting nicely paid to do it.

5. Having the freedom to take short trips, and to choose when I want to go.

6. Talking with my friends and neighbours.

7. Learning about something completely new and different.

8. Thinking about the spirituality of humanity, picking the parts that make sense to me, and using them as a guide for my daily thinking and actions.

9. Having a new project on the go.

10. Going to the theatre.

11. Enjoying dinners in a good restaurant.

12. Watching my children and grandchildren develop their talents as they grow.

13. Having good health – not having to endure pain or any major health challenges.

14. Spending time outdoors – hiking, gardening, taking photographs.

15. Maintaining a loving relationship with those who are part of my past and present daily life.

16. Feeling needed and worthwhile.

It is also important for practitioners to understand that many individuals require encouragement to look beyond what they have been accustomed to doing. Just as life itself is changing continuously, so too the sources of quality in life change to some degree. An important component of successfully leading a quality life in an ongoing way is using one's individual ability to search for, recognize and adopt new sources of quality and to leave behind old ones that are no longer as relevant. George very much enjoyed skiing expeditions when he was a young man, but as he grew older he found his interest in skiing waning. He began instead to spend his leisure time in the colder months reading and vacationing. Occasionally, he regrets not skiing, but he recognizes that things are different now. Helping others with their life gardening entails encouraging them to develop the ongoing habit of starting to search, recognizing what to select, and easily incorporating into their lives the results of their selection.

Summary: Life gardening

Life gardening is the process of applying quality of life concepts to promote living in a quality way.

How large? Your garden should be enjoyable and fulfilling to you, but not overwhelming.

What to select? Select things that add quality; eliminate, control or minimize things that detract from quality.

How extensive a search? Long enough, far enough and frequently enough to fulfil individual needs, and to see what else there is.

Developing quality through everyday experiences

How do we apply quality of life concepts to our everyday experiences to promote living in a quality way? We do this by looking at opportunities, activities and daily routines that reflect our own values in the lives we already lead, and that add both to our enjoyment of life and our sense of self-worth. We also do this by looking at opportunities and activities that we could be doing to help us live through time in a quality way. Purposely engaging in this type of self-examination and development may not be a habit with many people, but a quality of life approach encourages us to do so. In this section, we provide three main strategies to help with this process: cherish the everyday things we value; cherish aspects of our daily life; and cherish things outside our daily routines. Within each of these three main strategies, we provide several sub-strategies. Taken together, these will help us to understand the links between quality of life and everyday experiences.

1. Cherish the everyday things you value

> My family and friends are the most important thing in my life. I care so much about them, and it makes me very happy to see them enjoying their lives and doing the things they want to do. (Ellen)

The most important part of life gardening is to enjoy and enrich those aspects of life that have developed value and meaning. These are somewhat different for each person, and it is essential to recognize them at a personal level because they determine the kinds of things that add quality to life. The best way to uncover personal values is to take sufficient time to honestly ask yourself and to ask others what they are. This is easier than might be imagined, for it is a rare person indeed who cannot identify what he or she values most in life.

(A) IDENTIFY VALUES OF EVERYDAY LIVING

Individuals often surprise themselves with their own responses, because they have seldom stopped to think seriously about this before. Moreover, practitioners who support others and help them improve their lives are often quite surprised by those others' responses. One of the authors, Ivan Brown, experienced such a surprise when he posed a question about values to Martin because he had no idea at all, based on their 'helping' relationship, what Martin valued most in life. Understanding this value was essential to helping Martin enjoy his life more.

IB: What is the one thing that is most meaningful to you in your life?

Martin: My enjoyment of the outdoors and nature.

IB: How is this meaningful to you?

Martin: I get intense pleasure from hiking, camping – in fact, any activity that takes me away from the city and 'back to nature'. I love the smell of the ground when the dew is still on it. I love the damp smell of leaves in the fall, and the beautiful colours of the trees. I love summer rains when you just have to stop what you are doing and enjoy the pitter-patter on the roof. I love looking at the contrasts of the dark blue clouds in the fall when the sun is shining brightly. I just feel really happy when I am having anything to do with nature.

Explore one of the things that is most meaningful in your life by asking yourself, a family member and a friend. Compare the three responses and ask yourself which rings the most true.

Ask yourself: What is the thing that is most meaningful to me in my life?

Ask a family member: What do you think is the thing that is most meaningful to me in my life?

Ask a friend: What do you think is the thing that is most meaningful to me in my life?

(B) LOOK FOR VALUES IN DAILY ACTIVITIES

People attempt to do what they value, and practitioners should develop the habit of observing daily activities to help identify values. They might be surprised to find that most people have arranged a considerable part of their lives – knowingly or unknowingly – in such a way that the things they value most already add quality to their lives. Martin, mentioned above, not only had done so, but also appeared to be comfortable with the decisions he had made based on a value that was important to him.

IB: How do you make sure this continues to be meaningful to you?

Martin: Every chance I get, I take time to explore nature and to let my relationship with plants, animals and the outdoors flourish. I spend quite a lot of my money on this, I know, but I can hardly think of anything better for me to spend my money on.

Practitioners need to recognize, however, that people need to develop an awareness of life factors and behaviours that frustrate quality, and to make decisions that work to reduce such frustration. Anne provided an example:

> Lately, I have started to become discouraged and irritated with the amounts of time that I have to heave myself out of my warm room and walk down to the barn to look after the horses. There is so much work to do, and the daily grind can really get me down. But then I reminded myself of why I do it. I don't do it for me, but rather for my love and passion of horses. I do it for all the fun times that are involved, not all the stresses that go along with it. If I ignore all the bad, then I am sure to see the good, and the good is the best part of anything.

Practitioners also need to recognize that some of the people whose lives they are supporting have already arranged their lives in such a way that they appear to derive quality from things based on what the practitioner considers to be negative values. Two examples are provided in the following boxes.

Fedor received assistance from a community agency because of a number of difficulties he experienced related mainly to difficulty managing money, staying sober, and keeping out of physical fights. He had been to court several times on various charges, and was on probation for the third time. The main condition of his probation was that he was not to buy alcohol or go into any establishment that served alcohol. A few days later, his support worker was walking home from work and noticed Fedor sitting in the front window of a pub drinking beer. Fedor waved and motioned for the worker to come in. The worker went in.

> Worker: Fedor! What are you doing in here? You aren't supposed to be drinking!

> Fedor: [laughing] Want a beer?

Let us assume that Fedor's enjoyment of his beer in the pub occurred because being free to enjoy a beer when he wants is something he values, and because following the conditions of his probation is something he does not value. Fedor is responsible for his own probation. The role of the worker is to help and support him. What should the worker do?

Maria had experienced several failed relationships with men and with living arrangements when she sought assistance from a community agency. At that time, she had recently met another man and moved into his apartment. Soon, he was in trouble with his boss because Maria was causing him to leave late for work, with his landlord because Maria created a number of loud outbursts and disturbances, and with his male friends because Maria was flirting openly with them and causing jealousies to emerge. In counselling, it became clear that Maria recognized her role in what were troubling consequences to her new partner and his friends, but that she very much enjoyed such a role.

If the consequences of Maria's behaviours are something she enjoys, and presumably add quality to her life, how should the counsellor respond?

(C) SELECT VALUE PRIORITIES

We value many things simultaneously, but most people can identify several things they especially value that have come to have a strong impact on the way they live. It is helpful to develop a comprehensive list over time, but for most people it is best to start by identifying the one thing that is most meaningful (as in the box on p.86), and then the five things they value most (see example below). These things should be the focus of enjoyable and enriching life experiences, because valued things are there that add the most quality to people's lives. In fact, there is a kind of 'built-in' thrust to things that are valued, because they almost demand to be the focus of enjoyable and enriching experiences, and because problems emerge if this thrust is not heeded. When selecting value priorities, practitioners need to be careful to help people identify if an aspect of life identified truly adds positive quality and is truly valued. Humans do not necessarily value or enjoy the things they spend a great deal of time doing, or the things that have become habits, rituals or obsessions. Thus, thoughtfulness, balanced insight and judgement are required when examining the things we value most.

Carine: The five things I value most	Jonathan: The five things I value most
1. My religious faith	1. Being able to look after my own life
2. My family	2. Having a supportive family
3. Good health	3. Being able to experience success
4. Ability to earn a living	4. Having nice people around me
5. Feeling safe and secure	5. Feeling on top of life

(D) RANK THE RELATIVE 'VALUE' OF YOUR VALUES

The example showing the five things most valued by Carine and Jonathan should represent only a beginning. This initial list can be expanded and amended regularly for a more complete list of values. In addition, though, some values are more important to our lives than others. For this reason, as time goes on, the items on a list of valued things should be categorized according to their degree of importance so that we can remain aware of their relative 'value'. An example is provided from Doug's life:

Very important::	My children's well-being	Having a comfortable home
Important:	My sex life	Being able to play sports with my friends
Somewhat important:	Being in good physical shape	Spending time with my partner
A little important:	Support from my family	Being able to do well in my career

(E) DEAL WITH CONFLICTING OR UNREALIZED VALUES

Some of our values underlie activities that conflict with each other. For example, most parents value pursuing a career, but they also value spending as much time as possible with their developing children. Thus, a decision around the length of time to take for maternity or paternity leave is influenced by two strongly held values that pull parents in opposite directions. Most humans are adaptable and are able to deal with such conflicts quite well, settling for solutions that are most responsible, that appear to be most important at the time, or support their most important values, while leaving some others at least temporarily unmet. This occurs when a woman who enjoys the social use of alcohol does not drink at all during her pregnancy, or when a father gives up spending money on vacations so that his daughter can attend university. Typically, then, a compromise is reached.

When a valued or important activity is set aside, it needs to be recognized that this has occurred or problems may surface after it lies dormant for many years. One woman, who valued her promising career as a teacher, set it aside after she learned her infant son had autism. This was a conscious decision on her part, because she considered the care of her son to be more important than working. However, when she reached mid-life and found herself still caring for her son, now in his 20s, she experienced bitterness and depression that she attributed primarily to the loss of the career she had given up. What is particularly important to remember is that valued things of all kinds are the things that add quality to people's lives. If compromises need to be made because of conflicting values, the loss of life experiences that would have emerged from the suppressed values may have a negative impact on quality of life.

2. Cherish aspects of your daily life

> Every weekday morning, when my alarm clock awakens me, I hit the snooze button. I roll over and think the very same thought: 'I am SO grateful to have a warm, soft bed.' This puts me in such a good mood, I am always in a cheerful mood when I get up. (Sally)

All of us have many routines that we do throughout the day that we enjoy and that add quality to our lives. There is also a great deal individuals can and should do to change how they deal with their daily routines to improve their lives. Three ideas are given below: cherish routines that give pleasure; cherish small everyday pleasures; and cherish everyday life's surprises.

(A) CHERISH ROUTINES THAT GIVE PLEASURE

A good place to start is to recognize, then cherish, the routine things that you already purposely do and that already add quality to your life. Dawn, a student, provides a good example of this: 'Every night I get into bed a half-hour early, freshly exercised and showered, and I write email messages to people. This allows me to turn off my "work brain" and turn on my "sleep brain" in a way that I enjoy and that makes me feel connected to the people I like and love.'

Henry says: 'I go fishing by myself and enjoy the scenery and wildlife.'

Sam calls up his friends Michael and Rob every Friday to see if they're having cocktail hour. He says: 'Usually they are, so I drop over. We all have a couple, tell funny stories, and sing really loud – all the while laughing a lot.'

Randy and Cynthia go out to the theatre, to a symphony, or to a movie once a week. Peggy's routine is a little more active: 'About two or three times a week, I love to go horseback riding through the trails in the late afternoon. This is especially enjoyable in the late fall or early winter when there is a thin layer of frost covering the countryside. I just let myself go with the exhilarating feeling, knowing that I do not have to think about anything serious for the rest of the day, except make myself a hot cup of tea when I get home.'

(B) CHERISH SMALL EVERYDAY PLEASURES

You can also identify sources of quality that emerge from any number of other everyday events and activities in the usual environments where you live and work. These sources of quality are there for the taking. Aaron, an avid gardener, takes great pleasure in giving the vegetables and fruits from his large garden to neighbours and relatives. For Barbara it is 'Jeff waving to me from the door as I drove off to work this morning', and for Donald it is 'the warm feeling I get from putting on my favourite old sweatshirt'. Jay is struck by the sudden rush he gets when he goes out for a walk on a warm sunny day.

Such everyday pleasures occur many times a day or come up occasionally for most of us. When all of them are recognized and cherished for the positive influence they have on our lives, they can represent a very strong source of quality for us.

(C) CHERISH EVERYDAY LIFE'S SURPRISES

Many pleasant 'little' surprises pop up constantly from our daily routines and other experiences that need to be recognized and cherished because, together, they too can comprise a significant part of positive living. Many unpleasant surprises occur as well, and all of us have to find ways to deal with these. But an important contribution of a quality of life approach to the rehabilitation process is its emphasis on encouraging things that add quality to life, and minimizing or eliminating things that detract from it (see box on p.82). One way to put this into practice is to develop a mindset that looks for and cherishes the positive effects of life's pleasant surprises.

While carrying out her life around the house, Louise loves to pick up the phone and hear 'Hi Mom!' on the other end. To others, surprises to cherish include such things as: 'having my sister join me on my daily walk when she is visiting'; 'a toddler suddenly smiling up at me'; 'looking out the window and seeing the ground covered with freshly fallen snow'; 'learning something new and challenging when I am not expecting to'; 'a long warm hug from someone when I am not expecting it'; 'having Linda come out and start helping me when I am working in the garden'; or 'coming across a wonderful documentary or movie on television'.

Some of these 'little' surprises can give unusual, and sometimes inexplicable, amounts of pleasure, and their value is very real indeed. Janet admits: 'This may sound corny, but I look out my window every night and I just love to see sunsets and rainbows. Every time I see either one, I stop and stare and feel like the world is a much better place.' William tossed some nasturtium seeds into an empty flowerpot that was sitting on his windowsill at work one afternoon, and was totally delighted to come in the next Monday morning and see six seedlings popping out of the soil. 'I can't explain why that made me so happy,' he said, 'because I am a gardener and I plant lots of seeds. It seems kind of silly, but for some reason those seedlings made me really happy for about two weeks!' Recognizing the importance of such sources of pleasure and cultivating them are critical to carrying out effective rehabilitation programmes.

3. Cherish things outside your daily routines

> Doing anything that is out of the ordinary from the everyday routine enhances my quality of life. (Selina)

All of us routinely do a number of things over and over because we enjoy them, and we continue to draw upon the people and things that have become important and meaningful to us. But no matter how much we cherish the things that occur within our daily lives, most of us like to do things that are outside our routines.

(A) EXPLORE LIFE

It is part of our human heritage, a characteristic that has advanced the human race so dramatically to date, to enjoy exploring new places, new ideas and new people. Many people explore through numerous activities that we call leisure – travel, play, humour, entertainment, and many others – and this may be essential to an enhancement of quality of life. We explore through our imagination, our own creative eyes and our dreaming. We also explore through the more 'serious' aspects of life, such as formal and informal learning, work, caring for our homes and families, discussing ideas with other people, and following, and sometimes even participating in, new events and ideas that emerge throughout the world. Such exploration is rarely the focus of traditional services and service agencies, yet promoting them in people who have lost opportunities to do so themselves is critical.

We have learned in previous chapters that things change in our lives and so do our sources of quality. Exploration allows us to try out many new things, once or a few times, and then abandon them, postpone them, or adopt them into our lives. Things that were tried and not enjoyed can be abandoned. On the other hand, things that were tried and enjoyed are sometimes incorpo-rated into our occasional or routine life activities. We also incorporate some things into our lives that are not enjoyed, since new learning is sometimes dif-ficult and even painful but we accept short-term pain for long-term gain. Things explored once or a few times, then postponed or abandoned, might have been enjoyed, however, since the quality may have arisen primarily from the novelty of the exploration. We often have very stimulating conversations that we never explore again. We travel to places that we thoroughly enjoy, but do not repeat the experience. We imagine great successes, but do not come back to them. Harold attended the opera only once in his life and thoroughly enjoyed the experience, but did not pursue it because he had several other entertainment activities that he already enjoyed with friends. His one opera experience was a source of quality that he might repeat some time in the future or never repeat.

(B) USE NEW EXPERIENCES AS A SOURCE OF NEW LIFE ROUTINES

Whether we choose to adopt experiences that result from new exploration into the routines of our lives, or to enjoy the exploration for the quality it provides and move on, is an interesting tension within the life experiences of humans. All new routine activities have emerged from exploration at some earlier point, and, as we have seen, many of these continue to contribute to our overall well-being by acting as strong sources of quality. Yet, we cannot incor-porate every possible source of quality into our daily routines. We must enjoy many temporarily, then leave them behind. For successful quality living, individuals need to find a balance among garnering quality from established routines, from new things they explore then forget, and from new things they explore and adopt for their own lives. For successful life gardening, individuals need to cherish the routine aspects of their lives that they already value and enjoy, but they also need to seek out and explore new life experiences that they can enjoy temporarily and that will prove to be valuable sources of future routines that they may choose to adopt.

Life has literally millions of enjoyable things to explore. In fact, when you stop to think about it, there are far more enjoyable things to explore in life than you could possibly do in a lifetime. Life's garden has flowers of many varieties, shapes, colours and sizes. You can pick a few for your bouquet, but you can't pick them all. Nor would you want to. You want to pick those that appeal to you particularly. You will probably select a few that you enjoy most of all and seek out the seeds to plant in your garden.

When the rains come

Some days it rains. In our lives, too, we have dull, dreary days when we are slowed down, get inconvenienced, and sometimes get drenched to the skin. This sometimes makes us grumble to ourselves and complain to others. Sometimes, we even allow ourselves the luxury of having a 'bad day'. How many times have we all heard a friend or a co-worker groaning the familiar phrase 'everything that can go wrong is going wrong today!'?

Our metaphor of life gardening suggests that every garden needs rain along with sunshine to make it grow. An interesting philosophical question that has been pondered throughout human history is whether or not our lives, too, need the occasional rain or even a whole rainy day. In simple words: Do we need to have experienced and emerged from the lows of life to truly appreciate the highs? Can we understand what it is to be happy unless we have experienced and grappled with sadness? Can we know the love, trust and loyalty of those close to us unless we have met and wrestled with dislike, distrust and disloyalty in others? Do we appreciate our good fortune if we have never encountered and overcome misfortune in ourselves and others?

For quality of life, which recognizes the importance of variation and comparison, rainy days are necessary because they help us to feel real joy when the sun comes out from behind the clouds. In addition, though, the challenges of life help us to gain a positive mastery over our lives, and to feel increased levels of self-control. They also help us to understand what in life has special meaning, what things are deeply felt, and what things provide for us the spiritual sense of transcending the usual of life.

We need to recognize in quality of life work that such things as sadness, misfortune and even catastrophe do occur throughout life. Life is full of many sad and tragic events. Even a life that is most carefully planned for effective quality can suddenly face misfortune such as illness, accident or trauma at any time. When these do occur, they can reduce or destroy our sources of quality by gradually eating away at them or by delivering one quick blow. Some are bound to happen to us personally, and others occur to people who are part of our lives. Some of us become ill or less able. All of us do grow older and eventually die. We need to understand and appreciate these difficult aspects of life if we are to understand and appreciate the human condition, but we do not purposely need to let them become overwhelming or permanent parts of our lives.

A quality of life approach, in fact, assumes that difficult and negative aspects of life occur to us all, and that, in spite of our best efforts to do otherwise, they will continue to occur. A main advantage of the approach is its help in finding ways to decrease the number and intensity of difficult and negative experiences of life to what the individual finds acceptable over the short and the long terms, and to balance those against an increase in the number and intensity of positive, quality-providing experiences. Even in the most difficult life situations, such as severe illness or death, the strategies we have learned can be used to deepen quality and add meaning to life. When Nature gets carried away with itself and seems out of control – as it occasionally does – and the gentle rains we usually cope with nicely become a storm, seeking out sources of quality can help us restore balance within our everyday lives.

The quality of life

Grace has been dead for several years now, but she remains one of my life role models. During the years I knew her, she was legally blind, had some trouble getting around physically, did not know the meaning of numbers (not even 1–2–3), could read nothing, and signed her name by copying a sample that she carried in her purse. In spite of these apparent drawbacks, she was one of the most successful people I have known at living life to her fullest potential. She simply enjoyed to the upmost her most common daily routines – shopping for food, going to the bank, getting together with a friend. She was always eager to try something new, even though she had many disabilities and was more than 80 years of age.

The thing that was so fascinating about Grace's successful quality of life was that it was not just for her. Whether you helped her out or were just a part of her circle of friends and acquaintances, you always seemed to get back as much as – or more than – you gave. She had the knack of recognizing where quality came from in her own life and sharing that with other people. In doing so, she not only treated others well and made them feel good, but also, perhaps unknowingly, provided them with a way to explore through her experiences new things that they had never experienced themselves. I'm not even sure Grace knew that she was so successful at quality living. Certainly, she was never able to say so. But she taught me an important lesson: choose your path through life's garden as you go and enjoy its fruits and blossoms, but sharing these with others enables them to explore and enjoy what you are also enjoying.

Ivan Brown

The quality of death

Most of us have little experience in how to help another person have a quality death. My sisters, my brother and I were no exception to this, yet we were fortunate to have the time and support that allowed for much quality when my Mom died. During the last few months of her ten years with Alzheimer disease, Mom's eating and walking began to slow down markedly until she had to be helped. A week before she died, she stopped eating and getting up altogether. The nursing home where Mom lived the last year of her life provided us with privacy and all the material things we needed during that last week. The nursing and medical staff were attentive to her physical needs, but did not intrude otherwise.

As Mom lay in her bed those last days, she was surrounded by photos of her family and a number of her personal belongings that had special meaning to her. She was dressed in some of her favourite clothes, and was covered by a beautiful pink and blue patchwork quilt that she herself had made. It was a few weeks before Christmas, so we played Christmas carols softly as we talked, read, and told stories of her life. We laughed and we cried. Someone slept in the room with her every night, nodding in the chair by her bed, so she would not be alone. Throughout the day, two or three of us were always there. We chatted with her about her favourite and familiar things, or about whatever we were doing or thinking at the time. She would open her eyes at times, and her expression sometimes suggested she was joining in, although she could not talk.

When the end came near, those who were present told her stories of the afterlife that were consistent with her religious beliefs, repeated familiar passages from scripture, and sang her favourite hymns. As she took her last breath, we were around her bed, holding her hand and stroking her forehead gently.

Death is not easy to accept, especially when it is one so close. But Mom's death did occur, and it is gratifying to think back and realize that all the things we did that last week had deep and personal meaning for her and for my sisters, my brother and me.

Ivan Brown

For thought and discussion

1. To what extent do disabilities deprive or prevent exploration of new sources of quality?

2. Image three disabilities and list major quality of life impacts and the minor quality of life impacts – both positive and negative. What makes them major or minor?

3. Do professionals have a role in promoting the aspects of quality of life presented in this chapter? How does your response alter your understanding of professional practice?

4. Reflect upon your own life garden. How can you use the strategies presented in this chapter to achieve the quality of life purposes presented at the end of Chapter 1, namely to:

    (a) Focus attention on what is most *important* to you?

    (b) Help you feel *satisfied* with those aspects of life that are important to you, and not unduly *dissatisfied* with life?

    (c) Look for *opportunities* in your life?

    (d) Increase personal *choice* in your life?

    (e) Improve your *self-image*?

    (f) Increase your sense of *empowerment*?

5. How do you deal with recognizing that negative experiences may be part of the process of improving quality of life? What lessons does such recognition suggest for practitioners?

CHAPTER 5

Quality of Life
A Model for Practice

In the first four chapters, we have introduced concepts central to a quality of life approach that takes a whole-life perspective. We have also provided an opportunity to consider those concepts within the lives of several people, and referred to the historical and social context of disabilities and quality of life. Now, we need to introduce a more formal model for the quality of life approach, before we begin applying it more broadly to people's individual and family lives, and to assessment, measurement and interventions.

What is an approach? What is a model?

In simple terms, an approach is the general way we go about doing something. A quality of life approach for practitioners refers to practitioners understanding and using quality of life principles and ideas as they carry out the work they do in their own practice.

A model is a more formal way of outlining the main principles and ideas of an approach. Often, models are set out as diagrams, charts or tables so that they are easy to see and understand. Two other features of models are frequently, but not always, included. First, models frequently show the relationships between its components. Most commonly, such relationships are shown by using arrows or lines that lead from one part to another. In other models, relationships are understood by the use of table headings. In yet others, the shape or structure of the model, when viewed, implies relationships. For example, readers may be familiar with Maslow's hierarchy of needs, which is in the shape of a pyramid, implying a hierarchical relationship among the items stacked on top of one another. Second, many models include an action component. Sometimes arrows or lines imply action, and at other times action words or phrases are written in to show key actions of the approach, or action that is expected to occur as an outcome. Thus, models differ in their construction, but each serves the same purpose – to draw together the main components of an approach and show them in a way that most people can understand readily. A model is, by necessity, brief and general, but it serves as the overall blueprint for how to understand and use the approach.

In this chapter, we present a quality of life model for practice. This model is a simple, overall blueprint to help practitioners understand and use a quality of life approach in their work. Later in the chapter, this model is expanded and reshaped to focus on assessment and intervention because these are central to the work practitioners do. This model does not compete with other quality of life models, rather it is a slightly different way of looking at applying quality of life to practice. In fact, this model builds upon concepts and models developed by a number of researchers from several countries, and we have referred to some of these researchers in the sections below that describe evolving definitions and concepts.

A model is conceptual in nature, and our experience is that practitioners differ in how comfortable they are reading about concepts. For this reason, we have purposely designed a straightforward visual approach, and we have made every attempt to keep our discussion of it applicable to the range of interests of most practitioners.

Quality of life concepts: From glass to prism

Before we set out the quality of life model for practitioners, it is useful to take a look at some ways that quality of life work has evolved to date. First, we will focus on the prism as a metaphor to help us understand how quality of life can help us see things in an expanded and more 'colourful' way. Second, we will consider whether or not quality of life should be defined. Finally, we will outline some of the key ideas that have emerged from early definitions and descriptions of quality of life, and some of the domains that have been suggested for looking at quality of life.

The prism as a useful metaphor

Quality of life has been viewed as a sensitizing concept that enables us to see our lives and disability in new and various ways. It is rather like passing light through a prism. When we do this, we see that white light has many component parts of many colours. We can also rotate the prism, and each time we rotate it we see different colours and patterns. We can look at life in general and disability in particular through a quality of life prism to enable us to see their many aspects and to alert us to their many challenges. In doing so, we come to see life issues and disabilities in different colours and patterns, and usually to understand them more clearly over time as a consequence. At first, our understanding may be somewhat like passing light through glass, rather than a refined prism, and we may realize that we need to develop the glass into a more effective prism.

Should quality of life be defined?

People who are new to this concept often ask: 'What is the definition of quality of life?' Tight and clear definitions can, at times, be helpful to our understanding of how a new concept fits in with other concepts and knowledge that has become familiar to us. But they are not always helpful, nor are they always advisable.

A new concept emerges and develops over a period of time, and during this developmental period we do not want to limit the ideas that may arise within it, nor do we want to embed errors within an early definition that cannot easily be rectified later on. Francis Crick (famous for his co-discovery of the molecular structure of DNA), when later considering consciousness, indicated that it was unnecessarily restricting to define the concept precisely during its early and critical stage of development, for doing so would not enable us to explore the broad nature of a process or model and to refine our understanding over time. To define quality of life precisely early on would have limited us too much to the original concept. Such a view proved to be a wise one. The concept of quality of life is still developing, and research and practice illustrate ways in which new aspects need to be accommodated.

For the same reason, in the early part of the 21st century, still a critical period of development for the concept of quality of life, we shall follow the example of Crick. The approach we take to understanding the meaning of quality of life, rather than attempting to define it conclusively, is to describe how the term is used in this book.

Key ideas from early definitions and descriptions

It might be quite helpful to look at a number of proposed definitions early in the development of the concept of quality of life to abstract the content involved. They are likely to suggest key ideas, principles and foci for the concept, and they provide at least a temporary framework within which other ideas can be explored, and to which others can be added. In many ways, early definitions function as 'working' definitions or hypotheses, as ideas to be tested by further reflection, cogitation, inspiration and practical evidence. This activity, in turn, enhances further development of key ideas, principles and foci. It is in this sense that the many early definitions of quality of life can be helpful. Some of those that are referred to in the literature on disability are included in Table 5.1. See also Cummins (1997) for a review of different forms of quality of life definitions.

Table 5.1 Early definitions and descriptions of quality of life	
Source	*Definitions and descriptions*
Bach, M. and Rioux, M. (1996)	The social well-being enjoyed by people, communities and their society.
Cummins, R. (1997)	Is both objective and subjective, involving material well-being, health, productivity, intimacy, safety, community and emotional well-being.
Felce, D. and Perry, J. (1997)	A multidimensional concept involving personal well-being. Is concerned with intimate relationships, family life, friendships, standard of living, work, neighbourhood, city or town of residence, the state of the nation, housing, education, health and self.
Goode, D. (1988)	Is experienced when a person's basic needs are met and when he or she has the opportunity to pursue and achieve goals in major life settings.

Goode, D. (1990)	When an individual, with or without disabilities, is able to meet important needs in major life settings (work, school, home, community) while also satisfying the normative expectations that others hold for him or her in those settings, he or she is more likely to experience a high quality of life.
Goode, D. (1997)	An emphasis on promoting general feelings or perceptions of well-being, opportunities to fulfil potential and feelings of positive social involvement.
MacFarlane, C., Brown, R.I. and Bayer, M. (1989)	The discrepancy between a person's unmet needs and desires. Referring to the subjective or perceived as well as objective assessment. Relates to all life domains. Recognizes interaction between individual and environment.
Parmenter, T. (1988)	Represents the degree to which an individual has met his or her needs to create their own meanings so that they can establish and sustain a viable self in the social world.
Renwick, R. and Brown, I. (1996) and Rootman et al. (1992)	The degree to which an individual enjoys the important possibilities of his or her life.
Schalock, R. (1997b)	Person's desired condition of living (primarily related to home and community living, school or work, health and wellness).
Taylor, S. (1994)	A useful sensitizing concept that focuses research on the broader life-defining issues by attempting to comprehend the perspectives of the person with a disability.

Adapted with permission from R.I. Brown (1999) 'Learning from Quality of Life Models.' In M.P. Janicki and E.F. Ansello (eds) Community Supports for Aging Adults with Lifelong Disabilities. *Baltimore, MD: Paul H. Brookes Publishing Co.*

The early definitions and descriptions of quality of life listed in Table 5.1 provide us with a number of quality of life goals, ways to reach those goals, and ideas on how quality of life functions. These include:

Quality of life goals

- achieving physical, emotional and material well-being
- being satisfied with life
- developing positive self-concepts
- enhancing personal meaning
- enhancing various areas (domains) of life
- enjoying life
- improving social and environmental conditions
- meeting needs.

Ways to reach quality of life goals

- perceiving needs
- recognizing individuals' feelings about the good things of life
- recognizing ways a person wants to live
- responding to what is important to individuals
- ensuring opportunities are available
- improving social inclusion and social involvement.

How quality of life functions

- as a sensitizing concept
- as an interaction between the individual and his or her environment
- as a complex of objective and subjective measures
- as the discrepancy between what one has and what one would like.

The ideas that have emerged, and continue to emerge, from definitions and descriptions of quality of life provide us with valuable knowledge about the most effective ways to enhance quality of life. They help to shape and reshape, over time, our ideas of aspects of life that are important to most people, the role of the physical and social environments in personal quality of life, ways to achieve improved quality of life for individuals, and how we know when that improved quality of life has been achieved.

Suggested domains for quality of life

As we have seen already, quality of life focuses on an individual's whole life, but life can have many aspects to it. Practitioners have often found that it is easier to concentrate on one or two specific aspects of a person's life at a time, rather than on his or her whole life. Although we must not ignore the holistic nature of people's lives, it is usually easier to identify objectives that people want to achieve, and to describe the ways they want to achieve them, when dealing with only the aspects of life that are considered to be most crucial.

Many researchers, too, have recognized that, although life must ultimately be considered as an interrelated whole, it is often more practical to address specific aspects, or domains, of life at any one time in isolation. Moreover, most researchers see quality of life as *multidimensional* because they consider it to comprise several domains that can be viewed separately or put together to form a whole. For these reasons, domains of life have been described that researchers and others, often after consultation with people with disabilities, consider most important to focus on for quality of life study. Table 5.2 lists the most commonly described domains from a variety of researchers, although it should be stressed that there is not a set of domains that is firmly agreed upon. It should also be stressed that, in using domains, we are assuming that these are the most important parts of most people's lives, and that when we describe or measure these parts, we consider the quality of a person's whole life to be described well enough.

SUB-DOMAINS

At times, domains that have been described as useful for quality of life have been sub-divided into more specific sub-domains. For example, material well-being may be divided into such things as income, possessions, food security, and accommodation security. Similarly, interpersonal relations may focus on such things as family, friends, acquaintances, belonging to social groups, and socio-cultural identity. The assumption, when using sub-domains, as when using domains, is that when the most important sub-domains are described or measured separately, then aggregated, the domain is described or measured reasonably effectively (for more informa-

Table 5.2 Some suggested domains of quality of life

About the individual	About what the individual does	About the environment
• Material well-being • Physical health • Psychological well-being • Spiritual well-being • Social well-being • Self-image • Self-determination	• Work • Leisure activities • Personal development • Interpersonal relations • Intimacy • Education	• Social inclusion • Rights • Safety • Societal well-being • Home life/housing • Community resources

tion, see Cummins 1997). One measurement method that is sometimes used to try to ensure that this is more accurate is to weight the sub-domains according to the person's indication of their relative importance and value to themselves.

INDICATORS

Domains and sub-domains narrow attention to specific aspects of life to be examined, but the question that remains is the degree to which quality has been attained. Indicators are one or more ways that we can address this question. Let us assume, for example, that within a *work* domain, a sub-domain *work in a community setting* has been identified. Indicators of quality of life for this sub-domain might be wages, hours of work, length of time on the job, how much the person likes the job, or co-workers' perceptions of the person as a worker. For each indicator, researchers and practitioners can directly describe the degree to which quality has been attained for a specific aspect of life. But they can also describe other information for each indicator that is highly related to quality of life, such as the importance or relevance to a person's life, how much control the person has over this aspect of life, how many opportunities for improvement are available within the person's environment, or how much initiative the person shows to take advantage of opportunities.

DOMAINS, SUB-DOMAINS, INDICATORS AND HOLISM

The domains listed in Table 5.2 and the sub-domains and indicators that emerge from them could be added to or changed, depending on aspects of life that are most important to humans at particular times in their history. They could also be organized using different words or different columns because they overlap and interconnect. Such interaction is the reason we have to think of quality of life in a holistic way. For example, the sub-domains of physical well-being are relevant to all other domains. Those under psychological well-being influence other domains, such as social well-being and work. What we do at work and how we feel about it affects our social and physical well-being. Further, our physical recreational activities are likely to influence our emotional well-being and our work habits. This holistic aspect of quality of life means that we especially need to:

- look at the individual across all areas of functioning and in all domains of life

- remember that there are many points for intervention, not just the obvious ones

- broaden what our service systems do so that the current emphasis on specific domains, such as housing and work, is expanded to other aspects of living.

A quality of life approach for practice: Its concepts

The theoretical and practical work concerning quality of life outlined above has been carried out by numerous people in several countries of the world. Much of this work has contributed to the concepts of a quality of life approach to practice, as described below.

What are concepts?

Concepts are the general ideas we form in understanding things or classes of things and processes. For example, transportation is a concept, or a general idea, about ways of moving around. Frequently, concepts contain sub-concepts, such as ideas about automobile, air or rail transportation, and are connected to feelings, such as enjoying driving a car or feeling relaxed and comfortable on a train.

Transportation is one example of a large number of concepts that we have formed from our daily life experiences. But we also form concepts to understand ideas that we create. Such concepts are known as *social constructs*, because they do not really exist independently, but only exist because we consider them to and describe them in ways we think best. For example, intelligence, normalization and inclusion are concepts that have been created by human thinking. Social constructs emerge out of our daily life experiences, frequently because they are considered to have useful application. We can usually find indications of them in our physical world, but they would not exist on their own had we not created them.

Quality of life concepts

Quality of life is a concept that is a social construct. It is a general idea that we have created because it appears to be useful for enhancing human life. Some researchers, such as Renwick and Brown (1996), have described quality of life as an overarching concept, since it contains several important sub-concepts. In this book, following the lead of some others in the quality of life literature, these important sub-concepts are referred to collectively as *quality of life concepts*.

The quality of life concepts that are most important for practice, in our description of a quality of life approach, come from the main principles and ideas of a quality of life approach, first introduced in Chapter 1. These are summarized again in Table 5.3, now with the corresponding concepts which are interrelated. It is these concepts that together comprise the term 'quality of life concepts' in the model introduced in the next section.

Table 5.3 Main principles and ideas of a quality of life approach and corresponding concepts

Main principles and ideas	Corresponding concepts (interrelated)
Guiding principle All humans are entitled to enjoy quality lives	Human entitlement to quality living
Key ideas	
1. Quality of life addresses aspects of life that all humans share	Universality of human characteristics
2. Quality of life also addresses aspects of life that are unique to individuals	Uniqueness of human needs, behaviour and performance
3. Individuals can indicate what quality means for them and how they wish to achieve it	Human ability for self-actualization
4. All parts of our lives and environments are interconnected	Holism within human life
5. Quality of life is ever-changing	Dynamic nature of human life
Application principles A quality of life approach:	
1. Focuses most on what is important to the individual	Personal meaning and value
2. Supports action that increases personal satisfaction and decreases dissatisfaction	Personal enjoyment of life and happiness
3. Stresses that opportunities to improve must be within the person's grasp	Human needs satisfied from environments
4. Insists that personal choice should be exercised, wherever possible, in selecting opportunities	Utility of personal will
5. Improves the person's self-image	Utility of positive view of self
6. Increases levels of personal empowerment	Self-generated ability to act
7. Considers life span implications.	Framing living as a long term prospect
8. Recognizes inter- and intra-individual variability.	Uniqueness of individuals

Using a quality of life approach In general, progress from 1–3: 1. Attaining the basic necessities of life	Meeting primary needs
2. Experiencing satisfaction with aspects of life that are important to the person	Personal pleasure from life
3. Achieving high levels of personal enjoyment and fulfilment	Higer order fulfilment in life
Using domains and sub-domains A quality of life approach: 1. Uses a broad range of domains and sub-domains	Common human characteristics. Can be indicated in a variety of individual ways
2. Uses domains and sub-domains that describe individual needs; they may also describe the population group or population in general	Relative importance or relevance to individuals' lives See Table 5.2 for examples

Goals (end points)

Personal needs met

Enjoyment/satisfaction

Personal meaning

Positive self-image

Social inclusion

Improved well-being

The quality of life approach: An overall conceptual model for practice

An overall conceptual model for practice, using a quality of life approach, is shown in Figure 5.1. This is a simple model that illustrates the relationships among quality of life concepts and five foundations of practice: assessment (often including measurement), intervention, policy, professional practice, and research.

Quality of life and five foundations of practice

A quality of life approach holds that quality of life concepts should overarch, and be applied to, five foundations of practice, as shown in Figure 5.1. Below, each of these five is briefly described separately, and this is followed by four features of their relationship to one another and to the quality of life concepts.

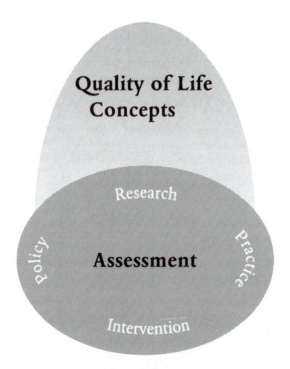

Figure 5.1 The quality of life approach: An overall conceptual model for practice

ASSESSMENT

Assessment includes the practice of listening to the perceived needs and wishes of individuals, and understanding them within the context of the environments within which individuals carry out their lives. Such assessment uses a number of sources of information, although the voice of the individual is critical, and there are a number of methods of listening to, gathering, synthesizing and interpreting information. Both formal and informal assessment methods are useful. More formal methods may include the use of one or more measures of quality of life that have been developed.

INTERVENTION

Intervention refers to action purposely taken by the individual or a practitioner to address an issue or set of issues. Typically, intervention takes place after a need has been identified and the practitioner has, with the individual concerned, appraised the need and made a commitment, carried out some initial assessment, and planned action that is both feasible and likely to produce positive outcomes. Consultation with the individual who is being assisted is seen as a central aspect of quality of life intervention, although it must be stressed that intervention without consultation may be warranted in instances where serious harm is occurring or likely to occur to the person or to others.

PROFESSIONAL PRACTICE

Professional practice is the set of functions that practitioners carry out. This includes assessment and intervention, as well as a number of other activities. Professional practice also includes the structure and rules that govern what functions are carried out and their methods of implementation. This occurs within a context of other practitioners carrying out similar work, and very often within organizational structures that both help and set limits. Professional practice evolves over time in response to changes in the knowledge upon which it is based, the experiences of practitioners, and changing social and environmental conditions. It is governed by ethical rules of behaviour.

POLICY

Policy, in the context of professional practice, means recognized plans of action or ways of doing things. Formal policy may be set out in laws or legislation, documents, or professional constitutions or by-laws. Less formal policy may be described for the rules or sets of procedures by which organizations or groups of people operate.

Research refers to creating new knowledge or extending current knowledge using sound, recognized methods. Research may create or extend theoretical knowledge from reasoning and argument, or practical knowledge from examining something in a systematic way. Knowledge that emerges from research can set the stage for professional practice and policy in a general way or it can provide ideas for specific professional activities or policies. In turn, professional practice and policy can suggest areas that require further knowledge development through research.

The five foundations of practice are related to one another, and, in a quality of life approach, reflect the quality of life concepts.

- Quality of life concepts should shape all the objectives of practice and the way practice is carried out for all five foundations of practice: assessment, intervention, professional practice, policy and research.

- A quality of life approach provides concepts and specific ideas for shaping current and emerging practice. It does not provide a completely different system for practice. Practitioners can and should apply a quality of life approach within the environments where they now work, doing the work they now do, and using the general practice methods that have been established as effective. A quality of life approach offers a method of shaping that work in ways that will further enhance quality of life for those receiving support.

- The five foundations of practice are interrelated. Each affects, and should affect, the others. Policy and professional practice should work together to set out an environment within which assessment and intervention methods that are most helpful to supporting the quality of life of individuals can be carried out. To do so, they need to respond to the assessed needs and wishes of individuals as well as to the requirements for effective intervention. Theoretical and applied research should be integrated into practice as one of its essential components in order to help policy, professional practice, assessment and intervention understand their interrelationship more clearly. In addition, all research should be influenced by the assessed needs and wishes of individuals, and their findings, in turn, should be relevant to individuals' lives.

- Although the five foundations of practice are interrelated, assessment (which may include formal assessment and measurement) of the perceived needs and wishes of individuals is a central requirement. Intervention follows and emerges from assessment. The other three foundations of practice should both

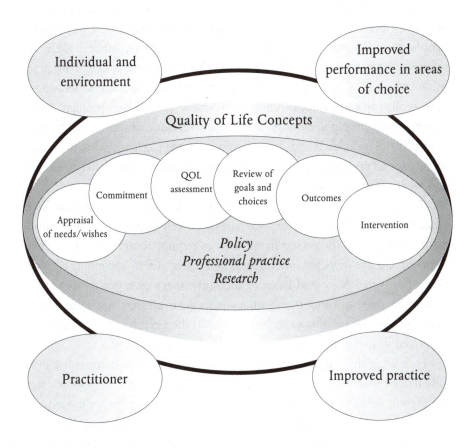

Figure 5.2 Using the quality of life model in assessment and intervention

respond to it in an ongoing way and set an environment within which it can be carried out effectively.

Assessment and intervention as the main activities of practice

As practitioners begin to take a quality of life approach to their work, they use the key ideas that are central to quality of life to shape how they carry out their work. It is important to do this for all five foundations of practice, but assessment and the intervention that follows from it are the main activities of practice for most practitioners. For this reason, the model is expanded in Figure 5.2 to show the components of assessment and intervention.

Typically, in practice, an individual comes to the attention of a practitioner with a presenting issue or set of issues through a variety of ways. Some people come to practitioners for assistance themselves, other people are referred by other professionals, while still others come into contact with practitioners because they are in an emergency or crisis situation. For some people, there is already a practitioner–client relationship when a new problem arises. Other people simply need ongoing support from one or more practitioners. However the individual and the practitioner come together, what is initially required is an appraisal of what the individual perceives his or her needs are, and what his or her wishes are.

Two aspects of the quality of life approach are particularly important here. First, the practitioner needs to understand, as well as possible, the environment within which the person lives. This can require observation of the environment and the ways the individual functions within it. Second, the practitioner needs to ask for and listen to the individual's own perspective of the presenting issue, and understand what wishes are expressed. Any intervention that is put in place will have to be relevant to the person's environment and expressed wishes if the outcomes are to lead to optimum effect.

Following the initial appraisal, the practitioner and sometimes the individual need to decide whether or not they will move forward. In some cases, the presenting issue is such that the practitioner is not the best or most qualified person to help, and in other cases it is outside the mandate of the practitioner's organization and thus deemed not appropriate to address. It may also be that the practitioner is not willing to proceed unless the context can be changed. For example, Leila came to her community support worker with a request to help her move, because she was experiencing problems with other people who lived in her boarding home. The problem for the worker was that she had helped Leila move three times previously for the same reason, and was working on an intervention to support Leila in getting along better with others. She decided to make it clear to Leila that she was willing to help her move, but first wanted to set Leila the challenge of learning how to get along better with her neighbours. Individuals, too, may decide not to proceed after a discussion with a professional. They may decide that too much effort is required to change the presenting issue, or that the activity they originally had in mind would not be a good choice after all.

If there is a commitment by both the practitioner and the individual to proceed, an assessment based on a quality of life approach should follow (described in detail in Chapter 6). An assessment almost always leads to some revisiting of the goals and choices that were established when the practitioner and the individual made a commitment to proceed. The reason for this is that the assessment usually provides some new information that sheds a somewhat different light on what was originally intended. Saeed, for example, who has night blindness, sought a volunteer who could support him in going out at night two evenings a week. During the assessment, it became clear that this would be too onerous on Saeed since he had a demanding job during the week, and he decided that once a week would fit his lifestyle and energy level better. In other circumstances, Saeed might have chosen to seek a volunteer two or even three evenings a week.

Intervention, described more fully in Chapter 7, should begin with setting clear goals and methods of achieving those goals. It should proceed, as far as possible, following the wishes, choices and perspective of the individual, working at every opportunity to empower the individual and support increased self-image. Outcomes of the intervention should be carefully evaluated, to determine how effective they are in improving the individual's performance in the area that he or she wishes to improve. If an intervention has been successful, its resulting improved performance should lead to improved quality of life for the individual within the environment where he or she lives. A second important outcome of intervention is that it should improve practice. A successful intervention for one person provides goals and strategies for other people with whom similar interventions can be undertaken. For example, Sonya experienced numerous successes with a ten-week programme that helped people with obsessive compulsive disorder to be able to leave their homes and attend work. Her method became a best practice within her organization precisely because of its record of success. This improved practice was beneficial for her as a practitioner, but also to her colleagues who benefited from her successful method.

Blending quality of life concepts into assessment and intervention

Practitioners who carry out assessments and plan subsequent interventions using a quality of life approach need to blend quality of life concepts into all their work. To help practitioners begin to do this, some ideas that were presented earlier in Table 5.3 are combined with the six oval steps of assessment and intervention of Figure 5.2 and some areas of focus of later chapters. This combination is presented in the box overleaf. Details from later chapters, as well as practitioners' own thoughts and experiences over time, can be added to make it more applicable to specific work environments.

Practitioners need first to look at the presenting issue in terms of the person and the environment within which he or she lives and consider, both for the individual and the environment, which aspects are unique to the person and which aspects are shared with other people. For example, a person who wishes to express herself in music shares a life goal with people from all cultures across time, while a person who wishes to learn to play a very specific instrument, such as the bagpipes, is expressing an idea that is unique to only a few. This quick process will help the practitioner understand the category of the presenting issue.

Next, the practitioner needs to ascertain priorities. Priority usually needs to be first on basic necessities, second on satisfaction with aspects of life that are important to the person, and third on high levels of fulfilment and meaning in life. With this knowledge – which sometimes can be attained very quickly – the practitioner can make a commitment to go forward to further assessment.

How to carry out an assessment is a crucial question, and one that needs to respond to the presenting situation. For example, a simple interview may be sufficient for a person who seeks some support finding physical mobility devices, but a comprehensive assessment may be helpful for a person who is having difficulty coping with life in general, cannot express wishes clearly, and appears to have several presenting issues. The degree to which objective or formal indicators and personal perceptions are explored is a clinical

Blending quality of life concepts into assessment and intervention

Look at the person and environment
- Person's own life experiences
- Personal domains common to most people
- Environmental, social and historical conditions in which the person lives
- Environmental domains common to most people

Set priorities for action
- First: Basic necessities
- Second: Satisfaction with what is important
- Third: Achieving high levels of fulfilment and meaning in life

Carry out initial appraisal
- Determine needs
- Determine wishes
- Determine if short/long-term and immediate/distant

Determine how to assess
- Objective indicators
- Personal perceptions
- Importance and value to the person
- Personal goals

Consider two key aspects
- Holism/domains
- Changing nature of life over time

Focus on what to assess and apply
- What is valued, relevant, important
- Perceptions of satisfaction
- Opportunities for improvement
- Personal choice
- Self-image
- Empowerment

Consider other practice factors
- Effect on families and close others
- Professional considerations
- Ethical issues
- Policy and management issues

Look to goals (end points)
- Improved well-being
- Enjoyment/atisfaction
- Personal meaning
- Positive self-image
- Social inclusion

decision of considerable importance. Usually, several sources of assessment information are helpful, but all should be interpreted in terms of how important and relevant they are to the person's life and the stated goals of the person. The principles and ideas in Table 5.3 provide a framework for deciding what to focus on in assessment and for formulating plans for intervention. In doing so, however, it is essential to consider the effects, or potential effects, of these on the person, his or her family and other people, as well as the relationship between them and standards of professional practice, ethical standards, and policy and management. Finally, it is important in carrying out assessment and planning intervention to think forward to consider their possible impact on improved well-being, enjoyment of life activities that are important, satisfaction with life in general and specific aspects of life, personal meaning of life, improved self-image, and increased opportunities for social inclusion. Achieving these goals is the very purpose of undertaking a quality of life approach in practice.

A few last words

This chapter has introduced a simple model for using a quality of life approach in practice. This model has been expanded for assessment and intervention, because these functions are central to the work of most practitioners.

In subsequent chapters, numerous ideas are presented that should help practitioners to consider and use specific aspects of this model: assessment and measurement, intervention with individuals, intervention within a family context, and professional practice, including policy, ethical and management issues. As explained in the preface, the fifth foundation of professional practice that was described for the model, research, is not a focus of the present book, although the importance of its relationship to the other aspects of the model should not be underestimated.

For thought and discussion

1. Formulate arguments for and against the following proposition and summarize your conclusions: 'Conceptual models have little to do with the work practitioners do on an everyday basis.'

2. In this chapter, we have taken the position that a definition of quality of life should not be given at this time, since the concept is still emerging.

    (a) For each of three other concepts that were also mentioned in this chapter – transportation, holism and social inclusion – consider whether or not a definition should be given, and, if so, whether or not it might change over time.

    (b) Next, revisit the question of defining quality of life. Provide reasons for and against defining it at the present time.

3. Make a quick list of all the different aspects of your life and the different environments where you live and work.

    (a) To what extent is your overall quality of life influenced by your quality of life in each of these areas separately?

    (b) What preconceptions does this analysis give you for thinking about holism and the use of domains?

4. How central is assessment to the work you do as a practitioner? How much emphasis does your work structure place on assessment?

Selected bibliography

Bach, M. and Rioux, M.H. (1996) 'Social well-being: A framework for quality of life research.' In R. Renwick, I. Brown and M. Nagler (eds) *Quality of Life in Health Promotion and Rehabilitation: Conceptual Approaches, Issues, and Applications.* Thousand Oaks, CA: Sage.

Brown, R.I. (1999) 'Learning from quality of life models.' In M.P. Janicki and E.F. Ansello (eds) *Community Supports for Aging Adults with Lifelong Disabilities.* Baltimore, MD: Paul H. Brookes.

Brown, R.I., Bayer, M.B. and MacFarlane, C. (1989) *Rehabilitation Programmes: Performance and Quality of Life of Adults with Developmental Handicaps.* Toronto: Lugus.

Brown, R.I., Brown P.M. and Bayer, M.B. (1994) 'A quality of life model: New challenges arising from a six year study.' In D. Goode (ed) *Quality of Life for Persons with Disabilities: International Perspectives and Issues.* Cambridge, MA: Brookline Books.

Cragg, R. and Look, R. (1992) *Compass: A Multi-perspective Evaluation of Quality of Life.* Birmingham, UK: Cragg.

Cummins, R. (1997) 'Assessing quality of life.' In R.I. Brown (ed) *Quality of Life for People with Disabilities: Models, Research and Practice, 2nd edition.* Cheltenham, UK: Stanley Thornes.

Cummins, R.A. (2000) 'Objective and subjective quality of life: An interactive model.' *Social Indicators Research 52,* 55–72.

Dossa, P.A. (1989) 'Quality of life: Individualism or holism? A critical review of the literature.' *International Journal of Rehabilitation Research 12,* 2, 121–136.

Felce, D. and Perry, J. (1997) 'Quality of life: The scope of the term and its breadth of measurement.' In R.I. Brown (ed) *Quality of Life for People with Disabilities: Models, Research and Practice, 2nd edition.* Cheltenham, UK: Stanley Thornes.

Goode, D.A. (1988) *Quality of Life for Persons with Disabilities: A Review and Synthesis of the Literature.* Balhalla, NY: Mental Retardation Institute.

Goode, D.A. (1990) 'Thinking about and discussing quality of life.' In R.L. Schalock (ed) *Quality of Life: Perspectives and Issues.* Washington, DC: American Association on Mental Retardation.

Goode, D.A. (1997) 'Assessing the quality of life of adults with profound disabilities.' In R.I. Brown (ed) *Quality of Life for People with Disabilities: Models, Research and Practice, 2nd edition.* Cheltenham, UK: Stanley Thornes.

Heal, L.W. and Chadsey-Rusch, J. (1985) 'The Lifestyle Satisfaction Scale (LSS): Assessing Individuals' Satisfaction with Residence, Community Setting and Associated Services.' *Applied Research in Mental Retardation 6,* 475–490.

James, O. (1997) *Britain's on the Couch: Why We're Unhappier Compared with 1950 Despite Being Richer: A Treatment for the Low Serotonin Society.* London: Century.

MacFarlane, C., Brown, R.I. and Bayer, M.B. (1989) 'Rehabilitation programmes study: Quality of life.' In R.I. Brown, M.B. Bayer and C. MacFarlane (eds) *Rehabilitation Programmes: Performance and Quality of Life of Adults with Developmental Handicaps.* Toronto: Lugus.

Parmenter, T.R. (1988) 'An analysis of the dimensions of quality of life for people with physical disabilities.' In R.I. Brown (ed) *Quality of Life for Handicapped People.* Beckenham, UK: Croom Helm.

Parmenter, T.R. (1994) 'Quality of life as a concept and a measurable entity.' In D.R. Romney, R.I. Brown and P.M. Fry (eds) *Improving the Quality of Life: Recommendations for People With and Without Disabilities.* Dordrecht, The Netherlands: Kluwer Academic.

Parmenter, T.R. (2001) 'Intellectual disabilities – Quo vadis?' In G.L. Albrecht, K.D. Seelman and M. Bury (eds) *Handbook of Disability Studies. Thousand Oaks, CA: Sage.*

Renwick, R. and Brown, I. (1996) 'The Centre for Health Promotions conceptual approach to quality of life: Being, Belonging, and Becoming.' In R. Renwick, I. Brown and M. Nagler (eds) *Quality of Life in Health Promotion and Rehabilitation: Conceptual Approaches, Issues, and Applications.* Thousand Oaks, CA: Sage.

Rootman, I., Raphael, D., Shewchuk, D., Renwick, R., Friefeld, S., Garber, M., Talbot, Y. and Woodhill, D. (1992) *Development of an Approach and Instrument Package to Measure Quality of Life of Persons with Developmental Disabilities.* Toronto: Centre for Health Promotion, University of Toronto.

Schalock, R.L. (1997a) 'Can the concept of quality of life make a difference?' In R.L. Schalock (ed) *Quality of Life, volume 2: Application to Persons with Disabilities.* Washington, DC: American Association on Mental Retardation.

Schalock, R.L. (1997b) 'The concept of quality of life in the 21st century disability programmes.' In R.I. Brown (ed) *Quality of Life for People with Disabilities: Models, Research and Practice, 2nd edition.* Cheltenham, UK: Stanley Thornes.

Schalock, R.L. and Verdugo, M.A. (2002) *Handbook on Quality of Life for Human Service Practitioners.* Washington, DC: American Association on Mental Retardation.

Schalock, R.L., Brown, I., Brown, R.I., Cummins, R., Felce, D., Matikka, L., Keith, K. and Parmenter, T. (2000) *Quality of Life: Its Conceptualization, Measurement and Application: A Consensus Document.* Document for the WHO-IASSID Work Plan. The Special Interest Research Group on Quality of Life. The International Association for the Scientific Study of Intellectual Disabilities. Available online at www.iassid.org

Schumaker, J.F., Shea, J.D., Monfries, M.M. and Groth-Marnat, G. (1993) 'Loneliness and life satisfaction in Japan and Australia.' *Journal of Psychology 127,* 65–71.

Taylor, S.J. (1994) 'In support of research of quality of life, but against QOL.' In D. Goode (ed) *Quality of Life for Persons with Disabilities: International Perspectives and Issues.* Cambridge, MA: Brookline Books.

World Health Organization (1999) *International Classification of Functioning and Disability (ICIDH-2).* Geneva: Author.

CHAPTER 6

Assessment and Measurement of Quality of Life

We have learned a great deal about what quality of life is and how it is a useful concept in the lives of people. For professionals, a quality of life approach needs to go beyond this – it needs to be useful to the work they do. We began to see in Chapter 5 how quality of life concepts could be used in assessment and intervention. We turn our attention here to a more detailed look at assessment using a quality of life approach, and, within assessment, the place of measuring quality of life. The application of assessment to intervention is addressed in more detail in Chapter 7.

What are assessment and measurement?

Assessment using a quality of life approach in professional practice with people with disabilities is the process of:

1. looking at a situation that has come to our attention for a particular reason

2. gathering as much information as is feasible about the situation

3. analysing what aspects of the situation are working well (sources of quality), and what aspects are not working well (needs)

4. understanding the factors that help improve well-being, and the factors that hinder its development.

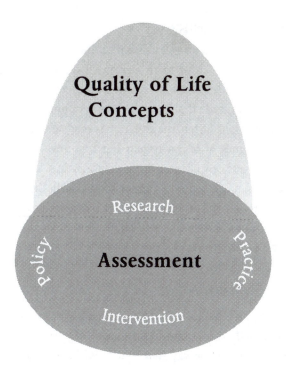

Figure 6.1 The quality of life approach: Assessment

Each of these four assessment steps is important, but the second, gathering information, is crucial to understanding how best to proceed using a quality of life approach. For this reason, it is the main focus of this chapter.

Information may be gathered in many ways, but it is usually much better to do so in a systematic way. *Measurement* is the term used to describe gathering information in a systematic way. There are many types of measurement. In everyday living, for example, we measure volume of ingredients when we bake a cake, we measure our financial success by tracking our assets in such places as bank accounts and real estate, and we measure the effect of our words and actions on others by noting within a mental framework how they respond. Each type of measurement has its own characteristics that are tied to the purposes for which it is intended. When baking a cake, for example, we need to measure the ingredients using measuring cups and measuring spoons to ensure that we are inserting the correct proportions so that it will taste good. No matter what type of measurement we use and for what purpose, the common feature is that it provides a structure, or system, within which information can be gathered and recorded.

Step 1: Looking at a situation

Practitioners who work in areas related to disabilities become aware of situations that require assessment for many reasons. Typically, though, there is a particular reason, and this reason is usually a problem or challenge that has reached sufficient magnitude that it requires some support, intervention, new direction or practical help. Often, the situation is acute and requires immediate attention; at other times, it is not urgent but requires attention to allow a person's life to progress or to keep it from deteriorating. When beginning to look at the situation, it is essential to understand clearly the reason for doing so and the degree to which it is urgent. It is also essential to understand how the person feels about the situation, and about how he or she will participate in assessing and reacting to it.

Step 2: Gathering information

Gathering information about a situation that has come to our attention for a particular reason is the most important aspect of assessment. Information should be gathered in such a way that it has two main characteristics:

- It is *authentic*. The information is correct, and reflects the reality of the situation. It is reliable, that is it can be verified at another time and by another person.

- It is *unbiased*. The information describes the situation from the perspective of those most closely involved in the situation.

Information is gathered in many ways. We talk with people to learn facts about situations, the feelings they have about those situations, and their opinions on what factors contribute to them. We observe the environment and the behaviours of people. We listen to stories, events and responses from others. We note how things change over time, and how people react to those changes. Three main ways of gathering information using a quality of life approach are described below: adding quality of life ideas to traditional methods of information gathering, assessing the quality of life of individuals directly, and measuring quality of life systematically.

Adding quality of life to traditional assessment methods

Practitioners are familiar with gathering information because it is an integral part of their training and professional practice. Some common methods of gathering information used by practitioners that have stood the test of time include:

- interviewing or talking with the person

- interviewing or talking with other people who know the person well

- listening to the person interact with others

- observing the person's behaviour alone or with others

- observing the person's environment

- asking the person or another person to respond to surveys or questionnaires

- asking the person or another person to respond to standardized instruments

- reading reports completed by such people as other professionals or family members

- consulting sources kept for the purpose of recording information in an ongoing way, such as journals, charts, weekly summaries, file notes and databases.

- carrying out formal assessment procedures, such as administering standardized tests.

Practitioners with experience are already familiar with gathering information using these methods. Students and newly trained practitioners will have begun the process of gradually building skills to use them effectively. Gathering information using a quality of life approach makes use of these same procedures, but incorporates additional ideas. When using each of the methods listed above, practitioners should evaluate their own work in an ongoing way by asking themselves how well they are incorporating these eight key ideas:

General ideas:

- *Holism*: Look at the person's whole life and environment, rather than simply the presenting issue.

- *Life stage appropriateness*: Consider the life stage of the person, and explore the person's own recognition and perception of that life stage.

Person-specific ideas:

- *Person-centredness*: Look at the situation from the person's point of view and consider what is of value and importance to the person.

- *Emotional perception*: Take careful note of the feelings of the person, particularly their level of satisfaction and dissatisfaction with the situation.

- *Perception of availability of options*: Understand the degree to which the person sees that there are options available for action, and that these are realistic and accessible.

- *Personal decision making*: Weigh the degree to which the person will probably find decision making in the situation empowering, and the degree to which decision making might be stressful or otherwise challenging.

- *Self-enhancement*: Consider carefully how the person's self-image needs to be, and can be, enhanced.

- *Empowerment*: Understand how the person needs to be, and can be, empowered through action taken in response to the presenting situation.

Assessing quality of life directly

A second way to gather information using a quality of life approach is to assess quality of life directly for an individual. Here, it is assumed that it is important to address the quality of life of the person in a holistic way, not necessarily just the presenting problem, because the various aspects of life are interconnected. The presenting problem may be related to other issues that have not come to the practitioner's attention; on the other hand, it may be supported by a number of positive sources of quality already present in the person's life. An assessment that looks at the quality of life of the whole person can uncover these, and can suggest some relationships among various aspects of the person's life that might be very helpful (see the following box for an example).

Quality of life – an example of assessment

Joan came to her community living worker when she found that she was pregnant. Because she had a number of cognitive disabilities, she felt unsure of her ability to have the baby and care for it without assistance from others. A quality of life assessment uncovered other more troubling aspects of her situation: her husband was physically abusive, and she was about to lose her job due to staffing cutbacks. But the assessment also revealed several sources of quality in Joan's life: she had several supportive friends in her apartment building, her parents visited regularly and helped her in practical ways, she had a plan for moving away from her abusive husband, she welcomed help from other professionals to learn about her pregnancy, she had spiritual beliefs that supported her life, and she was strongly motivated to make the best of things. In spite of some quite serious presenting problems, Joan's sources of quality were such that she and her community living worker were able to prepare a useful plan to correct them.

CONCEPTUAL FRAMEWORKS

A quality of life assessment uses a specific conceptual framework. A number of these have been developed in recent years. One such method was developed and used by the Centre for Health Promotion at the University of Toronto by one of the authors, Ivan Brown, and his colleagues, and is presented here as an illustration of how it and other methods work (see Brown, Raphael and Renwick 1997).

Three main domains of life:

1. Being – who the person is

2. Belonging – the people and places in the person's life

3. Becoming – things the person does through life

Nine sub-domains of life:

1. Physical being – body and health

2. Psychological being – thoughts and feelings

3. Spiritual being – beliefs and values

4. Physical belonging – the places where the person lives and works

5. Social belonging – the people in the person's life

6. Community belonging – the resources in the person's environment

7. Practical becoming – the practical things done in daily living

8. Leisure becoming – the things done for fun and enjoyment

9. Growth becoming – the things done to cope and develop

Six questionnaire items for each sub-domain (54 questionnaire items in total):
Example: Physical being

1. My appearance – how I look

2. My exercising and being fit

3. My hygiene caring for myself

4. My nutrition and the food I eat

5. My physical health

6. My sex life

For each item, four key questions:

1. How important is this to the person (or how relevant is it to his or her life)?

2. How satisfied is the person with this aspect of life?

3. Are there opportunities for the person in this aspect of life?

4. Does the person make the decision wished for in this aspect of life?

This quality of life assessment framework provides a way to collect a great deal of information about a person's life. It may be collected over a period of time or all at once. In either case, it should be reviewed regularly and altered through an ongoing and continuous assessment process to ensure that it accurately reflects the changing circumstances of the person's life. Remember, quality of life is ever-changing, and quality of life assessment needs to adapt to its changing nature.

ATTEMPTING TO EVALUATE INTERESTS, ACTIVITIES AND NEEDS

Brown and Bayer (1992) developed a quality of life questionnaire for their Rehabilitation Programmes Study into quality of life. This turned out to be qualitatively very informative, and is now used by a variety of practitioners in different countries. It is easy to administer in a casual and relaxed environment and provides a wealth of information concerning the issues relevant to quality of life. The interview protocol is a guide with both ratings and comment sections covering 11 major life domains, including home, employment, leisure and recreation. The content covers the kind as well as the quantity of activity. Although reliability is dealt with – repeated interviews were carried out on more than two hundred people – there is no attempt to provide data comparing information with other individuals. Rather, it is considered that quality of life is an issue for the person. The same questionnaire can be given to parents or other primary caregivers so that direct comparisons can be made to highlight differences in perception.

Measuring quality of life

Measurement, gathering information in a systematic way, has been an area of quality of life work that has been strongly emphasized over the past several years. There are several excellent examples of quality of life measurement available for use.

Before we describe some of the measurement methods and measurement tools that have been developed, it is important to understand two aspects of measurement: objective and subjective measurement, and quantitative and qualitative data. These two aspects, described below, will help you judge what type of measurement is most appropriate to a particular situation.

OBJECTIVE AND SUBJECTIVE MEASUREMENT

Objective measurement is a term used to describe measurement that has a 'truth' or external validity to it because it can be done the same way by different people at different times. The distance between two city centres using kilometres, for example, does not change no matter who is measuring it or when they measure it. Objective measurement makes use of a wide variety of types of measuring scales for such things as weight, height, population size, voting results, blood pressure, number of people who use wheelchairs, and literally thousands of other things in the broad spectrum of our lives and work. Objective measurement is also useful to verify whether or not a person understands the 'truth' of something; again, because all people viewing the same situation should be able to respond to the question the same way. For example, one questionnaire asks: 'Is it snowing outside?' It is expected here that people who do not have problems with reality or with severe perceptual impairments would say yes or no in response to what they could see or feel.

Subjective measurement, on the other hand, records a different kind of 'truth' or information. It is a term used to describe ways of recording people's perceptions of things, their thoughts, their feelings, their attitudes, and their values. Subjective measurement records information that is centred in the expressed thoughts and feelings of the person, but can be reliably collected using standardized methods by different people and often on different occasions. Many attributes of humans and human life change can be measured subjectively, and these are attributes we need to measure. For example, Johann felt cheerful when he left for work in the morning, whistling on his way to catch the bus. But by mid-morning, he was knee-deep in a crisis at work that made him feel extremely anxious. Subjective measures of his emotional well-being at 8:00am and at 10:30am would have produced very different results indeed. Thus, there is not necessarily an expectation that subjective information should remain the same over time. The 'truth' lies in how authentic the expression of thoughts and feelings is.

Subjective measurement may use scales (e.g. ratings on a scale of 1 to 10) or any other systematic way of recording information (e.g. daily journal entries or weekly files notes), but it may not be appropriate as evidence for some types of questions such as programme evaluation (see Cummins 2002 for a fuller discussion).

Is objective always objective? Is subjective always subjective?

Measurement that we think of as objective always has some degree of subjectivity to it. The very fact that one thing is chosen to be measured and not something else brings an initial subjectivity. The methods selected for measuring, analysing and reporting represent other types of subjectivity. Objective measurement sometimes has more direct subjective elements as well. For example, the rainbow is commonly understood, from an objective point of view, to consist of seven basic colours: red, orange, yellow, green, blue, indigo and violet. Yet, some people are colour blind to various degrees and do not see all of these colours, or see them in different ways from the majority of people. Such people naturally describe the rainbow differently, from the subjective point of view of their own vision. Another possible subjective aspect of this is that we do not have evidence that even the majority of people see colours in exactly the same ways. Thus, the rainbow might be seen in literally thousands of different variations.

Likewise, measurement that we think of as subjective can sometimes be thought of as objective. For example, two researchers who hear the same opinion or expression of feeling from someone can record it in the same way. Some questionnaires are validated in this way and also can have considerable reliability, two attributes of objective measurement.

Objective and subjective information working together

In practice, we very often use objective and subject information together. Marika told her mother at home that she had a high temperature and felt feverish. Her mother took her temperature with a thermometer, and found an above-normal reading. She concluded that Marika's subjective information was correct because it was verified by the objective measurement of the thermometer.

Andre was in the hospital, and the nurse routinely took a temperature reading. One morning she found an above-normal reading, and wondered if the thermometer was accurate. She felt Andre's forehead and asked him if he felt warm or had aches anywhere. When he replied that he felt hot and his legs ached a little, she concluded that the thermometer's objective reading was correct because it had been verified by subjective information.

Just to make sure, both Marika's mother and the nurse took a second thermometer reading a little later and asked Marika and Andre how they felt again. They knew that for information to be reliable it must be accurate and repeatable.

Whose subjective information should you record?

Jane, who lived in a nursing home, was being assessed on a quality of life scale by a student, and told her 'I am frightened at night'. She also stated that she had concerns for her safety. The student researcher recorded this subjective feeling. On hearing this, a passing nurse replied: 'No you are not, Jane. You are perfectly safe here because the doors are locked.' The student erased Jane's remark and recorded the one by the nurse because it appeared to the student that the nurse was correct – the home was perfectly safe.

In class at a later time, another student thought Jane's comment should have been left, and a third student thought both comments should have been recorded.

The students debated these questions: 1. What is the 'true' subjective information in this case? (a) Jane was frightened, or (b) Jane was not frightened – she was perfectly safe. 2. Can (a) be accepted as 'true' subjective information even if it is inconsistent with the objective reality observed by the student? 3. If both (a) and (b) are credible as subjective information, can they be 'true' if they contradict one another?

PERCEPTUAL MEASURES

As early as 1974, Andrews, who was one of the first sociologists in the United States to focus on this issue, regarded people's perceptions as the driving force of their actions. This view is now generally accepted, and for quality of life it becomes essential that we measure individual perceptions. Perceptual measures can be reliable, valid, and certainly repeatable. However, they may not reflect an external reality. Perceptions are of a different order than external reality, and we are not testing whether or not they are accurate in terms of external reality, but rather we are taking them as measures of individuals' thinking and feelings. The experience of many researchers is that such perceptions can be extremely reliable. But changes in perception may frequently occur, and are not necessarily a reflection of unreliability but of changes in mood and thinking. People's perceptions are critical to an understanding of their quality of life. In the example of Jane, above, her perceptions of safety are likely to influence her behaviour, rather than the objective means of ensuring safety alluded to by the nurse.

Examples of discrepancies in perception from person to person abound. Tricia is a teenager with mild intellectual disability and hearing loss. Her mother requested that she sit in on a quality of life assessment, believing that her daughter would not understand and that she (the mother) would be able to express Tricia's wishes. By the end of the interview, however, the mother was in tears. She had heard all sorts of things of which she had never previously been aware: Tricia would like to walk the family dog with her sister in the evenings; Tricia is upset at school during lunch times as no one will sit with her. This new knowledge of Tricia's perceptions had a great impact on the mother's own perceptions. It is tempting to think we know children's needs and wishes, especially those of our own children, but reality checking can produce changes in perception that are to everyone's benefit.

In spite of this, when measuring quality of life a question that sometimes emerges, especially for people who do not communicate well, is whether or not we should accept another person's perceptions of an individual. One practice is to ask one or two other people for their perceptions of the person's life, as an alternative way of collecting information. Those others are called *proxies* because they speak, to the best of their ability, for individuals who cannot speak clearly for themselves. Practitioners need to recognize that information from proxy measures may well be very useful, but it is not the same thing as information from individuals themselves. Both are perceptual information, but it is different information because it is from a different person's perception. For this reason, proxy measures should always be identified as such, and never assumed to be the perceptions of the person.

QUANTITATIVE AND QUALITATIVE DATA

Quantitative data is information that records the 'how much' of things using scales that we have developed. Often, it is used in objective measurement. For example: 'What mark did you receive on your exam?' 'How fast did the sprinter run?' 'What percentage of people in a population have cerebral palsy?' 'What is the probability that it will rain tomorrow?' But quantitative data are also used in subjective measurement. For example: 'How do you like your job?' (responses on a 5-point scale, with 1 meaning 'not at all' and 5 meaning 'a great deal') 'I think the Prime Minister is doing a good job' (responses: strongly agree, agree, neither agree nor disagree, disagree, strongly disagree). Numbers, most useful for objective measurement, and ordinal categories, most useful for subjective measurement, can be generated to provide quantitative data for these and countless questions like them.

Qualitative data also record the 'how much' of things, but in a very different way. Assessment based on qualitative data tries to get at the true nature of a person, a situation or a thing by describing its qualities, its characteristics, its context and aspects of its environment. Qualitative data are also interested in the 'how' of things, such as relationships between people, how working conditions affect job satisfaction, how religious rites are meaningful to a specific cultural group, or the ways people with psychiatric difficulties adjust to community living. In contrast to the quantitative approach, which reduces something that may be quite complex and tries to record it as clear and comprehensible data, the qualitative approach tries to describe the details of a situation by deliberately probing into its richness and trying to document its complexity. Such assessment measures in terms of ideas and concepts, rather than numbers. The systematic collection of qualitative data has a credibility because it is authentic and thorough. Its truth lies in the breadth and depth of the description.

QUALITATIVE MEASUREMENT METHODS

Qualitative methods of research have become increasingly accepted in recent years. However, these have been applied to quality of life assessment and measurement only in a limited way. One excellent example of qualitative measurement used to investigate quality of life was carried out by David Goode (1994a), who explored in great depth the life experiences of a child who was both deaf and blind. Goode used a variety of qualitative methods over a considerable period of time to garner as much complete information as he could. Another study, focusing on family quality of life, was completed by Renwick, Brown and Raphael (1997). These researchers interviewed 38 sets of parents of children with disabilities for two hours each. Although this study yielded a great deal of information, it missed the perspectives of other family members and other people, the interactions of the family members with one another

Table 6.1 Examples of quality of life measurement instruments

Instrument	Description
Comprehensive Quality of Life Scale (Cummins 1993)	Measures both objective and subjective areas over seven domains using satisfaction and importance.
Lifestyle Satisfaction Scale (Heal and Chadsey-Rusch 1985)	Measures satisfaction of the individual in relation to life space, friends and community opportunity.
Quality of Life Interview (Lehman 1988)	Assesses the quality of life of people who are chronically mentally ill.
Resident Lifestyle Inventory (Bellamy et al. 1990)	Relates to people with severe intellectual disability and is only completed by a carer.
The Resident Satisfaction Inventory (Burnett 1989)	Has the advantage that it can be completed on a self-report basis.
Rehabilitation Questionnaire: A Personal Guide to the Individual's Quality of Life (Brown and Bayer 1992)	Assesses client and, separately, family responses to 11 categories including 'home living', 'things you do', 'family and friends' and 'self-image'. Uses trained interviewers.
Quality of Life Questionnaire (Schalock and Keith 1993)	Uses a 3-point rating scale in the areas of environmental control, social integration and community integration.
The Quality of Life Instrument Package for Adults with Developmental Disabilities (Brown, Raphael and Renwick 1998)	This assessment method is for adults with intellectual disabilities. It involves input from client, family and professional carer within the context of 'being, belonging and becoming'.
Quality of Life Interview Schedule (QUOLIS) (Oullette-Kuntz et al. 1994)	Covers dimensions such as support, access, participation and contentment; 12 domains, e.g. health, housing and safety, case management. Assessment by trained interviewers.
Quality of Life Profile: Adult Version (Brown, Raphael and Renwick 1997)	A quality of life questionnaire for general populations. Versions of this have also been developed for seniors and adolescents. Nine sub-domains covering perceived importance of each item to the individual's personal satisfaction and individual control.

Source: Adapted with permission from R.I. Brown (2000) 'Learning from Quality of Life Models.' In M.P. Janicki and E.F. Ansello (eds) Community Supports for Aging Adults with Lifelong Disabilities. Baltimore, MD: Paul H. Brookes Publishing Co.

and with other people, and the observations and experiences of the researchers over time.

These two examples illustrate one of the problems for qualitative measurement: When is it enough? Essentially, it is never enough until the person's entire life is understood fully. But since this is never possible, a compromise has to be reached between getting as much information as possible and what is realistic to achieve.

QUANTITATIVE MEASUREMENT INSTRUMENTS

There are now many quantitative quality of life measurement instruments (see Table 6.1 and Cummins 1997). Some of these also incorporate ways to collect qualitative data. They are abundant in the field of intellectual disability, there are some in the field of mental health, and a number in the area of physical disabilities such as multiple sclerosis. There are some instruments, but very few, in the field of aging and disability, and these tend to be oriented towards professionals rather than older persons. There are some questionnaires for older children but virtually none for young children with or without disabilities. Very little has been developed in the areas of inclusion and education.

Some of these tools stem from a conceptual framework, such as the one described in Chapter 5 for the Centre for Health Promotion, by asking respondents to judge each item addressed using a rating scale that is provided. The Centre for Health Promotion, for example, asks respondents to rate each of 54 items on a 5-point scale for both *importance* and *satisfaction*. Some item responses result in objective measurement and others result in subjective measurement. Tools developed by other researchers use different items and slightly different rating scales, but they all employ the same general method.

This method is widely used because it is fairly easy to administer and interpret. In addition, it is widely recognized that quantitative quality of life tools tap into a great many aspects of life that are important to most people. Researchers have debated for some time, though, whether such procedures can realistically be applied to anything as complex as quality of life. The fear is that quality of life differs so much from one individual to another, and is so complex, that measuring it in this way simply loses much of what is truly important to the quality of people's lives. There is valid logic in this argument, as readers of this book will realize from previous chapters; thus use of all quantitative measurement tools, especially for assessing individuals, should be supplemented by other sources of assessment information. Quantitative measurement tools are often used on their own for research purposes, but in credible research reports the limitations of the tools and methods are explained by the authors.

CRITERIA FOR CHOOSING THE BEST MEASUREMENT INSTRUMENT

When selecting the most appropriate quality of life instrument, it is best to choose one that fits best with the purpose of using it. (The reader should refer to Cummins 1997 for a thorough discussion of this.)

- *For individual assessment*: The instrument should provide information about lifestyle, personal well-being and the living environment that relate to the problem situation. However, the instrument should also provide additional information about a broad spectrum of the person's life.

- *For programme evaluation*: The information may be broader in scope and less focused on specific problems.

- *For research with groups of people*: In addition to considering the content, the researchers may want to choose an instrument that has been validated and for which there are normative data.

A set of criteria for good quality of life measurement instruments was developed for the World Health Organization by an international group of researchers who formed the Special Interest ResearchGroup of the International Association for the Scientific Study of Intellectual Disabilities (Schalock *et al.* 2000, quoted with permission; also see Schalock *et al.* 2002). These criteria are very useful for evaluating instruments when selecting one for use. The criteria are based on five core principles:

1. Quality of life measures the degree to which people have meaningful life experiences that they value.

2. Quality of life measurement enables people to move towards a meaningful life they enjoy and value.

3. Quality of life measures the degree to which life's domains contribute to a full and interconnected life.

4. Quality of life measurement is undertaken within the context of environments that are important to them: where they live, work and play.

5. Quality of life measurement for individuals is based upon both common human experiences and unique individual life experiences.

For each of the five core principles, the reader will find a number of consensus guidelines for measuring quality of life.

Principle 1: Quality of life measures the degree to which people have meaningful life experiences that they value.

- The measurement framework is based on well-established theory of broad life concepts.

- The theoretical framework is comprehensive and multi-disciplinary.

- It is recognized that the meaning of life experiences that are positively valued varies across time and among cultures.

- The measurement framework provides a clear way to demonstrate the positive values of life.

- Assessment methods provide categories or terminology that describe how life is valued.

- Measurement describes quality of life clearly, using terminology that illustrates the degree to which life experiences are positively valued.

- Quantitative measurement of quality of life represents placement on a continuum between the 'best' and the 'worst'.

- Measurement uses clear categories that have an ordinal relationship, or terminology that can be clearly related to a best – worst continuum.

- Measurement scales show life at its 'best' at one end of the scale and its 'worst' at the other end.

Principle 2: Quality of life measurement enables people to move towards a meaningful life they enjoy and value.

- Measurement focuses on key aspects of life that can be improved, such as:
  - the degree to which basic needs are met
  - the degree of material and social attainment
  - choices and opportunities available and acted upon
  - the degree to which environments enable people to improve
- Measurement is carried out for a clear, practical purpose that supports people moving towards better lives.
  - It sets out a clear purpose related to improved policy, service, or individual support.
  - It helps identify unmet needs, and suggests ways to remediate those unmet needs.
  - It helps determine those aspects of a person's life that are of very good quality for him or her so that quality can continue to be supported, fostered and maintained for these aspects of life.
  - It is used as baseline and outcome data in evaluation of service delivery or interventions with a view to enhancing the quality of people's lives.
  - It may differ according to the purpose for which it is being carried out (e.g. education, service, housing, employment).
- Measurement is described within a framework that is potentially positive, neutral and negative – suggesting that it is possible to move towards the very positive.
- Measurement scales clearly show positive, neutral and negative ratings/scores.
- Measurement methods describe categories or use terminology that are positive, neutral and negative.
- Measurement is interpreted within the context of an overall lifespan approach.

○ It is interpreted within the age range of those being measured.

○ It is interpreted with a view to supporting people in moving smoothly from one life stage to another.

Principle 3: Quality of life measures the degree to which life's domains contribute to a full and interconnected life.

- Measurement uses a broad range of life domains, which are widely accepted as key indicators of the fullness and interconnectedness of life.

  ○ Domains are validated by a consensus of a wide range of people.

  ○ Domains are relevant for all people being measured.

  ○ Domains encompass a substantial but discrete portion of the quality of life construct.

  ○ The main domains are the same for people with and without disabilities. Some domains (e.g. services to people with disabilities) vary according to the special needs of the group (e.g. people with behaviour or emotional problems).

- Quantitative measurement uses key indicators of the fullness and interconnectedness of life within specific domains.

  ○ There is consensual validation that key indicators adequately reflect the life domain.

  ○ Key indicators may vary for people at various stages of life.

  ○ Key indicators may vary for people within specific cultural environments.

  ○ Key indicators may vary for people with special needs.

- Qualitative measurement procedures explore and describe a range of aspects within each domain.

Principle 4: Quality of life measurement is undertaken within the context of environments that are important to them: where they live, work and play.

- Proxy measurement (measurement by another person for an individual with intellectual disabilities) is not valid as an indication of a person's own perception of his or her life.

- ○ Measuring quality of life from the perspective of people who are not able to speak for themselves should use methods such as observation and participant observation that are most applicable to such people.

- ○ Measurement of one person's quality of life from another person's perspective might be useful in some instances, such as where people are not able to speak for themselves and others make life decisions on their behalf, but such measurement should be clearly identified as another person's perspective.

- Measurement takes an ecological approach, viewing the individual in interaction with his or her living environments. Interpretation is carried out within the context of the individual's environment.

Principle 5: Quality of life measurement for individuals is based upon both common human experiences and unique individual life experiences.

- Measurement uses both objective and subjective (perceptual) measurement.

  - ○ Measurement uses either qualitative or quantitative methods or both.

  - ○ Objective measurement uses quantitative instrumentation that reports frequencies and quantities of observable indicators. Subjective (perceptual) measurement uses degrees of expressed satisfaction with aspects of life or other kinds of subjective evaluations or descriptions about people's lives.

  - ○ Subjective measurement has both cognitive and affective components.

- Measurement allows for weighting of domains and key indicators, according to individual or group significance or value. Where it is not possible to do this, interpretation of quality of life measures needs to be made in light of significance or value to the individual.

- Measurement allows for weighting to reflect individual or group cultural life experiences.

- In most cases, domain scores and descriptions are more useful and expressive than the total scores or descriptions that are aggregated from separate domain data.

Step 3: Analysing quality of life sources and needs

After gathering together information about the person and the situation, the practitioner needs to analyse it by thinking carefully about how the information helps us to make the best possible decisions on how to proceed. In general, this involves:

- *Understanding what needs to be done.* Typically, an individual and a practitioner have come together because a particular problem or set of problems needs to be addressed. Although these presenting problems should not be overlooked, the practitioner should also think of the person's life and the situation in holistic ways. There are often aspects of life related to the presenting problem that can add quality, or that need to be resolved because they are working against quality.

- *Understanding the best place to start.* Through discussion, the person will often guide the practitioner to the best place to start. In some cases, however, it may be necessary to start somewhere else, such as cases where there is harm or a danger of harm, where an ethical decision suggests starting elsewhere, or where preliminary steps need to be taken.

- *Understanding the person's point of view.* Understanding the person's point of view is critical to being able to take effective action. In general, resources used need to be directed towards activities that improve the situation from the person's point of view. There are exceptions, however, such as activities that are illegal, unethical or harmful. In these cases, the practitioner should not proceed, yet it is essential to any action that is undertaken that the practitioner fully understands the person's point of view and, where possible, that this is recognized by the person involved.

- *Understanding points of view of other people.* Such views are often helpful in gaining consensus for the best course of action. In addition, other people's views may affect the outcomes of activities, and thus need to be understood and taken into account.

- *Understanding the legal, policy, ethical and management frameworks.* These matters are dealt with in Chapters 10 and 11. For the present, it is important to understand that the work of practitioners needs to be in keeping with the laws of their jurisdictions and the standards associated with their organizations, and professional or other working groups.

Step 4: Understanding causal factors

A final step in assessment is to understand the factors that help improve well-being, and those that hinder its development. These factors emerge from the variety of sources of information, and use various assessment and measurement methods. It is essential to understand them because they may facilitate moving towards a solution or they may act as barriers. They may be:

- factors that are common to all people, or most people
- factors that are specific to the individual.

Final note: Human capacity for satisfaction

One characteristic of human beings that affects quality-of-life-based assessment and measurement is that we have a great capacity for making the best of situations and, at the same time, never being quite satisfied with situations. This characteristic is recorded in numerous studies of satisfaction of life. The problem with measuring life satisfaction is that people may simply be making the best of a bad situation and have found ways to compensate.

> Rob, a man with a mild intellectual disability, said he liked being in prison because the food was good and there were lots of people to talk to. Because he had previously lived in his own small apartment and had few friends, the food and opportunities for socializing probably did look good to him. In fact, it appeared that they looked so good that he overlooked the obvious, that he was locked inside a prison and had almost no control over his own life.

For quality of life assessment, this means that, although satisfaction with various aspects of life or life on the whole may be said to be good, other important aspects of quality of life – choice, self-image, empowerment and others – may not be assessed as highly. All the quality of life concepts need to be taken into account during an assessment and weighed carefully when thinking about how a person's life on the whole needs to be, and can be, improved.

For thought and discussion

1. How can assessing and measuring quality of life affect the ways in which enjoyment of life can be enhanced?

2. Think of someone you know who has difficulty expressing his or her own point of view. To what extent can another person speak reliably for that person (i.e. act as a proxy), and how could you develop an assessment approach that would access the individual's feelings and perceptions?

3. On your own, or in a group, select a specific problem associated with one person. First, use a variety of traditional methods you already know to assess the problem, then add a quality of life approach to those methods. Second, assess the problem using a quality of life conceptualization. What are the advantages of each method?

4. What are the best uses of quality of life measurement?

Selected bibliography

Andrews, F.M. (1974) 'Social Indicators of Perceived Life Quality.' *Social Indicators Research 1*, 279–299.

Bellamy, G.T., Newton, J.S., Lebaron, N.M. and Horner, R.H. (1990) 'Quality of life and lifestyle outcomes. A challenge for residential programs.' In R.L. Schalock (ed) *Quality of Life: Perspectives and Issues*. Washington, DC: American Association on Mental Retardation.

Brown, I., Raphael, D. and Renwick, R. (1997) *Quality of Life Profile: Adult Version*. Toronto: Centre for Health Promotion, University of Toronto (www.utoronto. ca/qol/profile/adultVersion.html).

Brown, I., Raphael, D. and Renwick, R. (1998) *Quality of Life Instrument Package for Adults with Developmental Disibilities*. Full Version. Toronto: Centre for Health Promotion, University of Toronto (www.utoronto.ca/qol). (Also see versions for children, adolescents and seniors.)

Brown, R.I. (2000) 'Learning from quality of life models.' In M.P. Janicki and E.F. Ansello (eds) *Community Supports for Aging Adults with Lifelong Disabilities*. Baltimore, MD: Paul H. Brookes.

Brown, R.I. and Bayer, M.B. (1992) *The Rehabilitation Questionnaire: A Personal Guide to the Individual's Quality of Life*. Toronto: Captus Press.

Burnett, P.C. (1989) 'Assessing satisfaction in people with an intellectual disability living in community based residential facilities.' *Australian Disabilities Review 1*, 14–19.

Cummins, R. (1993) *The Comprehensive Quality of Life Scale – Intellectual Disability, 4th edition (ComQol-ID4)*. Melbourne, Australia: School of Psychology, Deakin University.

Cummins, R. (1997) 'Assessing quality of life.' In R.I. Brown (ed) *Quality of Life for People with Disabilities: Models, Research and Practice*. Cheltenham, UK: Stanley Thornes.

Cummins, R.A. (2002) 'The validity and utility of subjective quality of life: A reply to Hatton and Ager.' *Journal of Applied Research in Intellectual Disabilities 15*, 261–268.

Goode, D. (1994a) *A World Without Words: The Social Construction of Children Born Deaf-Blind*. Philadelphia: Temple University Press.

Goode, D. (1994b) *Quality of Life for Persons with Disabilities: International Perspectives and Issues*. Cambridge, MA: Brookline Books.

Goode, D. (1997) Assessing the quality of life of adults with profound disabilities. In R.I. Brown (ed) *Quality of Life for People with Disabilities: Models, Research and Practice*. Cheltenham, UK: Stanley Thornes.

Hatton, C. and Ager, A. (2002) 'Quality of life measurement and people with intellectual disabilities.' *Journal of Applied Research in Intellectual Disabilities 15*, 254–260.

Heal, L.W. and Chadsey-Rusch, J. (1985) 'The Lifestyle Satisfaction Scale (LSS): Assessing individuals satisfaction with residence, community setting, and associated services.' *Applied Research in Mental Retardation 6*, 475–490.

Keith, K.D. (1996) 'Measuring quality of life across cultures: Issues and challenges.' In R.L. Schalock (ed) *Quality of Life volume 1: Conceptualization and Measurement*. Washington, DC: American Association on Mental Retardation.

Landesman, S. (1986) 'Quality of life and personal life satisfaction: Definition and measurement issues.' *Mental Retardation 24*, 141–143.

Lehman, A.F. (1988) 'A quality of life interview for the chronically mentally ill.' *Evaluation and Program Planning 6*, 143–151.

Ouellette-Kuntz, H., McCreary, B.D., Minnes, P. and Stanton, B. (1994) 'Evaluating quality of life: The development of the Quality of Life Interview Schedule (QUOLIS).' *Journal on Developmental Disabilities 3*, 2, 17–31.

Renwick, R., Brown, I. and Raphael, D. (1994) 'Quality of life: Linking a conceptual approach to service provision.' *Journal on Developmental Disabilities 3*, 2, 32–44.

Renwick, R., Brown, I. And Raphael, D. (1997) *The Family Quality of Life Project: Final Report.* Report to the Ontario Ministry of Community and Social Services. Toronto: Centre for Health Promotion, University of Toronto.

Schalock, R. and Keith, K. (1993) *Quality of Life Questionnaire.* Worthington, OH: IDS Publishing Corporation.

Schalock, R.L., Brown, I., Brown, R.I., Cummins, R., Felce, D., Matikka, L., Keith. K. and Parmenter, T. (2000) *Quality of Life: Its Conceptualization, Measurement and Application: A Consensus Document.* Document for the WHO-IASSID Work Plan. The Special Interest Research Group on Quality of life. The International Association for the Scientific Study of Intellectual Disabilities. Available online at www.iassid.org.

Schalock, R.L., Brown, I., Brown, R., Cummins, R.A., Felce, D., Matikka, L., Keith, K.D., and Parmenter, T. (2002) 'Conceptualization, Measurement, and Application of Quality of Life for Persons with Intellectual Disabilities: Report of an International Panel of Experts.' *Mental Retardation 40*, 6, 457–570.

Intervention Based on Quality of Life

Placing quality of life within intervention

In Chapter 6, we began to apply the quality of life approach more directly to practice by addressing assessment and measurement. We now move to the next step after assessment and measurement, applying its outcomes to interventions.

One of the challenges for developing and improving effective interventions in the field of rehabilitation generally is the process of moving from one set of outmoded practices to newer constructs, but retaining those aspects that have ongoing value. If we move ahead without doing this, there will be loss of concepts and knowledge that are critical to effective rehabilitation. Also, it takes time and energy to develop new sets of practices, and it is important not to spend some of this time energy in 're-inventing the wheel' or parts of the wheel.

Examples of sets of ideas and practices that have been at least partially left behind include:

- *Institutionalization.* This was once very popular but is now disgraced and substantially reduced around the world. This has left many parents and organizations facing challenges over support and appropriate intervention options.

- *Intelligence testing.* Such testing has found disfavour in many eyes, yet it had many advantages, such as providing evidence for cognitive changes over the first 30 years of life amongst individuals who came from adverse environments and were initially seen as intellectually disabled. (It is of interest that some of this work from the 1950s and 60s has been edited and republished by Ann and Alan Clarke, 2003.)

- *Social skills training.* Here, assessment packages and programmes were developed, but today they are much less used, despite requirements for successful social adaptation amongst a variety of persons with disabilities.

These and other sets of practices have been supplanted by normalization, social deconstruction, educational inclusion, and others, which are in themselves critically important. Yet, these too will pass. They will be restructured, and parts of all of them are likely to find a place in the network of services at some time in the future. The development, loss and subsequent restructuring of such ideas over time is amply exemplified by the book *A Century of Concern: A History of the American Association on Mental Deficiency 1876–1976* by Sloan and Stevens (1976).

What does quality of life bring to all this? Quality of life is an overarching concept, and as we have learned in this book, it comprises several sub-concepts and ideas. These are useful to follow when applying any set of practices. In fact, quality of life concepts and ideas can be used to advantage in the application of other sets of practices, because they are based on holistic and humanistic values that are relevant across time. Quality of life as an overarching concept ties together other sets of practices by threading through them a view that the purpose of all intervention is to attempt to maximize quality within people's lives.

In this chapter, we provide steps that practitioners can take when applying quality of life concepts and ideas to intervention: four person-centred action steps and three professional-centred steps. These steps are applicable to most of the broad array of interventions that are practised in fields related to disabilities. Readers are encouraged, therefore, to examine interventions commonly used in their practice, and undertake to understand how a quality of life perspective can be more effectively implemented within those interventions.

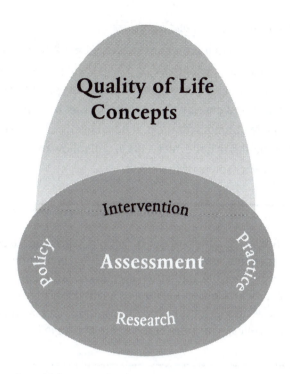

Figure 7.1 The quality of life approach: Intervention

In explaining the steps for applying quality of life concepts and ideas to intervention, we have included examples of situations drawn from a wide range of life experiences. The vignettes are descriptions of actual experiences of various people; although the reader may find some of them surprising, they represent for the most part reasonably common occurrences that we have recorded from several countries.

The success of any intervention that is carried out within an educational or service organization depends, at least to some extent, on the policies and management procedures that practitioners are advised to follow. Implementing a quality of life approach within interventions that were set up in a policy and management context that did not consider quality of life can present challenges. The issues associated with policy and management and implementing a quality of life approach to interventions are numerous and are dealt with in Chapter 11.

What is intervention based on quality of life?

Intervention is a term that is used in a variety of fields to describe a deliberate set of actions taken for the purpose of trying to help another person improve his or her life. It implies expertise, on the part of the practitioner or rehabilitation team, to find and develop the appropriate mix of concepts and intervention ideas that are optimum for the individual involved. Intervention based on quality of life implies that the intervention will follow the principles and ideas laid out in earlier chapters of this book.

> Intervention is an action or set of actions taken purposely to try to improve specified aspects of a person's life. Interventions are sometimes referred to as rehabilitation, special education, therapy, counselling or treatment. Concepts central to quality of life are natural parts of many interventions, but interventions based on a quality of life approach explicitly include these as core concepts.

Intervention based on quality of life also looks to improve people's lives to a greater degree, and sometimes more quickly, than is otherwise possible. In recent years, some practitioners and researchers have explored ways of doing this in a number of specific areas related to disability. Work of this nature has been carried out fairly extensively for people with intellectual and other developmental disabilities, but formal interventions involving a quality of life approach have also been described for people with head injuries, mental health problems, autism, physical and sensory disabilities, people living with HIV, older people, as well as other challenges. A sample of authors who have done such work can be found in the bibliography (see Brown, Bayer and Brown 1992; Janicki and Ansello 2000; Keith and Schalock 2000; Mercier 1994; Ory and Cox 1994; Renwick, Brown and Nagler 1996). Quality of life has been introduced as a useful concept for interventions within schools, a variety of healthcare and health promotion settings, vocational programmes, the fine arts, and leisure and recreational programmes. The reader should look at Brown and Brown (1999), Fidler and Velde (1999) and Warren (1997) for examples. Applications have been developed and are being recorded by a range of professionals, including frontline rehabilitation personnel, psychologists, rehabilitation counsellors, educators, physicians, nurses, and numerous allied health professionals such as nursing home and hospital personnel, occupational therapists and physiotherapists.

Four person-centred action steps

Intervention based on quality of life incorporates the values and principles that we have learned about to this point in the book. To help apply these best, we provide four person-centred action steps, which build on one another, and should be followed in planning and carrying out effective interventions. Real-life examples illustrate how the action steps can be implemented and what limits need to be placed upon them. In a subsequent section, we present three additional professional-centred action steps.

The four person-centred action steps are:

1. Begin from the place the person perceives as most important.

2. Follow the person's choices on how to proceed.

3. Encourage and support empowerment through self-management.

4. Shape interventions in such a way that they work to improve the person's self-image.

John: Beginning from the place the person perceives as most important

John worked on the railroad and was involved in a major accident on the track resulting in the loss of both legs. He spent considerable time in hospital, but there came a time when he could walk reasonably well on his artificial limbs. Hospital personnel then suggested that the time had come for him to consider new employment, which would have to be sedentary. John became very angry at this suggestion for he did not wish to consider work at all. He said that his life had changed dramatically during his time in hospital. He no longer possessed lower limbs, and his wife had left him and taken their two small children with her. He stated that he felt shattered and needed to get his emotional life in order before he could consider work.

To the healthcare staff, it seemed obvious that a change in job type was the priority. John's perception was quite different. He needed to address other issues and was not yet prepared to think about trying to improve his life through new employment options.

The quality of life approach tells us that it is important to begin where John himself perceives the beginning point to be. In this case, his emotional and personal life needed to be sorted out first. He may or may not have known how to do this, and this order of things might not seem to others the most appropriate way to resolve his problems. But that is not the point. John perceived major challenges in his emotional life that stemmed from personal mishap and family changes, and this is where intervention should begin.

Professionals who are helping people like John to start from his or her perceived point of beginning do three main things:

- *Solve practical physical problems.* Professionals in a helping relationship may need to deal as quickly as they can with some practical aspects of John's life, such as where he will live and how he will get the support he needs to lead an independent life. These kinds of things are pressing needs for John's physical well-being and must be part of the intervention, but they are not his most central concern at the present time. For this reason, professionals in a helping relationship should be sensitive to addressing John's practical problems in ways that respect the importance he places on his emotional problems, which he has identified as his central focus.

- *Take needed supportive action.* Professionals may have to take some supportive action, sometimes behind the scenes, to ensure that other considerations do not detract unduly from the focal point of the intervention. For example, the mandate of the service organization may be to secure employment – its funding may even depend on finding successful employment – but this mandate cannot override the need expressed by the person being helped, if quality of life is to be achieved in the best way.

- *Offer skilled counselling.* Skilled counselling is needed for three reasons. First, and probably most important, counsellors need to hear what people who require help say. Rehabilitation personnel, other professionals, family members, and others often prefer patients/clients/consumers who are quiet. Roy Brown and his colleagues have called this type of rehabilitation 'the art of keeping people quiet'. Hearing what people in need of rehabilitation have to say is an essential aspect of beginning to plan an effective intervention, although care should be taken not to place so much emphasis on listening to the person that the intervention itself is ignored. Second, John needs help to explore his emotional and personal problems and to develop effective ways of dealing with what he discovers. Finally, counselling may need to explore more basic problems that underlie his current emotional and personal problems. When people identify their own perceived starting points for intervention, they are frequently unaware that a more fundamental problem – a problem behind the problem – needs to be worked on first or simultaneously so that the effect of the intervention will be more holistic in nature. John has come from a particular background that, like all of our backgrounds, has strengths and weaknesses and hopes and disappointments. His current trauma may be the most shattering in his life so far, or it may be less important than other dramatic events that have occurred in his life. If it turns out that the latter is the case, intervention and services offered will differ quite considerably. In any case, this possibility needs to be explored in counselling. His current problems need to be seen in terms of his whole past and present life.

In some instances, other individuals involved in John's rehabilitation, such as parents and spouses, may also be involved in the counselling process, not just to seek their views and provide information, but also to help them understand the situation as perceived by John himself. Counselling may also be beneficial to individual family members by working through long-standing interpersonal issues, as this further benefits the individual undergoing rehabilitation by improving the degree to which he has supportive and understanding family around him.

In beginning from the place that is perceived as important to John, the team used a variety of intervention techniques that were known to them and that were based on a variety of philosophical perspectives. Their overall quality of life approach, though, kept them focused on valuing John's own perception and goals. By keeping their various intervention strategies centred on what was important, enjoyable and empowering to him, what his choices were, and what built self-confidence, their interventions were strengthened and more likely to achieve success.

Arthur: Following with personal choice, empowerment and improved self-image

Arthur experienced a cerebral embolism when he was 37. He had a supportive spouse and a young daughter, and, after the needed medical treatment, he wished to get his life going again. The surgeon involved believed he had done all that was possible from a physical perspective. Arthur had difficulty producing words, and the speech he was able to produce was cluttered. He had considerable hand and arm tremor and had lost motor power to a marked degree.

At the time of the accident, Arthur had been hoping to build a deck behind his house, a task that now seemed impossible. There was now a sadness that it could not be done, but he expressed the hope that he would some day be able to complete the deck. His rehabilitation team accepted this choice and set for themselves the challenge of working on it together. Rehabilitation was planned and initiated under Arthur's guidance around his goal of getting the deck built. Arthur's wife had some reservations ('He cannot do this now', 'He may have another accident'), and, further, the surgeon involved had doubts. The team needed to explain in detail how stress and risk would be contained, yet how he could direct and contribute to the building, while at the same time improving his physical and motor abilities. Of course, the focus on the deck, a dream he had been harbouring for some time, also gave him a tremendous emotional and spiritual lift.

Slowly the deck took shape. Assistants and volunteers, using Arthur's own plans, sawed the wood and did the hammering. Arthur assisted wherever possible, pointing, making comments, and indicating where others were going wrong. Gradually, he began to be more actively involved. A question from one of the volunteers, such as 'Where is the hammer?', was incentive for Arthur to stretch his motor ability by pointing and to stretch his speech ability by explaining. He began to use more actions and more words. As his involvement increased, his self-image improved alongside his physical abilities. By directing and participating in building his deck, he learned that he was not totally incapacitated. He also learned that he could still build upon values, ideas and dreams that had always been part of his life, although in a somewhat different way. Rehabilitation plans were built around a central activity that neatly represented the values, ideas and dreams central to how Arthur viewed himself. This helped him to improve physically, emotionally and spiritually, and at the same time he developed a positive sense of how his new self could direct and improve his own life.

All four of the action steps of the quality of life approach are illustrated very well in this intervention:

1. *The intervention began from the place Arthur perceived as most important –* the deck, rather than his own body. The decision to focus rehabilitation on building a deck must have seemed foolhardy to some, but it was how Arthur needed to start mending. Within himself, Arthur knew that it was important to the success of his intervention to concentrate on a rehabilitation activity outside his physical body that represented one of his future dreams and the value he placed on family and home in a clear and concrete way. Without asking Arthur, rehabilitation counsellors might have used several sessions coming to the same conclusion, but, in this case, all the rehabilitation team needed to do was listen carefully to what Arthur himself perceived and articulated, and respect his perception as the most valid course of action.

2. *The intervention followed Arthur's choices on how to plan and proceed.* To achieve this, rehabilitation personnel had to think very flexibly about what their role was, for, as they helped Arthur, they literally helped to build his deck. They also had to be creative, for they had to think how to encourage the physical movement and speech practice that were so important to Arthur's rehabilitation within the busy and ever-changing environment of deck building. Sometimes, they had to take non-verbal 'instructions' from Arthur, and they had to think how to respond in the best possible way. In all, they practised the art of good rehabilitation from a quality of life point of view. They threaded the procedures of their craft within the context of Arthur's overall choice and the many smaller choices he made along the way.

3. *The intervention was directed throughout towards empowering Arthur by putting him in control and thus encouraging his self-management.* The deck plan had been drawn up by Arthur before he experienced the embolism, and the rehabilitation staff were wise enough to install him as the 'boss'. All tasks were carried out to his specifications,

and under his direction. When they asked him 'Where does the railing go?', not only did they encourage him to speak and make physical gestures, but also reinforced the notion that he was in charge. Moreover, they simultaneously provided him with an opportunity to alter his plans as he wished. Thus, empowerment for Arthur came from two sources: the act of following one of his dreams, and the procedures that were followed during the building of the deck.

But individuals develop feelings of empowerment within environments that usually include other people, and the views of Arthur's wife within his home environment were an extremely important factor affecting his own feelings of empowerment. As the rehabilitation programme unfolded successfully through the deck-building project, Arthur's wife realized its benefits, and gradually allowed her own feelings of anxiety and the sense that she had to be in control to change to hope and recognition that major gains were still possible. In short, she became noticeably empowered as well.

4.   *The intervention was shaped in such a way that it worked to improve Arthur's self-image.* As a result, Arthur's fragile view of his new, post-embolism self improved dramatically. As his speech and physical abilities began to improve, he quite quickly saw himself as a man of still considerable capacity, and as someone who could direct his own life according to his own wishes. Such self-perception, in turn, gave him confidence to talk and move more, which further aided in his rehabilitation.

Improved self-perception also had a strong impact on Arthur's morale, resulting in a marked upturn of his spirits. As he became less consumed with negative thoughts, his ability to form and articulate positive thoughts and ideas increased. He began to think of new ways to access all the parts of his home where he had formerly easily walked. He began to experiment with different, but effective, methods of communicating with his wife and daughter. He began to think of alternative ways of completing daily self-care and routine household tasks that he had thought at first would now be impossible. People in quality-of-life-oriented interventions often improve aspects of their lives that are not targeted in the intervention at all. This is because successes that follow choices they have made themselves increase their self-image sufficiently to motivate them to try other activities, which they would otherwise ignore. A boost in self-image results in improved performance in other areas because the individual feels more confident.

The important aspect of such improvement in individuals' improved views of themselves is the realization that the environment in which they lived and worked is still filled with opportunities for them to live, work, grow and experience happiness. This is certainly the way it was for Arthur. He still had to deal with many frustrations and challenges, but his more positive self-image was a powerful tool in helping him to cope and move forward within an environment that he now perceived to have numerous opportunities. Such changes are beneficial not only in the short term, but also in the long term, for they no doubt will enhance Arthur's outlook on his family and home life for many years to come.

BECOMING INVOLVED

Arthur's story illustrates another aspect of the work of practitioners in areas related to disability, which readers may have been wondering about. Is it appropriate for practitioners to become directly involved as Arthur's team did? At times, it is absolutely necessary for the frontline professional to become directly involved in work or activities as a strategy to carrying out interventions. Simply put, there are times when they have to get their hands dirty. Arthur's team did this through modelling and demonstration, by cueing Arthur's behaviour, and by encouraging him to increase his use of his muscles and voice. In the process, they were able to help him work towards the realization of a dream, itself a tremendously fulfilling outcome.

Using the action steps judiciously

The action steps of the quality of life model need to be applied to interventions judiciously. Professionals, family and others who offer support to the person should be aware of risks, dangers and courses of action that will probably lead to negative results, and should weigh these carefully against the potential benefits of an intervention.

Donna wanted to leave hospital and return home after a serious physical accident to her limbs. Her rehabilitation called for intensive physiotherapy, but, as it was Donna's choice to return home, it was agreed that this wish should be accepted and that she could continue her physio exercises on her own there. Unfortunately, she did not follow her regimen and spasticity set in.

Providing the individual with choice of where to start and how to proceed is empowering and raises self-image. But sometimes choice cannot be followed, although it must always be openly acknowledged by members of the intervention personnel involved. Quality of life interventions based on the four action steps must be set within a sound and responsible rehabilitative structure. In Donna's case, her initial choice to leave hospital and return home might have been respected only on the condition that her physio programme be monitored and supported on a regular basis at home. Providing support of this nature may take some creative work on the part of professionals, especially if it is not typically within the mandate of the hospital. If it was not possible for the hospital to provide Donna with in-home support, it was inappropriate for it to accept her choice of going home. Personal choices are not acceptable when they are likely to result in breakdown of the kind Donna experienced. Those supporting rehabilitation have a responsibility not to accept personal choice when it is likely to be obviously detrimental to the person.

This raises a dilemma because recognizing what is detrimental is sometimes difficult and challenging. In some cases, we cannot know. It is better to go with the person's choices, if there is no reason to suspect harm, for many individuals will overcome obstacles with support if motivation is sufficiently high. The practitioner needs to rely on clinical judgement and experience in such contexts.

USE STRUCTURE THAT INVOLVES KNOWING WHERE THE INDIVIDUAL IS 'AT'

For interventions to be successful, they need structure to support them. Structure requires knowing the individual's functioning level, the degree of variability the individual demonstrates (people who function under stress or are learning new skills often show a high degree of variability in their performance), as well as a knowledge of the individual's strengths and challenges (e.g. how long an individual can function without becoming fatigued). These characteristics affect the amount of structure that should surround implementation of any choices. Practitioners will find they need to change the amount of support, control and other aspects of structure according to the person and the situation with which they are dealing.

There are major external components to structure that involve choice – when and where an activity will take place, who will work with the individual, and how they will work with the individual. For example, a person may work best in the morning. He or she is likely to work best in a familiar environment, but may choose another environment for personal reasons. The individual is likely to work best with someone familiar, chosen by the individual, thus providing 'person' structure. Some of these and related items are aspects of learning strategies, but here they are being applied in the acceptance of an individual's choices. Brown and Hughson (1993) have expanded on some of these aspects of learning.

Further acceptance of the individual's choice generally opens up further choices. For example, Leanne, who was 28 years old, wanted to learn to read. Previous history showed she had not been successful, but she insisted that this was her choice. Professionals thought that learning other skills might be more appropriate and acceptable, such as learning how to use the local transit system. But in the end Leanne's choice was accepted, and this opened up other choice requirements. Should she choose, through interview, who would teach her? Should she indicate the venue for this teaching? Both these aspects were incorporated into the programme. Leanne learned to read. However, she learned much more than reading. She gained experience in interviewing and selecting. She was proud of her achievement, and afterwards felt less disabled. Thus, accepting choices in their different forms into learning paradigms enhances the effectiveness of the intervention. There is some evidence that such choice involvement enhances the process of generalization, probably because self-awareness and self-image have improved. Brown *et al.* (1992) discuss this in some depth for readers who want further detail.

DO NOT RAISE FALSE EXPECTATIONS

The action steps outlined in this chapter, when used in interventions, can add positively to a person's life, but care should be taken not to encourage false expectations for the future. Overemphasizing the positive outcomes of an intervention is an inappropriate application of the quality of life action steps.

Those who support rehabilitation interventions have to learn to recognize the difference between real possibilities for further control of the environment and situations that raise hopes for things that are just not likely to occur. At the same time, individuals in need are often depressed in terms of their ability to believe that situations or performance can change. Experienced practitioners will indicate what they realistically believe can be achieved, even if this is above the individual's expectations. Concrete and visual expressions of such goals (such as graphical projections) are often important ways of demonstrating what can be expected, recognizing what the individual believes is possible. This is often less than what is possible, and seeing that the person can improve expectations is highly motivating and can improve self-image (e.g. 'Look, I did it – I didn't think I could!').

Three professional-centred steps

We now add three professional-centred steps for quality-of-life-based interventions to the four person-centred steps discussed in the previous section. Again, some real-life examples are used to illustrate how these work for practitioners in intervention.

The three professional-centred steps are:

1. Keep a philosophical focus.

2. Follow a logical implementation process.

3. Use sound professional skills.

Keep a philosophical focus

Quality of life provides a philosophical foundation upon which to build solid interventions. When proceeding with interventions that are based on this approach, it is essential that practitioners keep its ideas and principles centrally focused. Quality of life offers a broad, overarching approach that is largely consistent with other valuable philosophical ideas and principles with which practitioners are familiar. For example, a quality of life approach to intervention fits well with the view of disability as a social construction, which has very much influenced our current thinking. Michael Oliver, Len Barton and Marcia Rioux, representing advocates and disabiliy theorists from both sides of the Atlantic, are among the authors who have developed this theme that recognizes the social causation of disability. By way of another example, a great deal of what is understood as *inclusion* meshes very well with a quality of life approach. Thus, practitioners are encouraged, when focusing on quality of life as a philosophical approach, to be mindful of complementary philosophical approaches and to enfold these within their overall philosophical thinking. Some ways to do this are illustrated below, using the concept 'inclusion'.

INCLUSION

One of the major practice philosophies within the disabilities field today is that of inclusion. This concept includes a number of sub-concepts such as acceptance, access, equal rights, and social participation, as well as many others. Interventions based on quality of life can incorporate inclusion as a powerful philosophical tool, for it implies both the possibility for, and the right of, people with disabilities to experience life fully among the people and places in their environments. Over the last several decades, this has largely meant inclusion within normal or regular school systems of children with disabilities, and inclusion in the regular life activities enjoyed by the peers of people of all ages with disabilities.

It may be helpful to gain a better understanding of inclusion by exploring its opposite, exclusion. Exclusion has been practised by humans since time immemorial, and continues to be widely practised to varying degrees in today's societies. The box following illustrates that exclusion takes a number of forms. In general, though, exclusion is demonstrated by sets of rules and values that support social hierarchies and that limit participation of some people while providing rewards to other people, according to arbitrary positions within those hierarchies. Exclusion is undertaken purposively in order to provide benefits to some and not to others, and to allow exclusive access to some aspects of life for selected people only.

Inclusion is the antithesis of exclusion. Like exclusion, it is a set of rules and values, but this time for the opposite reason. Its aim is to break down hierarchies and to remove barriers so that people can participate fully in the life of the environments in which they live. Inclusion implies accessibility to places, equipment, ideas and people. Children who go to regular schools but are isolated from other children during classes, recess or mealtimes do not have

---

Aspects of exclusion

Exclusion can be:

- Physical

- Social

- Psychological

- Individual or group

- Inter-generational

- Short or long term

- Within homes, communities, services and institutions

---

access. A student who was deaf and used sign language stated she felt isolated because no one sat with her at school mealtimes. In addition, inclusion refers to concepts and practices that aim to enhance individual development and performance.

Aspects of inclusion

Inclusion requires:

- Accessibility

- Conscious awareness and insight

- Empowering, accessible and non-discriminating societies

- Interrelatedness

- Life span orientation

- Non-hierarchical social structures

- Personal choices and individual control

Inclusion has become a central value for numerous parent and professional groups, and places of service and learning, in recent years. Some of these are making forceful and dynamic contributions to the rights of children's education within school systems, and access to community resources, services and places for people with disabilities of all ages. This powerful philosophical tool is helping to improve the quality of life of many people.

Can all people with disabilities enjoy total inclusion? Some authors, such as J. E. Ysseldyke (a US authority on the educational needs of children with disabilities), believe that they can and should, and that a total inclusionary practice is required. Ysseldyke believes that if we stop short of total inclusion, it will be like putting a wedge in a door, resulting in the door being permanently only partially opened. If this occurs, people with disabilities will always be excluded. But not everyone agrees with this view, despite strong movements to inclusion in North America.

Inclusion requires accessibility at physical, social and psychological levels. Access to such an environment markedly increases quality of life because it enhances choice and gives individuals command over their environments. As a result, self-image and empowerment tend to be enhanced. But creating access also enables individuals to have a wider range of alternatives, improving the integration or holism of activities. For example, if banking information is in a form that can be easily accessed physically and can be personally acquired, and the tellers interact with people in a manner that is supportive and helpful (social and psychological access), individuals are more likely to use banks because they can select from a variety of services that meet their comfort level. This can increase their financial control, and the variety of activities in which they can participate. They are also more included in the community and therefore more likely to make contact with other individuals. A wide range of variables become possible once this type of access is available. The reader may wish to make a list of such activities and advantages, because these are the types of interactions that people with disabilities may not be currently involved with.

Community interaction also tends to promote appropriate barriers to negative or inappropriate interaction. For example, someone sophisticated in community interaction is less likely to respond to an inappropriate door-to-door salesperson than someone who is eager for contact but rarely receives it.

Doris is 55 years old and has Down syndrome. She lives in a house in the community with her friend, another woman with Down syndrome who is a little older. They function well in the house, but will open the door and invite in anyone who rings the bell. Their care workers feel they are vulnerable to inappropriate outsiders. The women have not learned how to discriminate or respond to different types of individuals, or to assess an individual's appropriateness. In their case, this may be because they have not lived in a home of their own for many years. They are used to group home attention with in-home care staff on duty. Thus, although the women can perform most of what is necessary to look after a home, and they are happy in their home, care has resulted in overprotection that has not allowed important skills to be developed.

If we apply quality of life to inclusion, the principles of quality of life cause us to view inclusion in a much more expansive manner than is usually done – in a holistic and lifelong way. Inclusion at school affects how a child is included at home and in the community, sometimes positively and sometimes negatively. These negative aspects, sometimes referred to as exclusion, need to be examined in some detail, for only then can we understand it fully and more holistically. We then need to see how such processes might be reversed to make them inclusionary. This is a challenging undertaking, as is illustrated by the reflections of one professional during a training course on using a quality of life approach in intervention:

> The aim of a disabilities support worker is to encourage and assist individuals with disabilities to identify their goals and desires, and to help them to work towards them. Today, in the course on quality of life, the discussions caused me to reflect on and examine my own value system. Do I practise inclusionary or exclusionary thinking and methods? One mother, whose child I work with, alarms me by her behaviour. But, like her, I know I have at times focused on why things won't work rather than explaining ways to make it possible. I also realize I share some of the exclusionary beliefs that are prevalent in my community. These beliefs are not from malice but from a desire to protect and nurture. The discussion forces me to examine these beliefs and will help me become a better support worker. The quality of life approach is very individualized, and change will have to be made in small communities to allow this to happen. We have had to focus on providing

services/programmes to groups of individuals in order to maintain fairness, but a shift in thinking will have to occur to allow for individualized plans.

A quality of life approach requires some adaptation to inclusion principles, for although quality of life recognizes the thrust to inclusion, it requires that certain processes relating to the individual and society are taken into account. For example, individuals may wish to make other choices depending on their own experience and wishes. Ultimately, quality of life follows the decisions that are in the best interests of the individual, even if that sometimes conflicts with principles of inclusion. Usually, there is little conflict, but exceptions will occur. It is the job of the frontline professional to seek out and provide a balance between the principles of quality of life and those of inclusion.

SOCIAL ROLE VALORIZATION

Another philosophical approach of the past two decades that has wide acceptance in the disabilities field is normalization, reconceptualized as social role valorization by Wolf Wolfensberger. The concepts within this approach have brought about many important changes.

It is now recognized that people with disabilities require normal experiences in their environment and should be treated in normal and socially acceptable ways. Concepts like deviancy juxtaposition have been recognized, whereby people or services for various disability groups and socially deviant groups are placed together, and much effort has gone into making changes right across disability groups. Although Wolfensberger himself does not accept the notion of quality of life being a development from social role valorization, many of the concepts are explicit within the quality of life approach we have described. However, as was the case with inclusion, the quality of life approach recognizes that choice, self-image and empowerment may require deviation from some of the principles of social role valorization. This is illustrated by the following example:

Beryl has Down syndrome. She met a man with physical disabilities within her training programme. He obtained work, but she did not. They were attracted to each other and eventually were married. For several years now, they have lived happily together in the community. He works while she manages the home. They share activities and take part in social events. They say they are happy and obviously support one another in a wide range of activities. She is more outgoing than he is, and thus does much of the talking in social situations. But she brings him into the conversations by asking him questions and supporting his self-image. When this marriage took place, some professionals argued that it was not 'normalizing' for her to marry someone with a disability. Freedom to choose and to find ways to enhance personal well-being while attaining one's goals are very important to Beryl and her partner, and critical to a quality of life approach.

Follow a logical implementation process

In addition to keeping a philosophical focus, it is also important for practitioners to follow a logical process when implementing quality of life based interventions. Practitioners need to take into account at least three basic principles of logical implementation: preparing a detailed plan for the intervention, implementing the intervention in an orderly and manageable way, and recording and evaluating ongoing changes in the person's behaviour. Each of the three is briefly described here for the purpose of highlighting some of the aspects of quality-of-life-based intervention that are particularly important.

PREPARE A DETAILED PLAN FOR THE INTERVENTION

It is essential to proceed from the person's own point of view and to follow this lead right from the beginning of the planning stage. Many practitioners formulate a plan quickly, because they are usually good at doing this, and subsequently try to include the person in the intervention and proceed from his or her point of view. It is sometimes a surprise, even to experienced practitioners, when they encounter some resistance. Sometimes, considerable effort is expended trying to overcome resistance. Yet, resistance frequently stems from the intervention not reflecting what is important to the person, what the person has chosen, and how the person wishes to proceed. Practitioners are aware of the importance of preparing detailed plans, but a quality-of-life-based approach also stresses the importance of including the person fully in the process from beginning to end.

There are times when practitioners need to be aware that they need to move quickly, and on their own, without consulting the person, such as when there is a crisis or an emergency. But there are other times as well. Too much choice is confusing and frustrating for some people, or taking too much time to develop a plan can take the focus too much away from what needs to be done. Some individuals, at times, simply want the practitioner to suggest a good course of action to which they can agree. Practitioners need to exercise good judgement to determine what degree of inclusion in planning is 'just right' for each individual.

IMPLEMENT THE INTERVENTION IN AN ORDERLY AND MANAGEABLE WAY

Besides following the person's choices, the intervention needs to be satisfactory to the person, it needs to enable the person to manage his or her own life better and to support positive self-esteem. In many interventions, this is best achieved through a series of positive steps that move in the direction of the overall goal. Above all, this series of steps needs to be seen as orderly and logical to the individual concerned. Because the person's sense of what is orderly and logical may differ somewhat from that of the practitioner, plans may have to be altered so that they seem orderly and logical to the person. In addition, each of the series of steps needs to be manageable to the person. Intervention change applied too quickly can lead to confusion and dissatisfaction, and perhaps to a lowered sense of empowerment and self-esteem. A judicious practitioner will monitor, in an ongoing way, the pace and logic of the intervention to ensure that it suits the person as closely as possible.

RECORD AND EVALUATE ONGOING CHANGES IN THE PERSON'S BEHAVIOUR

Practitioners realize that it is extremely important to keep detailed records of their procedures and the outcomes of their intervention on behaviour and functioning. They need to select a variety of functional and behavioural indicators appropriate to the individual and record data for each at regular intervals with the agreement of the individual. These should include measures of the perceptions of the person receiving intervention, as well as others affected, such as family members. In addition, they should keep detailed qualitative information, which is particularly useful as a rich source of information for description and explanation. It is crucial to keep such records with particular care in quality-of-life-based interventions that are innovative and person-centred.

Participating in one's own assessment can be an empowering experience, even if it is challenging. Where possible, it is suggested that the person also tracks and records procedures, perceptions and changes, and forms part of the team that interprets the outcomes. The person should be able not only to comment on the effectiveness of intervention, but also to ask for changes needed. This does not mean that practitioners should not give full attention to recording and evaluating, but rather that the person receiving the intervention needs to be part of the process.

Use sound professional skills

The quality of life approach offers numerous ideas for carrying out intervention, but these need to be done in ways that make use of sound professional skills. Two professional skill sets, counselling and service coordination (sometimes called case management), are discussed below as examples. After reading the examples, readers should think of other professional skills that can be used effectively in a quality of life approach to intervention.

COUNSELLING

Counselling is used to various degrees in nearly all interventions. Sometimes it is directed towards the individual, promoting personal quality of life, and at other times it focuses more on all members of a family, enhancing the quality of family life. In any helping relationship, ongoing emotional support is an important aspect of the relationship between client and professional, and appears highly relevant to a quality of life approach.

It is often assumed that individuals must be able to communicate effectively in order to indicate their preferences. But some people who have disabilities communicate in ways that non-disabled people are not skilled at understanding. Thus, a first step in becoming an effective counsellor and support worker is to understand the non-verbal as well as the verbal messages that the individual is conveying. A second essential step is to listen to and respect the messages and choices a person is making. In doing so, it is necessary to assess the degree to which individuals understand the choices they are making and the range of choices they may have considered. Restricted environments, with fewer opportunities, often result in less sophisticated choice. Counselling requires providing and promoting opportunities to explore alternatives and new experiences wherever feasible. Finally, the precise nature and likely impact of the choices needs to be understood clearly and explored with the person.

SERVICE COORDINATION

Coordinating the various aspects of most interventions takes considerably higher levels of skill than those of many people receiving intervention. For this reason, this responsibility must fall on the practitioner who is in a support position. The art of effective coordination is to draw together the needed aspects of the intervention in a timely way while including the person. In other words, the effective service coordinator acts on practical and often various small aspects of the intervention to ensure that they occur, but this should not be done without the full knowledge and consent of the person concerned. The practitioner should always be acting for or on behalf of the person, and in a way that offers support so that independence, self-reliance and increased positive feelings of self are enhanced.

Final comment

In this chapter, we have attempted to introduce some of the ways a quality of life approach can bring together a wide range of principles and practices while accenting some of the sensitizing and foremost principles of quality of life. The content is merely illustrative, but readers should examine their own examples to see how they would build an overriding and systematic quality of life approach in supporting individuals expressing various disabilities and challenges.

For thought and discussion

1. Using examples, illustrate how accepting people's choices can enhance intervention.

2. How does a quality of life approach add structure to an intervention? How does such structure help to ensure the success of the intervention?

3. How does a quality of life approach support inclusion of people with disabilities?

4. The aim of intervention is to help improve people's lives. Do all interventions do this? Are there times when interventions are justified that do not help people improve their lives?

5. We have learned that it is important to begin from the place the person perceives as most important. Think of three examples where the practitioner may choose to begin from another place for good reasons. Explain what those reasons are.

6. At times, solving practical problems that are not identified as important to the person can add important structure to the intervention and help in its success. Describe a situation from someone you know in your personal life where this was the case.

Selected bibliography

Barton, L., Ballard, K. and Folcher, G. (1991) *Disability and the Necessity for a Socio-political Perspective.* Monograph 51. Durham, NH: University of Hew Hampshire.

Brown, I. and Brown, R.I. (eds) (1999) *Exceptionality Education Canada,* vol. 9, special issue on inclusion and quality of life, parts 1 and 2.

Brown, R.I., Bayer, M.B. and Brown, P.M. (1992) *Empowerment and Developmental Handicaps: Choices and Quality of Life.* Toronto: Captus Press.

Brown, R.I. (1992) 'Challenges in counselling.' In S.E. Robertson and R.I. Brown (eds) *Rehabilitation Counselling.* London: Chapman and Hall.

Brown, R.I. (2000) 'Learning from quality-of-life models.' In M.P. Janicki and E.F. Ansello (eds) *Community Supports for Aging Adults with Lifelong Disabilities.* Baltimore, MD: Paul H. Brookes.

Brown, R.I., Brown, P.M. and Bayer, M.B. (1994) 'A quality of life model: New challenges arising from a six year study.' In D. Goode (ed) *Quality of Life for Persons with Disabilities: International Perspectives and Issues.* Cambridge, MA: Brookline Books.

Brown, R.I., and Hughson, E.A. (1993) *Behavioural and Social Rehabilitation and Training.* Toronto: Captus Press.

Clarke, A.M. and Clarke, A.D.B. (2003) *Human Resilience: A Fifty Year Quest.* London: Jessica Kingsley Publishers.

Fewster, G. and Curtis, J. (1989) 'Creating options: Designing a radical children's mental health program.' In R. Brown and M. Chazan (eds) *Learning Difficulties and Emotional Problems.* Calgary, Canada: Detselig.

Fidler, G.S. and Velde, B.P. (1999) *Activities: Reality and Symbol.* Thorofare, NJ: Slack.

Frazee, C. (2003) *Thumbs Up! Inclusion, Rights and Equality as Experienced by Youth with Disabilities.* Available online at www.laidlaw-fdn.org Children'sAgenda/Resources/ Working Papers series.

Hughes, C., Hwang, B., Kim, J., Eisenman, L.T. and Killian, D.J. (1995) 'Quality of Life in Applied Research: A Review and Analysis of Empirical Measures.' *American Jounal on Mental Retardation 99,* 623–641.

Janicki, M.P. And Ansello, E.F. (eds) (2000) *Community Supports for Aging Adults with Lifelong Disabilities.* Baltimore, MD: Paul H. Brookes.

Keith, K.D. And Schalock, R.L. (eds) (2000) *Cross-cultural Perspectives on Quality of Life.* Washington, DC: American Association on Mental Retardation.

Mercier, C. (1994) 'Improving the quality of life of people with severe mental disorders.' *Social Indicators Research 33,* 165–192.

Oliver, M. (1990) *The Politics of Disablement.* London: Macmillan.

Ory, M.G. and Cox, D.M. (1994) 'Forging ahead: Linking health and behaviour to improve quality of life in older people.' *Social Indicators Research 33,* 89–120.

Raphael, D. (1996) 'Quality of life of older adults: Toward the optimization of the aging process.' In R. Renwick, I. Brown and M. Nagler (eds) *Quality of Life in Health Promotion and Rehabilitation: Conceptualizations, Issues and Applications.* Thousand Oaks, CA: Sage.

Renwick, R., Brown, I. and Nagler, M. (eds) (1996) *Quality of Life in Health Promotion and Rehabilitation: Conceptualizations, Issues and Applications.* Thousand Oaks, CA: Sage.

Renwick, R., Brown, I. and Raphael, D. (1994) 'Quality of life: Linking a conceptual approach to service provision.' *Journal on Developmental Disabilities 3,* 2, 32–44.

Rioux, M.H. (1996) 'Overcoming the Social Construction of Inequality.' In R. Renwick, I. Brown, and M. Nagler (eds) *Quality of Life in Health Promotion and Rehabilitation: Conceptual Approaches, Issues and Applications.* Thousand Oaks, CA: Sage Publications.

Romney, D.M., Brown, R.I. and Fry, P.S. (1994) *Improving the Quality of Life: Recommendations for People With and Without Disabilities.* Dordrecht, The Netherlands: Kluwer Academic.

Schalock, R.L. (ed) (1997) *Quality of Life, volume II: Application to Persons with Disabilities.* Washington, DC: American Association on Mental Retardation.

Schalock, R.L. (2001) *Outcome-based Evaluation.* New York: Kluwer Academic/ Plenum.

Sloan, W. and Stevens, H.A. (1976) *A Century of Concern: A History of the Amercian Association on Mental Deficiency 1876–1976.* Washington, DC: American Association on Mental Deficiency.

Warren, B. (1997) 'Change and necessity: Creative activity, well-being and the quality of life for persons with a disability.' In R.I. Brown (ed) *Quality of Life for People with Disabilities: Models, Research and Practice, 2nd edition.* Cheltenham, UK: Stanley Thornes.

Wolfensberger, W. (1972) *Normalization: The Principle of Normalization in Human Services.* Toronto: National Institute of Mental Retardation.

Wolfensberger, W. (1992) *A Breif Introduction to Social Role Valorization as a Higher-Order Concept for Structuring Human Services.* 2nd (revised) edition. Syracuse, NY: Training Institute for Human Planning, Leadership and Change Agentry (Syracuse Universtiy).

CHAPTER 8

Quality of Life
in Families

Our family as a whole is so important to the quality of life of my son, but my son's disability also has a strong influence on the quality of life of the rest of us in the family.

Mother of Ryan, age 11

It is widely accepted today that children and adults with disabilities should be fully included in the home, school, work and community life that their siblings and peers experience. By basing our practice on the principles associated with such inclusion, we have a chance to move away from the serious problems associated with segregated care outside the family home, such as social isolation, exclusion from community activities, poor services, high cost and, most important, a perception that we support the view that disability is unwelcome in our communities. Principles of inclusion are increasingly accepted internationally, and now most children live with their families and attend schools in their own communities, and a large number of adults live in community settings either with their families or on their own.

Patricia is now 46, but when she was a girl she was sent to a special school for children with visual disabilities in another city. Although she enjoyed her school and still has several friends from her school days, she also regrets not being able to go to the school her sister attended. She also regrets that her parents 'were not real parents because they lived in another city'.

More inclusive community living has also meant that many family members now take the main responsibility for care of children and sometimes of adults with disabilities, especially adults with intellectual disabilities. Mothers, in particular, are most likely to feel the burden of additional responsibility. Families are almost always willing to accept the additional responsibility and often feel enriched by it, but many families need practical, emotional or financial support to meet their responsibility adequately. Services for families that include a member with a disability typically view their roles as providing support to families, rather than taking on the primary responsibility for care. This adds to the family's responsibility, for they have the added task of dealing with the support organization and support personnel. For this reason, it is all the more important for services to provide the right kind of support. Thus, for children and for those adults with disabilities who are supported by their families, the family is increasingly becoming the critical environment that affects quality of life and within which quality of life is experienced. This makes it particularly important to examine and support quality of life within the family.

Dennis and Shirley have a son, now 20, who has autism. They decided when their son was young that Shirley would stay at home with their son, rather than continue her career, because he required a great deal of care and attention. Dennis recognizes that Shirley needs a break from this routine, so every year for the past 20 years, he has spent his vacation from work looking after their son, allowing Shirley a few weeks respite away.

At the same time, having a member of the family who has a disability affects family life as a whole and the lives of individual family members in a variety of ways. There are many family stories, both in print and passed on informally, that illustrate this. It may seem surprising to readers, then, to learn that disability researchers and academics have only recently begun to turn their attention to studying family quality of life.

Family quality of life is such a new area that this chapter represents only an introduction. Study of family quality of life is no doubt complex, but we believe it is becoming a critical area for research and practice. Unless we, as a society, can recognize the impact of disability on the family and how it functions and take supportive action, the current trend to support people with disabilities who wish to remain in their homes regardless of age and across a wide range of disabilities is likely to be less than successful. We need to understand what supports are required for families to experience high levels of well-being. Knowledge about family quality of life will expand considerably over the next few years, so it is necessary to state that what is written here is likely to be expanded and modified in the near future. We present below some ideas about quality of life in families that have emerged in very recent years, and we also introduce some new ideas.

What is a family?

Families have existed in all human societies. There have been so many interesting variations of families that study of family and family systems is a major area of focus in some academic disciplines, especially anthropology, sociology and social psychology. Family is also a focus within disability studies, because families are a particularly important aspect of the life of many children and adults with disabilities. Full descriptions of family and family systems can be found in the texts of these disciplines.

The size and makeup of families, as well as the roles of family members, have varied considerably across various regions and across the centuries. These range from two-person bonds, such as two adults or a parent and child, to large complex systems. Whatever form it may take, a family is an arrangement between or among people that involves roles, responsibilities and privileges, and that is usually socially recognized by others, and certainly by its members.

All families tend to exist for the same general reasons. The present authors, in a chapter of the 2002 monograph *Family Quality of Life: An International Perspective*, suggested three main functions of families that have been stable across human cultures and over the millennia of human existence: to bring children into the world and to nurture them until they become independent; to provide a way in which physical and emotional attachments to others can be expressed; and to provide a basic structure around which other social and physical structures can be built.

In recent times, the structure of families, as well as the roles, responsibilities and privileges of family members, has increasingly been described in formal ways. These include laws and other policy documents that vary in scope, but that, when taken all together, set out who is entitled to be defined as a member of a family and what their financial and other responsibilities and privileges are. Such formal descriptions are added to or become obsolete over time, but, typically in most jurisdictions, some changes are made on a regular basis. By way of some examples, the right of adoptees to identify their birth parents, legal recognition of same-sex couples, maternity and paternity leaves from employment, and mandatory financial support for the care of children when a parent leaves the family home are relatively recent innovations that have altered how we think of family.

Researchers at the Beach Center for Family and Disability Studies at the University of Kansas have consulted extensively on the definition of family and found that both scholars and families themselves described family in diverse ways. The Beach Center group came to believe that it is critically important, when studying family quality of life, to ensure that there is a match between the researcher's and the family's definition of family. For this reason, they define family as follows: *A family includes the people who think of themselves as part of the family, whether related by blood or marriage or not, and who support each other on a regular basis.* In this view, people are a family because they *say* they are a family. Under some circumstances, they may not even live in the same household. But it is important that family composition is decided by members of a family itself, not the practitioner or researcher.

This definition seems very appropriate for practitioners who work with families that have a member with a disability. It is family-centred, in that it respects the family's own point of view and responds to the particular makeup and functioning of individual families. Practitioners who adopt a famlycentred perspective help to set the groundwork for positive family quality of life.

In following a family-centred definition, though, practitioners need to be aware that at times they may experience conflict between a family's own definition and a legal or service agency definition of family. At such times, the practitioner may need to advocate for special consideration or may need to make a difficult ethical decision about the best thing to do in the situation. More is said about ethical decisions in Chapter 10 of this book.

Understanding family quality of life

Family quality of life can be thought of in two ways – as a meeting place of individual family members' quality of life, and as a meeting place of factors that affect the whole family. In our view, it is better thought of as a combination of the two. Thus, building upon research conducted at the Beach Center, we describe below each of the two ways separately, then put them together.

A meeting place of individual family members' quality of life

Family quality of life can be thought of as the place where the individual quality of life of each family member meets. An example will help to illustrate how this works. Marnie lives with her husband Jim, her son Shane who has fragile-X syndrome, and her mother Peggy. She also works as a loans manager in a bank, has several friends of her own, and has a number of hobbies that she does not share with members of her family. In other words, part of Marnie's life involves her family, but other parts involve other people, activities and interests. Her own quality of life is influenced by both her family life and her life outside the family. The same is true of Jim, Shane and Peggy – each has a quality of life that can be described individually. This is illustrated in Figure 8.1. The four grey circles show that each individual's quality of life can be described partly by the family experiences they share and partly by the experiences they share in their lives outside the family.

But Marnie, Jim, Shane and Peggy each also bring at least part of their own individual quality of life back again to the family. Family quality of life can be thought of as the 'meeting place' within the family where individual members bring back and share their own quality of life (see Figure 8.2). Thus, the family contributes to the individual quality of life of each family member and each family member contributes to family quality of life in a continuous

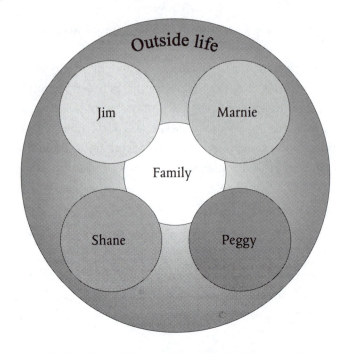

Figure 8.1 Individual quality of life comes from both family and outside experiences

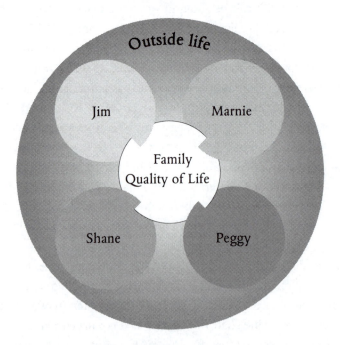

Figure 8.2 Family quality of life is the meeting place within the family where individual members bring back and share thier own quality of life

way. This creates a dynamic cycle of influence between the family and individual members of a family (see figure 8.2). As a consequence, it is usual for family members who experience satisfying individual quality of life to experience satisfying family quality of life as well. Of course, the opposite is usually also the case.

IMPORTANT ASPECTS OF INDIVIDUALS' LIVES FOR FAMILY QUALITY OF LIFE

What are the most important things for individual family members to bring back to the family meeting place? Work completed to date suggests seven areas of individual life that are particularly important for describing family quality of life. We have listed these in Table 8.1 and explained them in more detail in Chapter 4.

Table 8.1 Important aspects of individuals' lives for family quality of life

Individual well-being	
Physical well-being	Your physical health and activity
Emotional well-being	Your thoughts, feelings and adjustment
Environmental well-being	Conditions of the places where you spend time
Social well-being	The people in your life
What individuals do	
Advocacy	Participating in activities to promote things you believe in
Enrichment	Enjoying meaningful experiences beyond ordinary life
Productivity	The things you accomplish at home, school or work

For Marnie, Jim, Shane and Peggy, each of the seven areas of life is important or relevant to the family to different degrees. For example, Jim works as a chef in a hotel dining room and he brings back to the family a great many very good ideas for meals that he shares with the others, but Marnie brings little back to the family from her work as a loans manager. We have illustrated this in Figure 8.3, where it can be seen that the circle representing each person is divided into seven parts. But the seven parts are proportioned uniquely for each individual, indicating that the proportion of each of the seven areas of life that are brought back to the family meeting place varies from person to person. In addition, individual family members may choose not to bring back some aspects of their lives because they consider them private or not very relevant to the family experience. Peggy, for example, is experiencing some health problems, but she does not make these a central part of family, preferring to discuss the details privately with her physician. This all makes for a slightly complicated state of affairs, where individual family members bring back to the family meeting place some, but not all, of the things that are important and relevant to them. In addition, families all have their own unique patterns of 'bringing back'. To really complicate things, these patterns all change over time, according to a variety of influences.

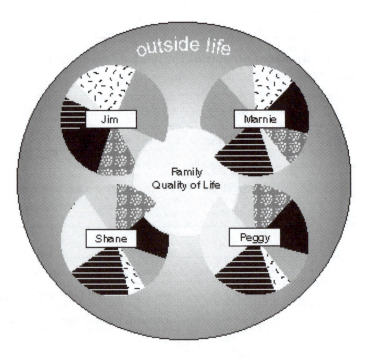

Figure 8.3 Seven areas of life are important to family members in unique proportions (see Table 8.1)

We can simplify this view of family quality of life to help us understand it. A more simplified view is especially useful for assessing the influence of each family member. To establish the contribution of each member of a family on family quality of life as a whole, we can ask each family member at a particular point in time for each of the seven areas of life:

1. How important or relevant to you is this area of life?

2. How satisfactory to you is this area of life?

3. How much do you bring this area of life back to the family?

A meeting place of factors that affect the whole family

A second way of thinking about family quality of life is to consider the influences on the family as a whole. Marnie and Jim both work at jobs that provide good income and they pool their money for everyone, so the family does not have to struggle financially or worry about how things will get paid. Marnie and Jim own a house that is large enough for all family members to have their own space. The family lives in a quiet neighbourhood that is close to shops, a park, transportation routes and Shane's school. But they moved to this city only recently, and, except for Peggy, both Marnie's and Jim's family and long-time friends live in another city. There is no one outside the family who can help look after Shane, and Marnie and Jim do not want to impose upon Peggy too much, so one of them is usually with Shane at all times. These considerations affect the whole family.

Seven important aspects of life for the whole family are outlined in Table 8.2. Again, these are drawn from the work of the Beach Center and the present authors' group.

Family quality of life, from the point of view of factors that affect the whole family, is illustrated in Figure 8.4. Here, the family quality of life circle represents that the family is influenced by each of seven factors.

But the seven 'pieces of the pie' are not always equally important within a family. For Marnie's family, support from other people, support from services, and parenting take on much more daily importance than family interaction, daily family life, and financial well-being. Moreover, the sizes of the 'pieces of the pie' are different for different families, because the seven factors are important to them to different degrees. This is illustrated in Figure 8.5 for Marnie's family and for her neighbour's family.

Table 8.2 Important aspects of life for the whole family

Family well-being	
Financial well-being	Having financial resources to meet family needs
Support from other people	Practical help and emotional support from people outside the family
Support from services	Having ready access to the services the family needs
Support from society	Laws, values, attitudes and accommodations supporting family needs
What families do	
Daily family life	The routines and activities the family shares
Family interaction	The way family members relate to one another
Parenting	Leadership and responsibility within the family

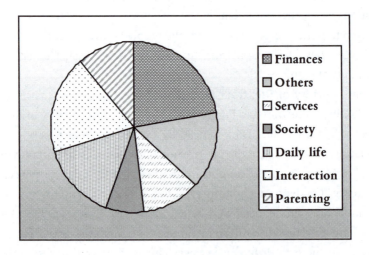

Figure 8.4 Seven important factors affect the wuality of life of the family as a whole (see Table 8.2)

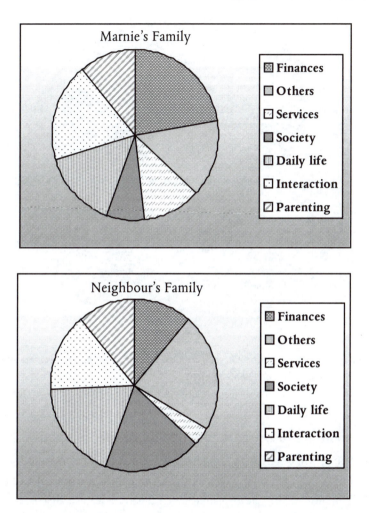

Figure 8.5 Unique influence of seven family factors on family quality of life for two families

Putting the two ideas together

The two views of family quality of life described above each show part of the picture, and they need to be put together to bring family quality of life into full focus. Family quality of life is partly the meeting place of the quality of life of individual members and partly a meeting place of factors that affect the whole family. The resulting interaction is likely to be unique to each family. Figure 8.6 represents graphically how these two ideas are put together.

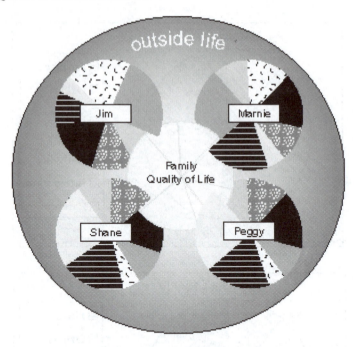

Figure 8.6 Family quality of life: The meeting place of individual family members' quality of life and factors that affect the whole family

Three examples of using family quality of life in practice

The section above describes *who* and *what* we look at in family quality of life. In the three examples below, we explore *how* family quality of life can be useful in practice. The same principles and strategies we discussed in the chapter on intervention also apply to families, but it is more complicated, essentially in two ways. First, it is necessary to take several people's points of view into account. At times, the point of view of one family member is different from that of others, and, at other times, it is the opposite. Second, an individual family member may choose to do something that affects the quality of life of the family as a whole (e.g. a parent choosing a career change that allows much less time for the family), or the family as a whole may choose to do something that is not perceived by an individual family member to be beneficial to quality of life (e.g. moving to another city and a teenage daughter loses daily contact with her friends). Thus, choices and compromises often have to be made within families, and these affect the quality of life of its members as well as the family as a whole.

Kathy and her mother

Kathy, a grade 12 student, who has a cognitive disability, also has had major emotional upsets when interacting with her mother. For her part, Kathy's mother has expressed the opinion that Kathy is too much for her, and she feels like killing her. This mother appeared to need some outside help, but the school counsellor to whom this information was reported did not feel comfortable in getting involved because this was somewhat outside her usual area of work. She was not fully confident that she had the training or skills to know how to handle the situation well. Still, she carried out a careful interview, after which she concluded that Kathy was not in danger, and recommended respite care service. She left the contact information with Kathy's mother, along with instructions, but the mother did not make any contact.

COMMENTS ON KATHY AND HER MOTHER

It seems clear from this case that Kathy's behaviour affects her mother in quite negative ways. As a result, it appears that their family quality of life is suffering.

When working with Kathy and her mother, a practitioner will immediately recognize, as the teacher did, that assistance and support are required for both Kathy and her mother. In doing so, it is always best from a quality of life perspective to proceed from the wishes of individual family members. In this case, the teacher did not do that, and there may have been a good reason for not doing so. She may have recognized that Kathy's mother had become so immobilized by the stress of her situation that she would not be able to seek out the help she required independently.

This is not uncommon. Frequently, we find that parents and other family members are not aware of the nature of stress, or the ramifications of disability, within the family. A graduate student studying quality of life and disability said, after reviewing several examples of problems within families followed by Kathy's story, 'This has helped open my eyes to the fact that even though a parent may say that things are okay at home, or not take up offers of support, there is a high probability that the levels of stress and anxiety are very high.' Practitioners need to be aware that this may be the case, and to monitor whether or not needed help has been sought out.

Practitioners who work with families such as Kathy and her mother need to ask themselves about each of the 14 aspects of life listed in Tables 8.1 and

8.2, but also a number of more specific quality-of-life-based questions that emerge directly from knowledge of the particular family situation. Some examples include:

- What are the most important aspects of family life to Kathy and her mother?

- How do Kathy's cognitive disabilities relate to the difficulties between her and her mother?

- What is Kathy's mother's life like outside her family? What are her sources of quality?

- What is Kathy's life like at school and with her friends? What are her sources of quality?

- Are Kathy and her mother able to bring back to the family positive aspects of their outside lives?

- Does Kathy's mother experience worries about her family well-being, such as financial worries or problems with her house?

- To what extent are Kathy and her mother supported by people and services outside the family?

- Would it help family quality of life for Kathy's mother to receive guidance in parenting Kathy?

- Would it help family quality of life for Kathy and her mother to learn more about Kathy's disabilities?

THOUGHTS ON GRANDPARENTS, SIBLINGS AND OTHER RELATIVES

Although it is not part of the vignette presented, it is possible that grandparents or other relatives could be a support to Kathy's mother. For some families, relatives are an extremely important aspect of managing to have a satisfactory quality of life.

Sometimes, though, grandparents, siblings and other relatives require some outside support too in order to be helpful to the family. For example, one grandmother thought her daughter was misguided and a poor mother because she would not allow her daughter, who had Prader-Willi syndrome, to have snacks. One of the main characteristics of Prader-Willi syndrome is a desire to overeat, and, at the same time, a tendency to gain weight even from a low intake of calories. The grandmother needed help to understand the consequences of overeating for such children. In another case, a sibling's quality of life was damaged when she felt harassed at school because she had a brother with a disability. She tried to ignore her brother and pretend she was not related to him. With counselling, she learned more about the importance of accepting disability and her brother. Slowly, she began to change her behaviour and to go out of her way to support her brother. As a result, she felt better about her own situation and considered that she had learned a great deal. For families, other relatives are reluctant to be involved for a variety of reasons, such as not knowing how to be supportive or considering disability to be a matter for the parents to deal with. They may not visit, may ignore the birthday of the child with a disability, or be unavailable for providing a few hours' respite. Family quality of life is often improved significantly by helping such relatives learn how they can be more helpful.

THOUGHTS ON COMMUNITY SUPPORT

Kathy's mother was not linked to any services, and may not have been receiving other community support. Such support is crucial to family quality of life for families that have a child with a disability. Supportive and understanding voices and actions are required from a variety of sources. Many such sources of support are available in almost all communities for the asking, although it sometimes takes an experienced practitioner or a persistent family member to seek them out and enlist their active support. At other times, advocacy is required for community organizations to provide the type of support needed. An example of this arose recently when interviewing parents in Australia (see Turnbull, Brown and Turnbull 2003). Families interviewed indicated that they did not feel their needs were well supported by their community groups and organizations. As one parent explained about her church: 'They do have a respite service so parents can attend church, but they have refused to take my child because he is said to be so difficult.'

Janice

Janice has diabetes, seizure disorder, and a mild intellectual disability. At age 37, she lives in a community residence owned by a social service agency that she shares with three other women. Neither of Janice's parents is living, but she has three sisters and two brothers, all of whom live a short distance away. Janice considers her family to consist of her five siblings and herself.

While she was growing up, Janice's family had numerous difficulties. Both parents had problems with alcohol consumption and maintaining steady work. The family moved frequently from one overcrowded rental unit to another. Both her brothers were sexually abused as young boys by a man who lived nearby. These and many other smaller problems added to one another until the family had difficulty maintaining the daily routines of a family, such as preparing meals and getting the children off to school. Relations among family members broke down, and Janice's family memories of this period are filled with people shouting at one another.

The family had special difficulty coping with Janice's disabilities. As a result, it was decided when she was nine years old that she would live in a residence for children with special needs. After that, Janice returned to her family home for weekends and holidays, but not to live permanently. The family's problems continued, and soon afterwards Janice's oldest sister ran away from home at the age of 15.

Today, Janice is in contact with only one of her sisters. Her eldest sister says she wants to re-establish contact, but has heard a family rumour that Janice does not like her. Janice claims this is not the case. Her two brothers and her other sister have substance abuse problems, and tend not to mix with the rest of the family.

COMMENTS ON JANICE

Where to begin? Janice was assigned a community support worker, Ted, whose responsibilities included assisting her with whatever personal and community needs she might have. During their first meeting, Janice made it clear to Ted that she very much wanted to establish closer ties with her family or, as she put it, 'to become a family again'. Ted did not know the other members of the family, but considered it important to try to support Janice's wish. So the question he was faced with was where to begin.

The practitioner needs to begin at the point of contact. Ted was assigned as a community support worker for Janice, not the family, and he needed to start by hearing Janice's story and understanding what her wishes and choices were. But, when supporting an individual, the practitioner is limited right from the beginning, since, in this case, he is representing Janice's wishes for closer ties, not the wishes of any other family members, which may differ quite considerably from Janice's wishes.

How to proceed? Because Ted was being paid to support Janice, he also had to proceed from her perspective, not that of any other family member or that of the family as a whole. Thus, Ted helped Janice develop a plan for moving forward. He understood that it would normally be best to follow both Janice's wishes and the path that was most likely to bring positive results. They planned first to meet with the sister who had been in contact, then to include the sister who had indicated a desire to have closer contact, and finally to reach out to her other sister and two brothers.

Proceeding from the perspective of the wishes of one family member raises interesting questions related to choice and the outcomes of choice for that individual and the family as a whole. When Janice attempted to develop closer ties with her sisters and brothers, they chose quickly not to respond, and Ted and Janice faced a negative result from their efforts. The quick negative choice from the siblings may have occurred because it was not their idea, because it is not important to them, or because they lacked confidence that closer ties would work out positively. What Ted realized was that the initial negative choice from the siblings may not have been their final choice, because they may have needed time and further opportunities to become accustomed to the idea. They may also have needed to experience small positive results from closer ties in measured steps. For this reason, he and Janice planned a series of small opportunities for Janice to share time with one of her siblings.

But an effective practitioner anticipates the possibility that choices may not work out, and that they may even have negative consequences. Janice's siblings might never agree to cooperate in establishing closer ties, because they consider Janice's wish to be a bad idea for the family. If this is their choice, it will ultimately have to be respected. Ted and Janice will then have to deal with the possibility that Janice will feel disappointed and dissatisfied with the whole endeavour to the extent that she will believe that her choices 'never work out', or that she will develop a lack of confidence in proposing other choice ideas. A good practitioner anticipates the possible outcomes of choice and plans for how to deal with them in constructive ways.

This vignette also highlights the lifespan aspect of the quality of life approach. Here, we have an example of family problems accumulating over time until it was impossible for the family to function as a unit. This state of affairs has long-lasting effects on Janice and, we might suspect, on her siblings. If the opposite had been the case – if Janice's family had accumulated positive family experiences over time – the effects would also have been long-lasting, and would have been an ongoing source of quality to Janice throughout her life.

Jane and John

Jane is in her 60s and has multiple sclerosis. Her husband, John, is several years older and is retired, and is the major support and caregiver for Jane. They are a devoted couple. Their children have left home and have their own families. Jane and John want to live in their family home as long as possible, but Jane is becoming increasingly concerned that she is deteriorating and becoming more and more of a burden for her husband. He does not complain, but it is obvious to Jane that he becomes increasingly exhausted by the extra duties he has taken on.

John does most of the shopping, and helps to physically support her in a range of daily activities, such as washing and bathing, dressing, and eating meals. They have some home help, but it is apparent that this is insufficient. Jane believes John will eventually break down. Their daughter visits when she can, but has her own family with a husband and three young children. She has suggested that her mother might need to go into a residential facility. Government services indicate they cannot at present provide more home support. Jane would like her husband to take a break. They do not have the funds to do this, though he could stay with his daughter, but then there is the issue of home or other support for Jane.

COMMENTS ON JANE AND JOHN

From a disability services point of view, this couple is functioning well. Their family is united, and although their daughter lives some distance away, she gives comfort and support when she can. Jane is getting by – the medical help is adequate – but it is the social and psychological aspects of her condition that are of concern, and that are largely unobserved by others.

There are several challenges here, but four are highlighted. First, for most people, physical health problems, such as Jane's, are a source of stress that act as a drain on emotional well-being for all members of the family. They also put physical stress on other members of the family, because of the need to carry out additional activities. Certainly, John spends a great deal of time caring for Jane and doing household chores.

Second, Jane recognizes that more and more of her discussion with people, and more of her activities and those of her husband, are associated with her disabilities. Such a situation is not uncommon. Similar scenarios occur in families where there is a child with disabilities or, for example, a father who has experienced severe head trauma. When someone has a disability in a family, family life becomes oriented more and more around the person with a disability. Quality of family life is profoundly affected, in this instance, gradually and chronically. The more complex the disability, the more likely it is that family life will become increasingly oriented around the needs of the person with a disability. When this occurs, family members simply do not have as much time available for social, productive, leisure or spiritually oriented activities, and this very often impacts negatively on family quality of life.

Third, when one member of the family has a strong health concern (or a disability), daily life of the family can change dramatically. The relationship between Jane and John changed to a considerable degree from equal partners to caregiver and care receiver. A great many of the routines of their daily life had to change because of the multiple sclerosis. Many of the things they did together changed, and they had to adapt to new ways of finding enjoyment from their leisure moments. The people they associated with changed as well. They began to see less of their friends because it was difficult for Jane to visit, and they began to see much more of healthcare workers. Even if all such new activities and relationships prove to be positive for families – although many do not – the energy required to adapt to them is itself an ongoing tension that impacts on family quality of life.

Finally, Jane's disability necessitated making a decision about her future. This was a difficult decision for Jane and John, and one that resulted in considerable anxiety for them. If Jane were to move to a long-term care home, where her physical needs might be better attended to, it would mean she would have to leave behind her home life and the many things that involved. The question of whether Jane and John would, on balance, be better off or not as well off following such a move was a matter they had to debate at length, even though it was an unwelcome burden to them at that time. Families that do not have such problems are free from the necessity of having to make such decisions.

There are instances where partners have divorced or separated, not because they wanted to, but because this was the only way to meet the requirements for service delivery (e.g. Cathy, who could only get geared-to-income housing and support services if she lived on her own). This is a clear example of how policy and necessary family quality of life support can be in conflict. In several well-developed countries like Australia and Canada there are numerous instances of aging spouses being separated as there was no suitable joint accommodation available.

What if a severe problem occurs in an unwilling family?

All practitioners who work with families encounter very serious problems from time to time. In some of these, family members do not wish to cooperate in addressing the problem. A recent case in Canada involved a family in which the parents disciplined one of their sons on numerous occasions so severely that he experienced very serious bodily harm. The parents did not want to work with the social worker who was assigned to support them and, in fact, hid many aspects of the problem from her. One set of actions by the mother, which was ignored by the father even though he was present, was so severe that the son did not survive.

Such examples are rare, but they do occur in all countries. Practitioners who encounter these troubling situations must take action, sometimes very swiftly, in accordance with the laws of their jurisdictions and the mandates of the organizations for which they work. Occurrences like this are examples of extremely negative family quality of life, and thus quality of life principles are relevant. However, practitioners sometimes need to set aside in part, or in full, their usual methods of supporting families to deal with the much more serious concerns of protecting children and responding to illegal activities.

Concluding commentary

The recent trend in most countries for children and adults to live, increasingly, with their families is making the impact of disability on family quality of life a particularly timely and important issue. From one perspective, this impact is not especially negative. The present authors and other researchers have found, from interviewing numerous families, that disability can add a richness to family life. Other research has shown quite clearly that human beings have a remarkable ability to adapt to the situations in which they find themselves, and that their quality of life remains reasonably stable over time. Robert Cummins's analysis on this suggests that about three quarters of all people in countries where studies have been undertaken seem satisfied with their quality of life, regardless of their circumstances. The same is probably true of families.

From another perspective, though, we need to be aware of the many additional strains on family members because of the presence of disability in the family. If too many challenging factors are present, families may lose some or all of their ability to cope with their situations effectively and find the richness in their situations. A recent Australian study with families conducted by Roy Brown and colleagues, for example, found that poor finances, poor access or knowledge about services, low community support, and unfulfilled spiritual and recreational needs were all found to be associated with a less than satisfactory perceived quality of life.

Even if families appear to be coping adequately, such challenges can detract considerably from their quality of life, and it should not be assumed by practitioners that they do not require supports and services. Most families that have a member with a disability do. Single-parent families may especially need them, because of the added responsibility. When assessing the need for support and services to families, practitioners need to be aware that mothers, fathers, siblings and other family members may perceive disability within the family in different ways. For example, there is evidence that some mothers show stress in different ways from fathers, and that stress may be particularly common where certain disabilities are present.

Family quality of life stresses how important it is for disability services to consider family needs as well as those of individuals with disabilities. Practitioners whose work with specific families includes such a focus can help improve family quality of life in a very personal way. Family quality of life also stresses the need to raise community awareness and support for disability in a more general way. In a variety of countries, 'good neighbours projects' and social action groups have provided practical examples of such action. Taken together, these appear to be an effective method of raising quality of life for families on the whole in an economically feasible manner. It is through ongoing advocacy and promoting such community action that the practitioner can help promote increased quality of life for families that have a member with a disability.

For thought and discussion

1. Who do you consider the members of your family to be? Why did you select those you did?

2. Consider your own life. What aspects of your family life and what aspects of your outside life contribute to your quality of life? What aspects of each detract from it?

3. Think of a family you know where one member has a particular challenge. How does this challenge affect the quality of life of the whole family?

4. Select a very large family known to you, and also a very small one. In what ways does family composition affect quality of life for the two families?

Selected bibliography

Braddock, D. (1999) 'Aging and Developmental Disabilities: Demographic and Policy Issues Affecting American Families.' *Mental Retardation 37*, 155–161.

Brown, I., Anand, S., Fung, W.L.A., Isaacs, B. and Baum, N. (in press) 'Family quality of life: Canadian results from an international study.' *Journal of Developmental and Physical Disabilities.*

Cummins, R.A. (2001) 'The subjective well-being of people caring for a family member with a severe disability at home: A review.' *Journal of Intellectual and Developmental Disability 26*, 1, 83–100.

Cummins, R.A. (in press) 'Normative life satisfaction: Measurement issues and a homeostatic model.' *Social Indicators Research.*

Cuskelly, M. (1996) 'Siblings.' In B. Stratford and P. Gunn (eds) *New Approaches to Down Syndrome.* London: Cassell.

Dale, N.O. (1996) *Working with Families of Children with Special Needs: Partnership and Practice.* London/New York: Routledge.

Darbyshire, P. (1994) *Living with a Sick Child in Hospital: The Experiences of Parents and Nurses.* London: Chapman & Hall.

Eacott, B. (2002) 'Family Quality of Life for Families who have a Child, or Children, with an Intellectual Disability between the Ages of Twelve and Sixteen.' Master's in Special Education dissertation, School of Special Education and Disability Studies, Flinders University of South Australia.

Egan, G. (1998) *The Skilled Helper: A Problem-management Approach to Helping, 6th edition.* Pacific Grove, CA: Brooks/Cole.

Greenberg, J.S., Seltzer, M.M., Orsmond, G.I. and Krauss, M.W. (1999) 'Siblings of adults with mental illness or mental retardation: Current involvement and the expectation of future care giving.' *Psychiatry Services 50*, 1214–1219.

Hoyert, D. and Seltzer, M. (1992) 'Factors relating to the well-being and life activities of family caregivers.' *Family Relations 41*, 74–81.

James, T.N. and Brown, R.I. (1992) *Prader-Willi Syndrome: Home, School and Community.* London: Chapman & Hall.

Mitchell, D.R. (1984) 'The family as partner – the parents and siblings.' Paper presented at the third Pacific Regional Conference of the International League of Societies for the Mentally Handicapped, Wellington, New Zealand.

Munro, J.D. (1999) 'Understanding and helping 'difficult' families.' In I. Brown and M. Percy (eds) *Developmental Disabilities in Ontario.* Toronto: Front Porch.

Nelson-Jones, R. (1984) *Personal Responsibility Counselling and Therapy: An Integrative Approach.* London: Harper & Row.

Park, J.Y., Turnbull, A.P. and Turnbull III, H.R. (2002) 'Impacts of poverty on quality of life in families of children with disabilities.' *Exceptional Children 68*, 2, 151–170.

Quinn, S. (ed) (1981) *What About Me? Caring for the Carers.* Geneva: International Council of Nurses.

Renwick, R., Brown, I. and Raphael, D. (1997) *The Family Quality of Life Project: Final Report.* Report to the Ontario Ministry of Community and Social Services. Toronto: Quality of Life Research Unit, Centre for Health Promotion, University of Toronto (www.utoronto.ca/qol).

Seltzer, G.B., Begun, A., Seltzer, M.M. and Krauss, M.W. (1991) 'Adults with mental retardation and their aging mothers: Impact of siblings.' *Family Relations 40*, 310–317.

Seltzer, M.M. and Krauss, M.W. (2001) 'Quality of life of adults with mental retardation/developmental disabilities who live with family.' *Mental Retardation and Developmental Disabilities Research Reviews 7*, 105–114.

Seltzer, M., Krauss, M., Choi, S. and Hong, J. (1996) 'Midlife and later-life parenting of adult children with mental retardation.' In C. Ryff and M. Seltzer (eds) *The Parental Experience in Midlife.* Chicago: University of Chicago Press.

Selzer, M.M., Krauss, M.W. and Janicki, M.P. (eds) (1994) *Lifecourse Perspectives on Adulthood and Old Age.* Washington, DC: American Association on Mental Retardation.

Singer, G.H.S. and Irvin, L.K. (eds) (1989) *Support for Caregiving Families: Enabling Positive Adaption to Disability.* Baltimore, MD: Paul H. Brookes.

Stancliffe, R.J. (2000) 'Proxy Respondents and Quality of Life.' *Evaluation and Program Planning 23*, 89–93.

Turnbull, A.P. and Turnbull III, H.R. (eds) (1978) *Parents Speak Out: Growing with a Handicapped Child.* Columbus, OH: C.E. Merrill.

Turnbull, A.P., Brown, I. and Turnbull III, H.R. (eds) (2003) *Family Quality of Life: An Introduction to Conceptualization, Measurement and Application.* Washington, DC: American Association on Mental Retardation.

Turnbull, A.P., Pereira, L. and Blue-Banning, M.J. (1999) 'Parents' facilitation of friendships between their children with a disability and friends without a disability.' *Journal of the Association for Persons with Severe Handicaps 24*, 2, 85–99.

Turnbull, A.P., Turbiville, V. and Turnbull, H.R. (2000) 'Evolution of family – professional partnerships: Collective empowerment as the model for the early twenty-first century.' In J.P. Shonkoff and S.J. Meisels (eds) *Handbook of Early Childhood Intervention, 2nd edition.* New York: Cambridge University Press.

Turnbull III, H.R. and Turnbull, A.P. (eds) (1985) *Parents Speak Out: Then and Now.* Columbus, OH: C.E. Merrill.

Selected websites (2002)

The Quality of Life Research Unit, University of Toronto – one of several research units within the Centre for Health Promotion in the Department of Public Health Sciences, University of Toronto
www.utoronto.ca/qol

Beach Center on Disability, University of Kansas
http://www.beachcenter.org/

The impact of childhood disability: A parent's struggle
http://www.pediatricservices.com/prof/prof-15.htm

Special needs family friendly fun
http://www.family-friendly-fun.com/

Quality of life, family services
http://www.ddc.dla.mil/qol/family/

CHAPTER 9

A Quality of Life
Case Example
Dealing with Grief

This brief chapter deals with a specific intervention that highlights several issues relating to quality of life. Barbara Matthews runs her own disability service in Australia, and is supported, at least in part, by government funding for specific individuals with disabilities. Barbara's work with Richard Gates, as documented here, is provided with the permission of Richard, Barbara, and Richard's father, Anthony Gates. You will note that real names have been used, and that is because of the wishes of Richard and others involved. Roy Brown met with Richard and Barbara and further discussed Richard's wishes. In recent research and writing in areas related to disability, it has become increasingly acceptable to include people in this fashion. They are the critical portion of the intervention, and where they wish, and it is acceptable, their involvement should, in our view, be recognized and their agreement recorded in writing and witnessed. Richard is keen for his story to be published, because he hopes it will help others who face a similar journey.

The specific topic of the intervention is Richard's grief following the death of his mother. The issues are sensitive and often difficult to deal with, particularly when the person with a disability is confronted with the loss of a family member who has been a major support. The account shows many aspects of intervention from a quality of life perspective with an emphasis on the well-being of someone who is helped to work through his grief. Many people with intellectual disabilities are discouraged from attending funerals for close relatives on the grounds that they will be upset and may upset others, or that they will not understand. In most cases, these views are incorrect. People with developmental disabilities, like others, benefit from mourning a loss and receiving support and sometimes grief counselling.

This intervention was selected for more than its relevance to people with disabilities, since it has a much wider resonance. It is also an example of how richness can grow out of adversity. It shows how a case worker supported Richard, who is 24 years old and has Down syndrome, through a difficult time, providing intervention that drew from him imaginative and poetic thoughts that were painful, insightful and growth enhancing. It might be helpful to note what principles of learning and counselling are involved, and how an overall structure relating to quality of life is engendered.

'Finding New Hearts on a Journey through Grief' by Barbara Matthews and Richard Gates

My life is so often enriched in my work with people with unique abilities, and their families. I feel certain, though, that I cannot express this fully by my words alone. For this reason, I am grateful that Richard and his family have agreed to let me use some of Richard's own words in telling his story.

This is the story of Richard's journey through grief. Richard's mother Ann died on 23 February 2001. From those who were closest to her – family, friends and working colleagues – I learned how much of herself she gave to other people, and how much she stood for, worked for and fought for people with unique abilities. I came to admire her courage and will through the many stories I heard about her.

I first met Richard in January 2001, when he was almost 24 years old. Ann's health was precarious, and there were major concerns about how Richard might deal with losing his mother. He has Down syndrome, and communicates in ways that are not always understood by others. He has four very favourite subjects that he just loves talking about. Also, Richard frequently focused on, and talked about, the things that he perceived to be the most negative aspects of his life. But the focus of our relationship was growing to understand grief and beginning to welcome happiness back into Richard's life.

I usually work closely with families, but the circumstance of Ann's health made it necessary for Richard and me to work alone together. To help keep the family informed, we tried to document everything we did in some way. We set up a folder for Richard that contained lists, charts, stories, letters and copies of his poetry. This was a special 'working folder' that he was very proud of.

Conversations around 'change' seemed natural and, as it turned out, quite useful. I learned that Richard had experienced many changes in his life, and we set about talking about how 'big' each one was in his life, and how he got used to them. Richard said he thought he managed the big changes because he was competent – being strong, like having 'inside muscles' and 'outside muscles' – and by having people on his side when he needed them. By this time, he began to understand that he had a *very* big change coming up, probably the biggest of his life so far.

Sharing life with grief

At first, I was not sure how much Richard understood grief. I wondered if he thought it was something like sadness that would go away fairly soon. We made a chart where we recorded his feelings about grief.

Richard wanted the following to be written at the top of his chart: 'Mum died at 7:30 on Friday 23 February at home. Dad held Mum's hand and so did I hold Mum's hand. Mum died of cancer and this made a big change in my life. Here is a picture of my life. The picture shows me the big change.' The 'picture' is a circle, with a line drawn across the circle about one quarter the way down. Inside the smaller part of the circle are the words 'This is the part of my life with Mum', and inside the larger part are the words 'The next part of my life will be without Mum. This is the biggest change in all my life so far.' Outside the circle there is an arrow pointing to the line. Here it says 'This line shows me that I was 24 when Mum died. When people lose somebody that they love, they usually feel grief. For me, my grief makes me feel lots of different things at different times.'

Richard spoke of many things that grief had him feel:

'Sometimes I feel lonely because of…'

'Sometimes I feel sad when I think about…'

'Sometimes I feel scared when I think about…'

'Sometimes I feel very tired…'

'Sometimes I feel confused…'

'Sometimes I feel angry…'

'Sometimes I feel proud when I think about…'

'Sometimes I feel happy and sad at the same time…'

Richard and I made a memory book about his mother, and had many rich conversations. These left me with many questions and thoughts about grief, which I began to write down in the form of letters to him. This helped him verbalize his own thoughts both as stories and poems. These reflected his journey, sharing his life with grief.

The letters and poetry of a journey with grief

Dear Richard,

I am writing you a letter because I thought it might be a good idea to write down some of the things we talked about, so that we can talk about them again if you want to. I hope this is okay. You told me there had been a few sad days lately. You said there are too many sad days, especially now because your sister and your dad have been sorting out your mum's clothes, and that this was making you feel 'heartbroken'. We then started to talk about how everybody does this kind of thing (sorting out clothes and things) when somebody that they love dies. This is because the person does not need those things any more. I am sure, Richard, that your dad would give you one of your mum's things, maybe a scarf or a hanky, if you wanted to keep something. Do you think maybe a scarf or a hanky might be something good to put in the memory book you are making?

And that beautiful letter that your mum wrote for you!! In the letter she asked you to help your dad because your dad would be missing her terribly, just like you. You thought it might be a good idea to ask your dad about the kinds of helpful things you could do for him. Maybe you could write some of the things down so that it's easier for you to remember them. I wonder how many things there will be Richard? See you soon.

Barbara

Dear Richard,

The last time we saw each other you told me that you helped your dad with your mum's clothes! You told me you actually helped your dad take the box of your mum's clothes out to the van. I was amazed that you could help your dad to do such an important thing. Taking your mum's clothes out to the van would have been a really hard job for your dad to do by himself. I bet he was really happy that he had you to help him. I am really looking forward to seeing you. A big smile for you.

Barbara

My Mum

by Richard Gates

Mum's Body Is Burnt
Mum's Coffin Is Burnt
My Mum Believes In God
My Mum Is Alive with God
My Mum Sees the Sun
My Mum Sees the Sky
My Mum Sees Polly, Cloud, Grandad and Jesus
My Mum Sees Jesus
Jesus Sees Mum
Pamela Told Me My Heart Is Beating
My Mum Is In My Heart Forever

Dear Richard,

Richard, I have to tell you how wonderful I think your new poem about your mum being in your heart is. I am really looking forward to hearing about your mum's place in your holiday heart and your work heart too...

Barbara

Mum in My Holiday Heart

by Richard Gates

Happy to have Mum in my holiday heart
I wished My Mum could have come
to Porepunkah with me and Dad
I wish Mum was with me and Dad on the plane
I wish Mum could come to Mannum
I wish my Mum could come
to the garden and home she Loved
I Love Mum so Much I Miss Mum so Much
Mum is such a character
Holidays bring happy sad memories about Mum back to life
My heart is still beating, because of happy memories of my Mum
I wish my Mum and Dad and I
could keep going on holidays together forever,
My Mum can't come on our flight on the plane
My Mum can't come to England
My Mum can't come to Dunstable in England
and see all of my cousins, aunties, and uncles living in England
My Mum can't come on any special holidays any more
and Mum can't come to the Royal Adelaide Show with Dad and I
But I can take Mum with me and Dad to all of these special places
because Mum has a special place in my holiday heart

Dear Richard,

Thank you so much for taking me to your mum's special memorial garden on Saturday morning. How was your mum's birthday night? I was so happy to hear you sing so happily – Happy Birthday to your mum – in the car, while we were having our sausage sizzle… Does it make you feel happy to know that your mum is staying in your heart FOREVER? Does it make you feel happy to remember the fun times you had with your mum at birthday parties or with friends?

Barbara

Forever Mum

by Richard Gates

Wanted my Mum and my family back together again
Just wanted Mum to come home
but Mum is not coming home forever
Can't have Mum at Stirling Hospital forever
Can't keep Mum's funeral forever,
Can't keep Mum at Centennial Park forever
Can't keep Mum's body forever,
Can't keep Mum's coffin forever,
Mum can keep her grandchildren forever,
Mum can keep her son Richard forever,
Mum can keep her husband forever too,
Mum can keep Alison and Ruby forever,
Mum can keep Andy and Keith forever,
Mum can keep all the family forever at home,
My Mum can keep Aunty Carol, Aunty Jean,
Uncle Mark, Uncle Roger, Uncle Steven,
my cousin Nicki forever,
I can keep Mum's Interchange family forever
I can visit Mum at the Memorial Garden forever
I can keep Mum's special memory boxes forever
I can keep Mum's memories and her love alive in my heart forever
I never need to lose my Mum from my heart

Dear Richard,

I enjoyed our time together so much last Saturday. It seemed that so much happiness was coming into your life all at once that it made you cry, but in a nice happy sort of way. Did you know, Richard, that tears aren't always sad tears? Sometimes people cry happy tears…

Barbara

Continuing to remember

Richard returned recently from an overseas holiday with his father. He is looking forward to speaking about his 'Christmas heart' and other things he says he has thought of as well. I am never quite sure, with Richard, where we will go, but am certainly looking forward to finding out.

This story is dedicated to Ann Gates 1936–2001

Some comments

It may be useful to underscore several issues. Barbara's work with Richard is very focused on his mother's death. But she was aware that her work was likely to influence Richard's overall functioning as well. This was very apparent to Roy Brown when he spent time with Richard over dinner at a community pub. Richard knew many people and was able to converse with them easily, and they came across to him and chatted with him about his life and what he was doing. The work Richard and Barbara did together appears enriching and empowering not only for Richard but also for Barbara, the professional. Effective involvement of this type is ideally reciprocal, bringing about positive involvement for all parties involved. The content is heavily based on Richard's perceptions – they are not questioned for their validity – and they are accepted in a straightforward way.

The aim of the intervention was clear and described simply – to encourage happiness back into Richard's life. The process involved keeping other family members informed of what was occurring. This was agreed to by all parties involved, and was necessary in terms of the emotional effects the intervention might be having. The structure around the quality of life goal involved not just thinking and talking but also visual charts and written material. In other words, Barbara chose media suitable to Richard's development and ones of which he approved.

Barbara, the professional, also took part in everyday activities with Richard, such as car rides and the sausage sizzle. In doing so, she was quite aware that she was blurring the border between professional and friend. The types of activities they undertook did contribute to a close relationship, but they were also important to the success of the intervention. They also demonstrated to Richard, in a very practical way, how he was valued by his worker.

Richard was strongly identified with the process. Self-image was discussed and was a central component of the involvement, moving from negative thoughts and feelings to positive ones. Interestingly, there is a clear division by Richard, with support, of external and internal processes. The context is present, yet the issues also are directed to longer-term issues, sometimes stated but often implicit. Both negative and positive feelings are involved. Reinforcement of Richard's activities in poetry and other activities are strongly and appropriately reinforced.

Finally, Barbara enters into Richard's belief and value system, which is not necessarily her own. Her respect for his values, including spiritual beliefs, and his feelings are overwhelming. Although Barbara's interventions are clear, we never feel her personal beliefs are intruding – in fact we never know what they are.

Interventions of this type, if carried out at this level for a long time, can often be stressful for the case worker. For this reason Roy Brown and his colleagues, in their 1992 book (see Brown, Bayer and Brown) on intervention and quality of life, found it important to ensure that such workers had ready access to counselling themselves. This support service is very important because, under stress, belief systems of the worker begin to intrude. Indeed, there is evidence that where the individual worker is under stress and does not have readily available supports, breakdown in such interventions seems more likely to occur. This is even more critical in community-based field work where personnel are often on their own, and trying to cope with too many cases of consumer need. On the other hand, it is very encouraging that many practitioners have a remarkable ability to carry out the complex work of an intervention well in order to achieve their objectives, as well as adding the extra value offered by the quality of life approach. Certainly, Barbara is achieving this aim.

For thought and discussion

1. Practitioners who work with people who have disabilities often feel enriched. Interview an experienced practitioner and discover ways he or she has been enriched. Share these views with others who have interviewed similarly experienced practitioners.

2. Richard has an intellectual disability. Consider how people with other disabilities, such as those with deafness or hearing loss, blindness or lower vision, mobility restriction or emotional difficulties, can be excluded from dealing with grief. What strategies might be useful to encourage greater inclusion in dealing with grief?

3. Where do the distinctions lie between a professional and a friend when using a quality of life approach with people with disabilities?

Selected bibliography

Brown, R.I., Bayer, M.B. and Brown, P.M. (1992) *Empowerment and Developmental Handicaps: Choices and Quality of Life.* Toronto: Captus Press.

Davidson, P., Prasher, V.P. and Janicki, M.P. (eds) (2003) *Mental Health, Intellectual Disabilities, and the Aging Process.* Oxford: Blackwell.

Delorme, M. (1999) 'Aging and people with developmental disabilities.' In I. Brown and M. Percy (eds) *Developmental Disabilities in Ontario.* Toronto: Front Porch.

Gordon, R.M., Seltzer, M.M. and Krauss, M.W. (1997) 'The aftermath of parental death: Changes in the context and quality of life.' In R.L. Schalock (ed) *Quality of Life, volume II: Application to Persons with Disabilities.* Washington, DC: American Association on Mental Retardation.

Ludlow, B.L. (1999) 'Life after loss: Legal, ethical, and practical issues.' In S.S. Herr and G. Weber (eds) *Aging, Rights, and Quality of Life: Prospects for Older People with Developmental Disabilities.* Baltimore, MD: Paul H. Brookes.

Prasher, V.P. and Janicki, M.P. (eds) (2002) *Physical Health of Adults with Intellectual Disabilities.* Oxford: Blackwell.

Webb, S.B. (1992) 'Disability counselling: Grieving the loss.' In S.E. Robertson and R.I. Brown (eds) *Rehabilitation Counselling.* London: Chapman and Hall.

Selected websites (2002)

The grieving process – Counseling Center, University of Buffalo
http://ub-counseling.buffalo.edu/process.html

Supporting a grieving person who has a developmental disability
http://www.npi.ucla.edu/mhdd/INFO/modules/grief.htm

Exceptional Parent Magazine – books about grieving
http://www.eplibrary.com/grieving/

'Children grieving: Grieving children'
http://www.familynetsource.com/news_views_parenting_grieving.htm

CHAPTER 10

Professional and Ethical Issues for Quality of Life

The quality of life approach sensitizes us to a number of different ways of looking at individuals with disabilities. We have noted that it encourages us to look at the wishes and choices of individuals and families, as well as at their strengths and needs. In doing so, we have considered how quality of life can be enhanced for individuals and families – but always within a broader physical and social context, for all of us live within environments that both influence the way we live and respond to changes that we make to them.

Service systems within which professionals and other practitioners work are one part of the environment that can have a considerable impact on personal quality of life. A number of factors – training and education of professionals, the policies that guide professional activities and behaviour, and the procedures of professional systems – can help people develop improved quality of life or can hinder them from doing so. Thus, there is a need to place the principles discussed in the previous chapters alongside known professional service systems, and to examine the professional and ethical questions that arise as a result of doing so. There will be no clear answers to some of these questions, but they do need to be considered.

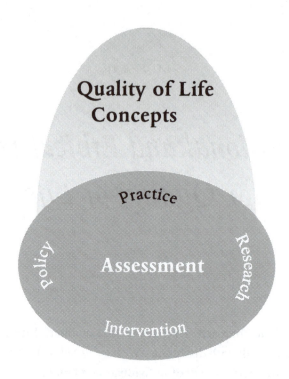

Fugure 10.1 The quality of life approach: Practice

What are professional and ethical issues?

Professional issues are aspects of the work of paid practitioners that are considered to be important in carrying out activities with or concerning clients. One of the interesting aspects of practical work in almost any field is that the things that constitute a professional role – its duties, responsibilities, limitations and boundaries – may not always be clear and straightforward when applied to everyday work situations. This results from practitioners assisting from the position of certain value systems and service mandates, duty-of-care requirements, professional codes of conduct, preconceived roles, knowledge and skills bases, and sometimes legal requirements. At the same time, those being assisted have needs to be addressed and perceptions of how they should be dealt with that are sometimes different from those of the practitioners. Angela, for example, lives in a home with three other persons with disabilities and often wishes her care staff person would give her a hug at night or when she is feeling down, but the care staff person feels she is not Angela's parent and does not wish to touch her. Besides, this type of touching is frowned on in the home because it is thought to be 'unprofessional' behaviour.

The professional–client gap illustrated above is sometimes confounded by another gap – the one between what professionals would do in their professional roles and what they would do in their personal lives. In our example, the care staff person is a devoted mother who readily hugs her own children when they need comfort at night or when they are feeling down. Thus, the reason that she does not hug Angela is not that she lacks compassion, rather that she thinks it is professionally inappropriate. But the end result is that Angela does not get hugged. She may or may not respond to the information or support she needs, and this may restrict her learning and development. Similarly, service restrictions about touching students in schools or adults who live in their own apartments may be helpful guidelines for limiting inappropriate activity, but such restrictions may have negative impacts on learning and emotional stability.

All professionals need to make decisions about how to deal with the gaps in fit between what they are willing and able to do in their roles and what really needs to be done to carry out their professional work well. When searching for ways to make these decisions, professionals are confronted by a series of ethical issues.

Ethical issues may be about many things, such as professional standards, how people are treated, the type of intervention followed, and whose choices are observed. However, the question for ethical decision making is always the same: What is the best thing to do in this particular situation?

Making an ethical decision is sometimes the same as making a decision based on generally held moral codes and religious beliefs, but there are many, many instances where making such a decision is not necessarily consistent with particular moral and religious beliefs. For example, hospital staff and family members who have strong personal beliefs in preserving life often choose to provide morphine to a terminally ill person who is in considerable pain because it is thought to be best for the person, even though it brings on death prematurely. In practice, ethical issues cannot be considered apart from professional issues, because the latter always have some bearing on the former.

Purpose of this chapter

Professional and ethical questions are ever-changing and so numerous that it is impossible to highlight all of them. Instead, we present some ideas to illustrate how important it is for practitioners to consider critical professional and ethical questions that emerge from their work using a quality of life approach. Many of the illustrations we use emerge from our own work – an approach to rehabilitation that is caring but allows for and encourages growth and development for the individual concerned and the supporting network.

The chapter serves three main functions: 1. to highlight some important professional and ethical issues and dilemmas for professional practice, 2. to stress the importance of practitioners recognizing and making decisions about ethical issues, and 3. to act as a list of topics for professional training. To address these functions we first focus on issues related to professional skills, and we then address numerous professional/ethical issues and dilemmas that are central to good professional practice that promotes quality of life.

Issues related to professional skills

Differing skill sets among practitioners

Today, there is a wide range of personnel entering the field of rehabilitation and they come from a wide range of professions. There is no guarantee that they will have covered similar topics in their education or have encountered the same experiences in their work. There are some advantages to this. One advantage is that multiple skills are available and potentially there is the opportunity for multi-disciplinary cooperation. There are also a number of worrying concerns. There is little guarantee that professionals can adapt to a wide range of situations if they have had only certain forms of education or experience. They may also have difficulties in using similar language and the possibilities of miscommunication or varied approaches because of different training values and philosophies are likely to arise. Here is an example:

> One of the authors, Roy Brown, recently completed a review of rehabilitation coordinators, where a wide range of training expertise among staff was noted. Senior management personnel were surprised that frontline personnel requested education and training in a wide range of skill areas, and that the variation among them was considerable. Even within professional disciplines, there was no guarantee that similar courses had been taught. For example, personnel with psychology degrees may not always

have had a course in counselling or disabilities. Social work personnel might have had considerable counselling experience, but know little of physical or sensory disabilities.

It is not surprising that most practitioners have not experienced courses that include quality of life as it relates to philosophy and practice in rehabilitation. These are not yet typically available in colleges and universities. Those who have knowledge of quality of life have usually gained it through training seminars and workshops, and these are often geared to specific applications within service organizations, rather than to the generic service needs of a range of people with disabilities.

The skills that practitioners have are not always the ones that are needed. When this is the case, three scenarios may occur: practitioners may learn the knowledge and skills and apply them to their work (as they are doing from studying this book); they may not learn the knowledge and skills but carry out the work anyway (sometimes with negative effects); or they may not carry out certain aspects of the work because they do not have the knowledge or the skills. The first scenario is the one that improves the situation, but the second and third serve neither the practitioner nor the person receiving support. Sometimes, the first scenario is not possible because of system constraints (e.g. lack of permission or funding, or professional boundaries), but, in this case, what is best for the system may not be best for practitioners or for service recipients. This results in a further ethical question: Should you choose what is best for the system, what is best for the practitioner, or what is best for the person receiving support?

Core skills set for disability practitioners

Practitioners who work with people who have disabilities need a core set of skills to carry out their work effectively. Some systematic way of ensuring that practitioners have such skills has several advantages, but the three chief ones are: practitioners have a similar understanding of the meaning and philosophy of disability; practitioners have a theoretical and academic background from which they draw on in their practice; and the service system has assurance that practitioners are using important strategies and skills such as empathy, listening, respect for individuals' values and wishes, and commitment to development and empowerment. Insisting on core skills has disadvantages as well, including the danger of practitioners in a particular field thinking too much alike, and a decrease in willingness to explore outside ideas and opportunities.

Practitioners who base their work on quality of life principles may wonder if a 'special' core set of skills is required for this. They may also wonder if they possess such skills. Below is a list of some of the knowledge and skills that we believe are necessary to ensure that the ideas and issues discussed in this book can be applied effectively:

- clinical knowledge of disabilities
- knowledge about family systems, dynamics and issues
- knowledge about the development of services
- knowledge of community and environmental factors that contribute to disabling conditions
- knowledge of community services and supports available
- knowledge of language development and common problems associated with language and speech
- knowledge of learning principles
- knowledge of legislation related to disability
- knowledge of lifespan development, including early life, transitions and aging
- knowledge of multicultural concerns
- knowledge of quality of life principles
- knowledge of social and emotional development
- knowledge of the main approaches to treatment and intervention
- understanding of the long-term nature of working with people with disabilities.

Skills that relate to *professional practice strategies* include:

- ability to judge issues for the best results
- appropriate interviewing skills
- basic knowledge and understanding of policy and management processes

- effective counselling skills based on eclectic counselling theory and practice
- effective interpersonal communication and collaboration skills
- effective observation skills
- effective oral and writing skills
- effective teaching strategies
- effective time-management skills
- organizational and coordination skills
- skills in understanding the perspective of others.

Skills that are helpful as *supplementary professional skills* include:

- knowledge about local community access and challenges
- knowledge about when to make referrals and suggest alternative methods
- knowledge of possibilities associated with adaptive and technical aids
- specialized knowledge in specific disability areas.

SKILLS AND HIGHER EDUCATION

An interesting question is the extent to which these skills are taught within colleges and universities to would-be rehabilitation practitioners. Some are part of formal education, health or other curricula, although there is sometimes little consistency among educational institutions. Many skills remain untaught, which means that they need to be taught at the in-service level, or picked up informally through practice experience. However, since services tend to provide what they want for their own needs, rather than what is ideally required, leaving the introduction of large amounts of teaching to in-service education is likely to restrict the breadth of knowledge and practice amongst personnel.

Proactive links between higher education and community-based service centres can provide for the innovative types of learning experiences that are desirable. Several Western countries have attempted to develop such links, but much is still wanting. Universities often do not always have access to service facilities, and, when they do, such facilities may not provide the types of innovative experiences that a progressive university programme should offer. For example, how easy would it be to apply a quality of life approach with choices in hospitals, community residences or institutions?

SKILLS AND PERSONAL CHARACTERISTICS

Carrying out work based on quality of life requires certain professional knowledge, attitudes and values. It also appears that certain personal characteristics may be necessary. These include:

- creativity
- emotional energy to change the environment
- flexibility
- innovation
- patience
- sense of humour
- stamina
- strong and positive values related to people in need
- understanding of own values, attitudes and beliefs
- warm personality.

It is also helpful for practitioners to possess the ability to:

- accept a variety of lifestyles and different options
- advocate effectively for those they support
- assess their own strengths and abilities, and to know when they need to seek outside assistance
- assume some risks
- discuss challenges and problems impartially
- feel comfortable letting others, especially people with disabilities, assume control
- make decisions regarding difficult ethical issues

- separate personal choice (i.e. the choices they would make for themselves or within their family) from the choices made by the people they support

- solve problems in a constructive way

- work well as a member of a team.

Ethical issues related to the main uses of the quality of life model

In Chapter 1, we addressed what a quality of life approach achieves for practitioners. We suggested that, when we use quality-of-life-based approaches, we put into practice six essential aspects of quality of life:

1. We focus attention on the processes that are most *important* to the person at the present time.

2. We help to ensure that people are *satisfied* with those aspects of life that are important to them, and that they are not dissatisfied with other aspects of their life.

3. We stress that *opportunities* to improve must be within the person's grasp.

4. We insist that *personal choice* should be exercised, wherever possible, in selecting opportunities.

5. We improve the person's *self-image*.

6. We increase levels of personal *empowerment*.

When we engage in actual practice, we find that applying these six essential aspects is not always straightforward. In fact, applying each aspect will result in some interesting, and sometimes quite challenging, dilemmas for the practitioner. Below, we describe and illustrate some of these dilemmas.

Personal values and interests of people being helped

Quality of life practice assumes that it is best to understand and base intervention on personal values and interests, except where harm to self or others is likely to be the consequence. Thus, quality of life practice puts the perceived needs of the person first, not those of the professional.

There are reasons why it is sometimes simply not possible for professionals to put the person's values and interests at the centre of a helping plan. Three main reasons for this are 1. they may not be allowed to do so, either by law or by the policies of their profession or organization; 2. they may have a conscientious personal objection, based on beliefs or knowledge; and 3. they do not think it is the best thing to do in the situation.

For each of these reasons, a real-life illustration follows that concludes with the ethical issue and an ethical decision that was made. Readers, like the writers of this book, may agree or disagree with some of the decisions made, and may want to discuss alternatives with colleagues. Such discussions should consider the needs and wishes of the person and the needs and wishes of others affected, including society at large, and should form views about the predominance of the various positions taken. They should also consider alternatives that might be satisfactory for all concerned.

ILLUSTRATION 1: THE PROFESSIONAL IS NOT ALLOWED TO HELP

Andrea has no family and only a few friends in the city where she lives. Her landlord had sold the apartment building where she had resided for about ten years, and it was to be demolished for reconstruction. Thus, Andrea had to move, but she used a wheelchair and needed help finding another place to live. Because she did not really want to move, she did not contact a case worker to help her until one week before the date when she had to vacate. The case worker visited her apartment, and found that it was badly overrun by cockroaches. She knew that they could not legally move any of Andrea's belongings because of a municipal law that prohibited people from knowingly bringing pests such as cockroaches into new lodgings. Both she and Andrea were facing the possibility of stiff fines, if convicted.

The case worker had to decide rather quickly what would be the best thing to do in this situation. She helped Andrea find another place to live quickly, but refused to move any of her belongings. The building was demolished shortly after, and all of Andrea's personal possessions were lost.

ILLUSTRATION 2: THE PROFESSIONAL HAS A PERSONAL OBJECTION

Bradley is a 28-year-old man with a mild intellectual disability who is married and lives with his wife and two preschool daughters. He was arrested and spent a few days in jail, following confirmation that he had a habit of spending a great deal of his time at home in the nude, and of engaging in sexual acts, both alone and with his wife, in the presence of his children. At the end of his trial, he received a sentence of probation and was allowed to continue living at home with supervision by a professional case worker and a parole officer. The case worker did not agree with this legal decision, because she thought his actions had been such that he should not be allowed to be alone with his daughters, and because she did not believe that he was committed to changing his behaviour. Her service organization had no mandate to ask for changes in his situation, unless further evidence of wrongdoing should emerge.

The dilemma for the case worker was whether or not to continue her work with this family under circumstances with which she did not agree. After consideration, she voiced her objections to her superiors and asked to be removed from the case. Her request was granted, and another case worker was assigned.

ILLUSTRATION 3: THE PROFESSIONAL DOES NOT THINK IT IS THE BEST OPTION

Kadir, a man in his thirties, has difficulty walking and also has problems with social and emotional control. He visited his counsellor every Tuesday to work on his goal of developing friendships and becoming involved in satisfying social groups. Kadir does not value personal hygiene very highly, and this results in unpleasant odours and an unkempt appearance. His counsellor helped him to understand clearly that others often view poor hygiene negatively. He counselled Kadir that improving his hygiene – even if he does not think it is important personally – was a stepping-stone towards developing relationships with others. However, Kadir did not want to improve his hygiene; he wanted to seek out people who would accept him the way he was and for the person he saw himself to be.

The counsellor, who follows quality of life ideas in his work, could not think how Kadir's idea would work to achieve his desired goal of having more friends, since it had never worked before. In the end, the counsellor just did not agree that looking for friends who would accept his poor hygiene was Kadir's best option, and helpfully explained to Kadir why he could not help with it. He refocused his counselling sessions on drawing new kinds of parallels between hygiene and lack of friendships.

Satisfaction with things that are valued by the person

The second essential aspect of quality of life is that individuals are satisfied with those things in life that are valued by them. For practitioners, this presents two main requirements: respecting the opinions of people receiving services when they indicate that they are satisfied and dissatisfied, and promoting quality of life for them by supporting those aspects of life that are satisfying to them.

RESPECTING OPINIONS OF SATISFACTION

We need to know what people find satisfying and dissatisfying. As simple as this seems, it is a core idea in quality of life practice, because we cannot help people improve their lives unless we pay close attention to their feelings and reactions towards the multitude of things that occur in their lives. Moreover, professionals need to make this an ongoing part of their work, because, for many reasons, what is satisfying last week may not be so rewarding this week.

People sometimes get pleasure from things that professionals find questionable. Josef, a 55-year-old man who had lived in an institution almost all his life, wanted to jump in puddles after a heavy rainfall. His care worker wondered if that was appropriate; she also realized he would become wet and dirty in doing so. Still, she let him do it. The activity brought him great pleasure, satisfied a curiosity he felt, and resulted in no harm at all to him. He did get wet and cold, though, and felt uncomfortable afterwards. If memories of this discomfort (dissatisfaction) are strong enough to outweigh the pleasure Josef received from the activity, he might not repeat his jumping in puddles again.

The example of Josef results in very little harm to himself, and no harm to others. A few years later, however, Josef wanted to learn to drive a car because he got a great deal of satisfaction from travelling around. Because he experienced seizures, however, his care workers and physician could not give him permission for duty of care reasons. Their professional opinion was that, in spite of the satisfaction he would get from being able to drive, there was too much risk involved for Josef himself and for others on the roads.

In respecting satisfaction and dissatisfaction, professionals need first to accept the expression as legitimate, and share this acceptance with an individual like Josef, especially if they are not going to be able to support a request because there is too much potential for harm (e.g. 'I know you would really enjoy being able to drive, if you could'). They also need to explore other options that Josef might like to do instead of driving, such as helping him travel in other ways, or being around cars for other purposes such as washing or repairing. In addition, the practitioner needs to be careful to make the professional/ethical decision separately from acceptance of the source of satisfaction. It is essential in quality of life practice to keep in mind that respect for satisfaction and the decision about the best thing to do in a situation are sometimes very separate processes. Thus, part of a practitioner's job is to recognize expressions of satisfaction and dissatisfaction as valid and explore other options, but another part of the job is to help make the best decision.

HELP SUPPORT ASPECTS OF LIFE THAT ARE SATISFYING

Practice in the human services typically exists because people have difficulties in their lives with which they need help. For this reason, the mandates, priorities and operations of organizational systems within which practitioners work are primarily concerned with helping people to do things they cannot do well themselves. Some of these things are satisfying to those being helped, but others are not. Sometimes, they are just necessary parts of life that need to be dealt with. For example, Sarah does not particularly like grocery shopping. But she needs groceries and, because she is unable to shop alone owing to her disability, someone comes by once a week to help her. Similarly, others do not get particular pleasure from being helped with transportation, personal finance, hygiene, or other aspects of life, but these things are necessary parts of their everyday lives. Thus, many things that service organizations tend to do with their resources may or may not have much to do with how much satisfaction the recipient of the support experiences.

Service organizations typically do not spend their resources just assisting people to promote those activities that bring pleasure, but also those that they cannot do by themselves. Nor do they usually do things only for the pleasure it adds to life, even though we almost always identify things that are fun and enjoyable as strong contributors to our own quality of life. An exception is a recognition in some healthcare facilities of the value of fun and laughter to rehabilitation. In some hospitals and nursing homes, for example, humorists and artists work with multi-disciplinary health teams to increase humour and fun for people who are sick or dying (for some accounts see *The Humour Connection*). However, many service organizations whose mandate is to help people show little recognition of the value of fun and laughter to people's quality of life. Yet, this is a crucial and central part of quality of life work. Helping others improve their quality of life involves assisting them to continue to experience satisfaction and enjoyment from all aspects of life they find pleasurable, to explore aspects of life in which they believe they might find pleasure, and to encourage them to express their enjoyment of life. This is one reason why leisure activity is so important.

Adam is a 26-year-old man who, because of his mobility challenges, cannot get into his local video shop, because it has steps. He asked his case coordinator for someone to go there for him and rent adult (sex) videos once a week so he could watch them. Since it is a common practice in his city, and perfectly legal, for other adults his age to rent such videos, he considered this to be a reasonable request. Adam's worker said she could not do it because of a policy in her organization. This practitioner was pulled between the wishes of her client and the mandate of her organization, and she readily decided in favour of the organization. Other practitioners who base their work on quality of life principles might make the opposite choice, or might consider another option.

Wherever possible, practitioners should support the maintenance and enhancement of satisfying aspects of life that are satisfactory to others. As this example illustrates, however, it is sometimes difficult to make decisions about the best thing to do in a particular situation. If the practitioner decides that he or she simply cannot provide such support, it is extremely important to help the person understand that the decision not to do so is not related to approval or disapproval of the request itself. It is also important, if requests cannot be supported, that the practitioner consider other possible sources of support and help initiate contact with them. For example, Adam's case coordinator might have directed him to a local community centre that has volunteers who run errands for people with disabilities.

Ensuring that opportunities to improve are available and within the person's grasp
The illustrations above already refer to the importance of ensuring that a number of opportunities are available to an individual from which the best choice can be made. In fact, providing a range of opportunities actually decreases ethical dilemmas to a great extent because if one option does not appear to be viable, another (even if it is a 'second choice') may be almost as

good. Most ethical dilemmas that practitioners face stem not from their ability to generate a number of opportunities and viable options, but rather from the policies and practices of their organizations that permit the use of just one or a very limited number of opportunities. For example, an organization may not offer the opportunity for an individual with disabilities to receive help finding the living arrangement best suited to his or her needs and wishes, but instead may offer a residence in a particular location on a take-it-or-leave-it basis.

A frontline worker, Janet, worked in one such organization, but during the course of her work she discovered that the woman she was helping, Mara, had no desire to live in a home with others but wanted to live with her boyfriend. Since the organization did not allow for this in its practices, Janet had to grapple first with the ethical problem of whether to help provide opportunities for Mara that were outside the normal function of her organization. Janet decided she did want to help Mara at least explore these opportunities, but then she had to grapple with the problem of how to do so as an employee of her organization. Such decisions may be difficult for an employee such as Janet, and the final decision may be out of her hands, but, in quality of life terms, she has shown she respects the individual's choice. One of the important roles of the practitioner is to create opportunities in which decision making can be carried out by the individual, and this may mean confronting the system to allow for more approaches.

There are also several judgement calls that the professional needs to make when providing opportunities. How many opportunities should be supported? Ideally, as many as the individual can be expected to consider. How much time should be allotted to creating opportunities, in relation to helping people solve practical problems? As much as possible, within the time available. Should the practitioner create opportunities that have some potential for harm, even if they bring considerable satisfaction? People with disabilities typically need to take risks just as non-disabled people do, but the degree of risk of harm needs to be understood by the person with disabilities as well as the practitioner. Should the practitioner create opportunities that he or she does not believe will bring satisfaction? Counselling can be helpful here to challenge the individual to lay out the options and look ahead to possible consequences of selecting each. Should the practitioner create opportunities that the individual wants and enjoys, even if they do not seem to be appropriate ideas? The level of potential harm to self and others needs to guide the decision here.

All these questions, and others, arise when ensuring that opportunities to improve are available. Decisions are not always easy to make, but confronting such dilemmas with the person with disabilities and resolving them, even if it is a compromise, can lead to important steps forward in the rehabilitation process.

Using personal choice

One of the most important things that practitioners can do in their work is to respect the choices that people with disabilities make from the options that are available to them. However, the practitioner will meet with some challenges here, and there are some risks.

CHALLENGES IN USING CHOICE

People with disabilities may on occasion want decisions made for them. This is sometimes appropriate, because all of us occasionally find the need for a decision to be made for us. At times, in the presence of too many options, having to make a decision can be stressful. Sometimes, individuals just want someone to make a decision so they can get on with it. Some people with disabilities have lived in ways such that they have not experienced making choices, so they may be hesitant, lack the necessary skills, or have little motivation to make a choice. They may need practice in decision making, but once they get the hang of it they usually demand choice. A difficulty for practitioners, then, is to know when to encourage choice-making and when to allow decisions to be made by others.

A second challenge is that practitioners do not always recognize that in many instances the choices only matter because the person is dependent. Raj, a man who needs a personal attendant, wished to interview and hire his own support worker. This sounds reasonable, but was difficult because of the way this wish was not supported by numerous support agency and funding agency policies. Raj's 'problem' only arose because he had a disability; non-disabled people simply do not face such difficulties. On the other hand, dependency provides literally hundreds of additional opportunities throughout the day for choice-making. An effective attendant listens to the numerous choices the person with disabilities makes about even small details of activity, and if they are not forthcoming, the attendant will sometimes prompt. Thus, dependency both demands and creates opportunities for additional decision making, and these need to be accommodated in the course of daily living in a way that supports the development of positive self-image and empowerment for the person with disabilities.

A third challenge, related to the second, is that some situations arise only because of a disability. The mother of a young man, Mike, injured in a motor-cycle accident, requested help from rehabilitation agency personnel to respond to his sexual needs and choices. Since Mike would soon return home, it was agreed aspects of the situation needed to be discussed with his mother. This was difficult for his mother, because open discussions about sexuality had not been part of the mother–son relationship. Mike had previously ful-filled his sexual needs outside the family life experience, and had kept his sexual activities private. Disability now required that they no longer be so private. The question of right to privacy and independent decision making thus became an issue within the issue of Mike's right to choice and wish for support.

RISKS INVOLVED IN USING CHOICE

There are also many risks in choice. When practitioners allow others to make their own choices, they are risking that the choices made might not be the ones they would make. At times, they might think the choices are just not appropriate, or even dangerous. Marion, a 53-year-old woman, wanted to jump up and down on a trampoline in her residential accommodation. The staff thought this might result in injury, or that there might be insurance or legal risks. They had to decide whether to respect Marion's choice.

At other times, practitioners risk their own values and better judgement. Eban wanted his girlfriend to move into his apartment, even though he had many times experienced negative consequences of her habit of creating con-siderable havoc in his life. His support worker's experience had taught her that this choice would almost certainly result in a great deal more trouble for both Eban and herself. Still, she risked her own doubts and respected Eban's choice.

Another risk Eban's support worker took was that, even if the move did not work out, there might be a way for Eban to develop life skills and choice-making skills. Only a few days after the move, Eban's girlfriend did create a great deal of trouble in his life and Eban had to call in his case worker. An opportunity presented itself to engage in some further counselling with Eban for the purpose of encouraging him to think more about the consequences of his choice. In spite of counselling, however, Eban did not want his girlfriend to move out. On balance, the pleasure of having her live there outweighed his disturbance at the chaos she was creating.

If choice is to be respected, it has to be recognized that some choices do not work out, and others do not work out the way the practitioner would like. But this does not mean the choice should be turned down, for there is learning and development potential in almost every choice. It is only by making choices and experiencing the results of those choices that people with disabilities learn to make better choices that are helpful to themselves and to others. Having choice promotes thinking and opportunities for learning.

Changes to self-image

In quality of life work, we enable people to exercise choice within a range of options that are valued and pleasing to them. People who do this typically experience improvement in self-image, because there is harmony between how their lives are going and how they see themselves. Such harmony is reinforcing to positive self-image. But creating harmony between people's lives and how they see themselves can also create some very interesting professional and ethical dilemmas. Two such dilemmas are explored below.

NEGATIVE SELF-IMAGE IS SOUGHT

Some people with disabilities may appear to prefer a negative self-image. Living in a world dominated by non-disabled people, they may, over many years, have come to believe that they are unworthy or that they will never live up to the ideal. When we stop to consider the life experiences of people with disabilities, it is easy to identify any number of social, environmental and systemic factors that add to this learning and act as barriers to the development of positive self-image. Such thoughts and feelings are also brought to bear on parents and relatives, sometimes resulting in challenging or tragic circumstances. Parents, other family members, and society at large often view both children and adults who have disabilities in non-positive ways. Recently in Canada, a mild-mannered farmer asphyxiated his six-year-old daughter who had severe cerebral palsy, because he did not envision her having a future in any worthwhile way. This case came to the attention of the public, but many forms of negative self-image are passed on quietly to both children and adults that result in their thinking of themselves in negative ways as well. As a result, a great many of the choices they make, and even the things that appear to give them pleasure, support negative views of themselves. Practitioners, especially those with a quality of life focus, face an interesting challenge when trying to support family members or individuals who make choices that may lead to poor experiences, which then may increase negative self-image.

Such a challenge faced Sarah, a community worker who supported people with disabilities and mental health problems. Sarah began to work with Marika, a 60-year-old woman who had a long history of making decisions that led to people taking advantage of her – sometimes rather extreme advantage. Sarah's plan was to help Marika develop a more positive self-image and make decisions based on that self-image. Before she could begin her work, Marika experienced a crisis. Her landlord had served her an eviction notice, because, two weeks previously, she had befriended a stranger from the street and let her move into her apartment. The problem for the landlord was that the new friend had littered the entire formerly neat apartment knee-deep with street litter, which was creating a very unpleasant odour throughout the entire floor. But Marika liked her new friend and enjoyed having her around. She made it clear that she did not want to ask her to move out, even though she clearly understood the several negative consequences of allowing her to stay.

Sarah's dilemma here was whether to respect Marika's choice and try to eliminate the negative consequences as much as possible, or to take direct action in an effort to begin to develop better decision making. She had little time to decide, but took the latter option, viewing it as an opportunity to demonstrate to Marika how to make decisions that make you feel good about yourself, make you feel more in control of your life, and make you feel the things you do in life are worthwhile. Sarah helped Marika clean her apartment, get new keys, and tell the new friend that she was not welcome to come in any more. In taking this action, Sarah was not without doubts, as she realized she was acting against Marika's expressed wishes, but felt hopeful that she was acting in her best interests.

One problem with negative self-image, which most practitioners already know from their work, is that it is sometimes very difficult to make it more positive. Self-image is tied closely to personality or character, which is quite stable over a person's lifetime even when serious efforts are taken by the person to bring about change. Still, changes to more positive self-image can be made, and they can be strengthened, as Sarah knew, by making choices that bring rewards. By strongly encouraging Marika to make a choice that could work out well, Sarah was hoping to show Marika how making certain choices would make her feel happy, more in charge of her life, and more important as a person. Sarah's hope was that this was a first step for Marika to learn that the harmony between a new set of choices and a different self-image is better than the harmony between the choices she used to make and her more negative self-image. The danger is that such a response by Sarah could, if not carefully handled, lead to decreased empowerment. Thus, this example illustrates some of the complexities in working in the field – issues that require careful discussion and documentation.

But self-image can change. Jane regarded herself as very disabled. She spoke in a whisper, and was usually silent when men were present. She had difficulty initiating activity. After many months of practical experience, working alongside her rehabilitation practitioner carrying out routine clerical duties, her self-image began to become more positive. One day, she indicated that she took a friend out to lunch. After some discussion, she was asked why she had decided to do this. She replied: 'Because Anne is handicapped like I used to be.'

THE 'WRONG' SELF-IMAGE IS SOUGHT

A second dilemma for practitioners concerning self-image is that some individuals may have an ideal view of themselves with which the practitioner simply does not agree. Jonas, a 42-year-old man with a physical disability, sees himself as a member of a street gang. He has dressed for many years in clothes that match this image as closely as possible, and he has adopted the language nuances of those with whom he identifies. Whenever he could, over the past 20 years, Jonas has developed friendships with 'street people' and has learned the ways of drug trade, prostitution, hustling for money, and some minor crime. In fact, he has many street skills and speaks proudly of his abilities.

Jonas's self-image is not negative for him. In fact, it is very positive. He makes choices about things he enjoys and that are meaningful to him, and these, in turn, make him feel very good about himself. But not all people share this point of view.

Jonas's support worker, who sees him occasionally when the need arises, is one of those. She simply does not agree with the self-image he has adopted. She believes that engaging in activities that are in harmony with his perception of himself is physically dangerous for him. An additional problem for her is that when she is assisting Jonas in various ways, she often becomes aware of activity carried out by him or by others he knows that is illegal or morally very questionable. Yet, even though he may be putting himself at risk, he has not brought direct harm to himself nor has he knowingly brought direct harm to others. So, although the support worker generally believes in encouraging activities that build whatever self-image her clients have, in the case of Jonas she does not believe that this self-image is positive.

This worker considered that she had several choices: to withdraw her support, to continue to support Jonas occasionally and overlook the fact that she did not think his self-image was positive, to continue her support and try to find ways to help Jonas change his self-image, or to continue her support and try to find ways that she could accept his choice of self-image better. Workers, and readers, will differ in which of these options they would select. Jonas's worker chose the second, although she felt less than certain that this was the best choice.

Empowerment to individuals and groups with disabilities

Empowerment occurs when control, or power, is passed to an individual or group. In rehabilitation, medicine, social work, psychology, education, and many allied disciplines, it is gradually becoming recognized that the healthiest and most effective individuals have personal control and make decisions for themselves with advice and input from others. The belief here is that, for best results overall, final decisions should be made by the individuals who are most closely affected by the decisions.

But professional standards and practices do not always mesh with personal empowerment. Many professionals find it difficult to pass control to their clients or patients. Sometimes this is because they assume that the people with disabilities whom they support are unable to exercise control. These include children, though teachers and youth workers are beginning to realize that children need a say in matters that concern them, either as a body of students or as individuals. Elderly people frequently lose control of their environments and even their personal lives because others believe they cannot cope. Adults with more severe disabilities, especially those who do not use language fluently, are often assumed, erroneously, not to be capable of being in control of their own lives.

There is some validity to such professional doubts. People with disabilities typically do need help in some areas of their lives, and some need help in many areas, because they cannot do certain things themselves. However, such professional doubts need to be reframed. Mary, whose cognitive development is such that she does not understand numbers, cannot be expected to control her own finances, but she can exercise control over such things as who goes to the bank with her, when they go, and how much time they spend there. She can sign her name to cheques and deposit slips, even though she does not understand the numbers she is signing for. Because Mary's support worker believes in empowerment, he encourages Mary to take charge of their weekly banking activities by controlling the decisions about these procedures. This often works out well, but sometimes Mary wants to go to the bank at times that are difficult for the support worker to fit into his schedule. In his work with Mary and the many others he supports, the worker needs to make ongoing decisions about how to balance his belief in empowering people with disabilities with the realities of his work schedule.

There are many instances where individuals can be given, or continue to have, control over some aspects of their lives, or where they can be given greater control in other parts of their lives. Many persons who are aging and experience dementia may function well in some aspects of their lives and function well some days. Unfortunately, it is sometimes thought easier for the care worker to take over entirely. This is not in the best interests of the individual or, in the long term, for the care workers themselves, since it encourages greater deterioration and dependency.

Many professionals by inclination, and frequently through training, like to be in control themselves. They feel comfortable when they are directing, organizing and practising what they believe in and what they are trained to do. Thus, a move towards client empowerment requires a change in their philosophical and practical approach, and this poses an ethical dilemma for many professionals when it conflicts with the historical approach of their own profession. Moreover, professional agencies and organizations typically like to feel that they are in control of their own activities, mandates and funding. This makes passing control to people with disabilities all the more difficult.

The quality of life approach to supporting people with disabilities values empowering people to take control over their own lives as much as possible. But at any point in time professionals have to do this in ways that are workable for them and the service systems within which they function. Service systems themselves need to adopt an empowerment approach, and a critical first step is to develop guidelines for the development of empowering models that promote consumer development. We need to plan opportunities for people with disabilities to exercise maximum control over their lives, protect against repeated failures that may occur, document our successes and failures, and share this information with one another. These are complex challenges, but ones that must be met at policy and professional levels if individual consumers are to develop and succeed.

Issues related to the value of disabilities in society

A number of professional and ethical issues emerge from time to time in disability work that have to do with the value we place on people with disabilities in our society. Five such issues are described below by way of examples.

Valuing people with disabilities

Practitioners with a quality of life focus accept disability in society, and respect and value people with disabilities along with non-disabled people as important and equal citizens. Indeed, disability frequently adds value to society, sometimes because it causes individuals to express their resources in new and creative ways, and sometimes because it causes society to reframe its goals and actions positively. All societies consist of people who have a wide range of skills and abilities, and there are many reasons for fully recognizing and respecting the full range. In everyday practice, however, not all professional groups or professional services demonstrate acceptance of disability well, even though their purpose is to provide services for people with disabilities. There are very practical ways that value for the person with disability can be demonstrated. These include the use of respectful, person-oriented language that is clear, non-condescending and non-technical but encourages understanding and decision making by the client, respect for private, physical space, and encouragement of personal social and psychological space.

Valuing equality of opportunity

Although practitioners with a quality of life focus support choices that bring desired and meaningful results from a range of options, few professional groups offer themselves as one of those opportunities. Ray was an employment counsellor in an organization that trained people with mild intellectual disabilities for work in community settings. Shortly after beginning his job, Ray interviewed Aaron who said that ever since he was a boy he had wanted to help other people by being a counsellor. In fact, he had been a camp counsellor for three years while a teenager. Ray saw an opportunity for Aaron to act as a mentor and practical helper to some of his peers, and sought out a 'junior counsellor' position for Aaron within the organization. But the answer was no. The organization did not hire people with intellectual disabilities, rather it helped them find employment elsewhere. Ray's organization acted as if it valued equality of opportunity for people with intellectual disabilities in the workplace, but it showed no willingness to demonstrate that value in its own functioning. This came as a surprise to Ray, and he had to deliberate over whether or not to oppose the position taken.

Valuing ability

Practitioners often act very effectively as advocates for people with disabilities participating fully in life experiences. The principle they act on is that people with disabilities have the right to lead a life that is similar to non-disabled people, even if they need considerable support to do so. For example, practitioners usually support the wishes of people with disabilities who choose to be parents. But valuing people's right to procreate and to be parents can clash with factors that work against this right, such as lack of local services to support parenting. When such clashes occur, the practitioner has to decide on the best thing to do in the situation: continue to support the wish of the individual as well as possible, or to choose another route.

Valuing bringing disability into the world

Considerable efforts are being taken by medical and other professional groups to prevent disabilities wherever possible. The search for genetic and other causes of disability is very strong, as is the view among both practitioners and people in general that it is better for newborns not to have disabilities than to have disabilities. Pre-natal counselling that includes the option of abortion, especially if there is a known or suspected risk for disability, is considered by most medical practitioners to be an ethical responsibility. All these efforts are typically explained and justified as necessary because they provide information families need to make the best choice.

The problem for practitioners is that these efforts also give the impression that professionals and others in the disability field devalue bringing disabilities into the world. But it is critical that every practitioner finds the ethical pathway between respecting and valuing people with disabilities, respecting the values of potential parents, and the work to prevent disabilities.

Valuing disability rights and entitlements

Much has been written about rights and entitlements. A quality of life approach supports legal rights and entitlements because they are frequently necessary to ensure that people are able to live the life they seek. This is more than just the right to live in an environment that is non-discriminatory and non-devaluing. There is a belief that people with disabilities should not have to fight for their rights more than other people. Rights should be a 'right' for everyone equally.

But equality does not necessarily mean equal. People with disabilities very often require more help and support than other people to attain similar goals, or to attain goals of their choice. The more they become empowered, the more likely this is to occur. The amount of help required for this leads us to consider where to stop. What is the appropriate kind of help? How much help is too much, or just simply not a good use of resources? Our value of rights and entitlements mingles with reality to produce difficult ethical questions.

Tonya wished to get married to a man with a physical disability, as is her right as an adult. She herself had an intellectual disability and had little facility with money concepts. Though Tonya had associated with her boyfriend for many years and they jointly planned to marry, her mother was against any wedding. Tonya was so forceful in her opinion, however, that her mother at length agreed to support it, but in arranging the wedding negotiated with the officiating priest to marry them in a fictitious wedding where no formal records would be signed. Tonya's mother was concerned that if Tonya were to marry this man she would be under his control, and that when she hesrself died, he would run off with her inheritance. Obviously, Tonya's rights were seriously transgressed, as were those of the young man.

Issues related to quality support for people with disabilities

All of the professional and ethical issues discussed so far in this chapter have links to the quality of support given to people with disabilities. Sometimes in professional work, though, ethical issues emerge that entirely focus on the quality of support. Three such issues are presented below.

Providing quality living for one at the expense of others

In most countries of the world, even those with the best services, the funding and personnel made available do not meet all the needs of all the people with disabilities. This creates a special ethical dilemma for practitioners who implement a quality of life approach: to what extent do we offer support to individuals so that they can live in quality ways, when these same resources are being denied to others who are also in need?

Joyce is a 78-year-old woman who has had mobility difficulties almost all her adult life. She has no family in the city where she lives and receives considerable support from an agency that assists older people to live independently. Over the course of a few months, she experienced four falls in her apartment where she lived alone. She was able to call the superintendent for help in each case, and was not seriously hurt. The agency, in keeping with its mandate to support independent living, increased the care it provided and made additional accommodations to her apartment to help her move around more easily. Agency staff took special care to listen to Joyce's point of view and to respect her choice. In particular, they made considerable effort to ensure that Joyce could continue to enjoy those aspects of her life that gave her pleasure.

Staff at the agency deliberated for some time over the decision to do this, however, since they had a long waiting list of other people needing support. The quality of Joyce's life was being enhanced, but it was at the expense of others going without any support at all. Ultimately, they solved their ethical dilemma by referring back to the mandate of the organization, and decided that supporting Joyce to live independently was acting in accordance with it. Others may not have agreed with their actions, however, and may have taken a very different approach.

Providing new supports because of medical advances

In recent decades, numerous scientific and medical advances have led to many more people being kept alive than was formerly the case. Infants are increasingly able to survive early life difficulties, teens and adults with a number of conditions are surviving very much longer than in past decades (e.g. Down syndrome, head injury), and older adults are living longer each decade. At the same time, patterns of known disabilities are changing somewhat, sometimes from new health concerns (e.g. HIV in children) and sometimes through the discovery of 'new' causes and contributing factors to disability through genetic and other scientific advances in knowledge (e.g. Asperger syndrome, foetal alcohol syndrome). Such advances mean that we have increased opportunities and capability to provide support, but we may not have the resources or capacity to do so.

In addition, we may not always consider that providing support is the best thing to do in particular situations. For example, the practice of keeping children or adults alive because we have the technology to do so poses some of the most difficult ethical dilemmas practitioners face. With such dilemmas, decisions need to be made on an individual basis, but usually involve the same three questions: What are the likely outcomes of our actions on the person being kept alive? What effects will our actions have on other people? and How many of our resources should we use for this purpose? Providing support because we have the technical ability to do so and providing support because it is the best thing to do are not always the same thing, but deciding upon the difference is a serious responsibility indeed. The principles of quality of life are well worth considering in such situations. For example, what are the lifespan issues for the person, the family, professions and services when a newborn child with profound disabilities is enabled to survive using extrordinary interventions?

Quality of care and quality of independence

In practical work with people who have disabilities, two principles sometimes pull in opposite directions: providing appropriate care, and enhancing self-care and independence. Family members, other informal support people, community groups, agencies and government funders all assume some responsibility, to varying degrees, for ensuring that care is provided. At the same time, people with disabilities strive for independence in their lives and usually welcome it, provided that it is accompanied by an ease of being able to carry out the activities of life of their choosing.

Practitioners recognize that, if desired by the individual, providing care and enhancing independence can each improve quality of life. The difficulty is that most people with disabilities require both care and independence, and the two contradict each other to a considerable degree. Ryan is an eight-year-old with cerebral palsy who uses a wheelchair and requires considerable assistance to carry out his daily activities. He wants to play with his friends and do many things on his own, but his care givers are sometimes hesitant to let him. The ethical struggle for the care givers is how much to provide him with care and how much to risk personal safety so that he can gain the independence he seeks. This is not a single decision, moreover, because the best thing to do depends on the particular situation he is in, and these situations change constantly throughout the day. Thus, his care givers need to make many decisions over the course of every day about the degree to which they will encourage care or independence. Such decisions are made by all effective practitioners many times each day as they carry out their work.

Finding the balance

Practitioners can rush headlong into providing opportunities and promoting choice around aspects of life that are important and satisfying to people with disabilities. Sometimes, these efforts work out well, but it takes skill to avoid such problems as too many opportunities in too short a time. Further, inappropriate risk taking can give rise to serious challenges. On the other hand, practitioners can proceed too cautiously, and so lose opportunities for effective development. Control can be easily justified under the guise of unnecessary risk taking, administrative restraint and insurance or legal risk. Being too impetuous tends to be more obvious and alarming to the outsider, but being too cautious, though less apparent, is usually not helpful and even harmful in the long run.

It is important for practitioners who want to take a quality of life approach to find the balance among their personal characteristics and abilities, the personal characteristics and abilities of the people they are paid to assist, what they are paid to do, and the professional controls from the organization for which they work. This is a complex balance to achieve. But it is within the context of this complex balance that a great many ethical decisions, some of which are very difficult indeed, have to be made.

For thought and discussion

1.   Bring to mind an issue that is of concern in your workplace, and describe it. Is it an ethical or a professional issue – or both? How is the issue being handled? Is it being handled in the best way?

2.   What are the most important ethical issues for your personal quality of life?

3.   What are your five priorities for recommended action that might emerge from considering ethical questions? Why is each of these of particular importance?

4.   George, a lonely man, has been supported by his care worker for several years. He brings her a present as a 'thank you'. The care worker's agency has a policy on personal gifts: no such gifts are to be accepted. What are the ethical and professional issues for the care worker? What are the rights and needs of the client?

5.   Gillian is a young woman who has poor speech skills and little understanding of speech. She responds well non-verbally (e.g. pointing; a light touch on the arm; a smile). The agency manager has sent a note to all staff saying touching of clients is unacceptable in the light of legal cases highlighted in the press. What is the professional and ethical issue (what is the *best* thing to do in this particular situation) from the points of view of the client, the professional worker and the manager? How might the situation be resolved?

Selected bibliography

Bain, R. (1993) *Fools Rush In*. London: Marshall Pickering.

Brown, R.I. (2000) *Evaluation of Options Co-ordination: Committee on the Evaluation of Quality Services for People with Disabilities*. Report to the Minister for Disability Services, Government of South Australia, Adelaide, Australia.

Dale, N.O. (1996) *Working with Families of Children with Special Needs: Partnership and Practice*. London: Routledge.

Egan, G. (2002) *The Skilled Helper: A Problem-management and Opportunity-development Approach to Helping.* Pacific Grove, CA: Brooks/Cole.

Franzini, L.R. (2002) *Kids Who Laugh: How to Develop Your Child's Sense of Humor.* Garden City Park, NY: Square One.

Garfat, T. and Ricks, F. (1995) 'Self-driven ethical decision-making: A model for child and youth care.' *Child and Youth Care Forum 24,* 6, 393–403.

Pettifor, J.L., Estay, I. and Paquet, S. (2002) 'Prefered strategies for learning ethics in the practice of a discipline.' *Canadian Psychology 43,* 4, 260–269.

Reinders, H.S. (2000) *The Future of the Disabled in Liberal Society: An Ethical Analysis.* Notre Dame, IN: University of Notre Dame Press.

Somerville, M.A. (2000) *The Ethical Canary: Science, Society and the Human Spirit.* Toronto: Viking.

Sullivan, B. and Heng, J. (1999) 'Ethical issues relating to consent in providing treatment and care.' In I. Brown and M. Percy (eds) *Developmental Disabilities in Ontario.* Toronto: Front Porch.

Tennyson, W.W. and Strom, S.M. (1986) 'Beyond professional standards: Developing responsibilities.' *Journal of Counseling and Development 64,* 298–302.

The Humor Connection. The newsletter of the Association for Applied and Therapeutic Humor. Available from www.aath.org or 1951 West Camelback Road, #445, Phoenix, AZ 85015, USA.

Towsen, J. (1976) *Clowns.* New York: Hawthorn Books.

Selected websites on ethics (2002)

Canadian Association of Disability Management Coordinators
http://fas.sfu.ca/fas-ce/cadmc/code.htm

Canadian Sociology and Anthropology Association
http://www.unb.ca/web/anthropology/csaa/englcode.htm

Disability Research Digest
http://www.smd-services.com/information/may2002drd.html

Ethics in Science and Scholarship: The Toronto Resolution
http://www.math.yorku.ca/sfp/sfp2.html

The Canadian Resource for Hospital Ethics Committees
http://www.ethicscommittee.ca/intl-inst.html

The Network on Ethics and Intellectual Disabilities
http://www.georgetown.edu/research/kie/intdisnews.htm

CHAPTER 11

Policy, Management and Quality-of-Life-Based Practice

As a frontline worker, I am often put in the position of saying, 'No. It can't be done because of my agency's policy.' I am looking forward to being able to ask instead, 'How can this be done?'

The role of policy and management

So far, we have said little about the impact of policy and management of services on practice based on quality of life. Yet the implications of these have been present throughout. If a quality of life approach is to be effective for practitioners, both policy makers and management need to understand the principles of a quality of life approach and incorporate them into the guidelines and procedures of service systems. In this chapter, we are interested in understanding how policy can help set the context for effective quality of life work by practitioners, and how management can set up and run programmes in such a way that a quality of life approach is supported.

This is particularly important in light of the dilemmas raised in the previous chapter about ethical issues. There, we learned that some of the ideas that are important to practice and use a quality of life approach can clash with the way service systems typically carry out their work. One reason for this is that the policy – the laws, rules and procedures that act as guidelines for how practice is carried out – is not always based on the same values and principles as those of a quality of life approach to practice. But policy is usually fairly general in nature and is almost always open to some degree of interpretation by service managers. Thus, another reason for such clashes is that those who manage services do not always interpret policy in such a way that it accommodates the ideas that are central to a quality of life approach. Developing policy and management procedures that are in keeping with quality of life principles should reduce the number of ethical dilemmas practitioners are presented with.

Practitioners are not specialists in policy, nor do they need to be. But they do need to understand the basics of what policy and management are for, how they might impact intervention, and what practitioners might do to minimize any possible negative effects.

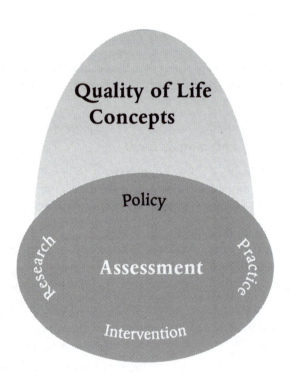

Figure 11.1 The quality of life approach: Policy

What are policy and management?

Policy, both formal and informal, sets the stage for how services are set up and what the scope of their activities is. Policy takes various forms, but it is helpful to think of three levels:

1. formal *laws and legislation* that set out the legal parameters within which action must be carried out

2. *statements*, written or unwritten, that provide overall direction to the way legislative bodies, funders and governance bodies function

3. *regulations*, written or unwritten, that provide rules for specific governance, funding and operational procedures.

Management of services involves putting policies into practice and running them in an ongoing way. It has numerous components, but, in general, management covers two main activities: it develops and uses a practical conceptual/philosophical framework that indicates why the service exists and what it does, so that policy ideas can be put into practice with rules and boundaries that are understood; and it creates and maintains a clear infrastructure within which the service operates in a continuous way.

The importance of understanding quality of life

Policy makers and managers should not use quality of life *only* because it is becoming popular. The danger is that the term will become policy and management jargon, but without being fully understood. For this reason, it is necessary for management and policy personnel to have first-hand knowledge, and preferably experience, of its application. Paul, the director of a government disability services unit, observing the frontline interventions of personnel over a period of days, learned a great deal, and came to understand what duties and issues faced the personnel working in the disability field. Such action is critical because our promotion policies often place successful people in management and policy-making positions, and the danger is that quite soon they become out of touch with the practical application of theory to practice.

Impact of policy and management on interventions

Both policy and management can have a strong effect on the way interventions are carried out, and even on how possible or impossible it is to implement them. Thus, they are very relevant to the work of all practitioners, but particularly to practitioners promoting personal values, satisfaction, personal choice, opportunities, and other ideas central to a quality of life approach. Two examples are provided below that serve to illustrate this: the experiences of Celeste with the policy and management of the healthcare system, and the experiences of Mark's attempt to become involved in decisions about his own education.

CELESTE AND HOME CARE

Celeste is a woman, 56 years old, who uses a wheelchair as a result of a car accident earlier in her life. She spent a few days in hospital due to a serious problem with blood circulation in one of her legs, but was discharged with her consent on a Friday morning. She was sent home by ambulance to her apartment, where she lived alone, with strict instructions to rest in bed and to let home care staff attend to her health needs.

When Celeste arrived home, she discovered that she had not been given specific information about the home care staff, and, perhaps due to some emotional difficulties, was not confident enough to call the hospital. She waited alone in her apartment until late Monday afternoon when she at last received a telephone call from the home care agency.

Celeste survived, but it is clear that the healthcare system did not support her over the first critical weekend after she had been released from hospital. What happened? The jurisdiction in which Celeste lived provided health care, including free hospital and home care, and it was clearly within the policies of both the hospital and the home care agency to approve service in cases such as this one. The problem lay in the important fact that policies of the jurisdiction, the hospital, and the home care agency, or even different policies within the hospital, did not always fit together. Further, management had not ensured that there were practical solutions to problems that arose from policies not fitting together.

Celeste's physician appropriately recommended home care, but in accordance with hospital policy left the arrangements to the nursing staff without ensuring that care was actually in place. The nursing staff, in accordance with policy that directs their work, made a reference to the discharge planner before assisting Celeste to go home. Hospital policy allowed for just one discharge planner for the entire hospital, and department policy stipulated that the discharge planner dealt with people partly in the order they were referred and partly according to their need for assistance. On the day Celeste was referred to the discharge planner, several other people were referred ahead of her and a few others jumped ahead of her in the queue because of more serious needs. A separate hospital policy allowed for reduced work hours in the summer months, and since it was the middle of the summer, the discharge planner had time only to make a quick telephone referral to the agency that provided home care before she left work at 4:00pm. The agency that took home care referrals had a policy that it did not accept new referrals after 3:00pm on Fridays, so they did not begin to process Celeste's referral until Monday morning. In accordance with other operational policies, they had to receive various other pieces of information from the hospital and from Celeste's own physician before they could proceed. This took most of the working day on Monday to accomplish, and it was 4:20pm when the agency telephoned Celeste to make arrangements for her home care.

The intention of policy is to set out clearly what the rules are for doing things, and the intention of management is to ensure that these rules are followed in ways that support the everyday work of the service. Home care for Celeste was a routine intervention, one that was both a legal entitlement and an established practice, yet the process of implementing it bounced around among numerous policies and management procedures that were not well matched. The result was an unfortunate and potentially dangerous outcome. Celeste's experiences clearly illustrate three things. First, policies of various kinds at various levels – many of which we may not even be aware of – have an impact, and often a strong impact, on the success of an intervention. Second, policies that act as the framework for practice do not always fit together perfectly in real-life applications, and sometimes they even contradict one another. Third, an important role for management is to understand and anticipate problems that might emerge because of the infrastructure they have set up, and to devise appropriate solutions.

MARK AND SCHOOL DECISIONS

Senior school officials and teachers decided that there should be a planning meeting to discuss and set goals and requirements for a young adolescent named Mark who had reading and writing difficulties. Mark's parents were asked to attend, and the matter had reached a stage where a lawyer was also representing the family. Mark was not invited to the meeting, even though he had requested to be present.

The meeting was to involve Mark's education, the choices to be made about his learning, and the methods the school would use to teach him. He had many views about these matters and was able to express them satisfactorily. The implications of any decisions made would affect several domains of his life. The issues were likely to cover the lifespan in terms of their effects. However, the educational policy and practice of the jurisdiction was that such students should not attend these planning meetings. Instead, legal representation was used to assert Mark's rights, as well as his need to be there.

This is a clear example where the policy is not consistent with the quality of life approach, but where things would probably work out much better if they were. Mark not only should have been allowed to attend the meeting, but also should have been encouraged to do so. Does this mean that such individuals should always be present? No, not necessarily, but it should be the usual position. Adopting such a usual position requires educational managers and teachers to be comfortable with it – which may involve some professional training – and it may also require that outside agents, such as lawyers, become aware of changing practices.

Integrating policy, management and practice
Four overall strategies for tying policy and management to practice

The quality of life model that is put forward in this book suggests strategies that can be used to ensure that policy, management and practice are all based on a quality of life approach and that they are in keeping with one another.

MAKE POLICY AND MANAGEMENT FIT THE FACTS

A basic strategy is that policy needs to fit the facts, rather than the facts fitting the policy. This may seem rather obvious, but circumstances of life for people with disabilities have changed so radically over the past few years that discrepancies between policy and practice often arise simply because of change.

A shift to a quality of life approach is one such change. For example, policy makers and managers frequently cite lack of funding as a reason not to meet the individual needs of many people who require services. However, using a quality of life approach, we often find the facts to be that many people have inexpensive needs that can be satisfied with creative, flexible supports. If policy and management could better fit the facts of the shift towards a quality of life approach, much better support could be offered to many more people.

LOOK AT THE LONG-TERM EFFECTS

A second strategy is to look at the long-term advantages of interventions, rather than simply at fixing the problem in the short term. Often, long-term intervention over the course of many years is necessary. For people who have experienced a head injury, neuronal recovery, including dendritic reconnection, may take many years, and steady intervention in inclusive settings with regular support can pay dividends. Individuals who later become self-supporting not only contribute to their society, but also are no longer largely dependent on the service system. The advantages to individual quality of life are obvious. Thus, policy and management need to direct attention not just to immediate problems but also to the ways they enable active quality improvements to occur over time.

PROVIDE FLEXIBILITY TO FRONTLINE PERSONNEL

Frontline personnel must have permission from management to try out things and to adapt interventions and supports within the general policies of the service system. A quality of life approach requires some reasonable risk-taking and experimentation at times. Alvaro, who lives in a community home with four other people with mild intellectual disabilities, is legally blind but enjoys going to a club he belongs to and other places of his choosing on his own. He understands clearly where he is going and has good skills to ask for any needed help. His support team worry that crossing streets may not be safe and that he will be misunderstood when he accidentally bumps into people, but they do encourage his independent behaviour because it is important to him. The agency they work for has in place policies that support risk-taking, and has procedures in place to deal with any problems that might emerge as a result.

DEVELOP WAYS TO ADDRESS THE NEEDS OF OUTSIDE AGENTS

As people with disabilities use community resources more and more, a problem that sometimes arises is that the policies of outside services or agents are not in keeping with the policies of the practitioner's own organization. For example, a particular insurance agency does not provide coverage to people with disabilities who are taken to a community recreation programme from their service agency because they are considered to be at risk of incurring injury. This is one illustration of a growing range of issues where insurance agencies, sometimes unwittingly, restrict critical rehabilitation interventions.

Practitioners can advocate for fair treatment from outside agencies such as this, but, ultimately, they usually cannot change an agency's policy unless they can show that it contradicts legal requirements. For example, should reasonable risk-taking be a right? In some countries, see-saws and roundabouts have been taken away from playgrounds because local councils are concerned that accidents can happen and that the council may be sued. But taking away such items may overprotect children, with the result that they do not learn how to cope with risks and therefore become more vulnerable. Many psychologists have expressed concern over such developments. The same issue arises in the field of disabilities. Management needs to have in place ways to explore and deal with the policies of external agents when problems like this arise.

Taking steps to integrate policy, management and practice

To this point, we have learned generally what policy and management do and how they sometimes impact on intervention. Here, we provide four steps that can be taken to reduce the frustrations that sometimes spring up from 'having' to abide by policies that systems have put in place.

STEP 1: BE INFORMED – ALWAYS ASK WHAT THE POLICIES ARE

Many practitioners and people who use services do not think to ask about the policies of an agency or an organization. Yet, becoming informed is one of the most important sets of initial questions, and they are never confidential or secret. It is just that many social service, health, education and other professionals have not been accustomed to sharing this information. The questions can be informal and do not even have to use the word 'policy'. Ask such questions as 'What are your rules about...?', 'What are your requirements for...?' or 'What process would you follow if...?' Most professionals are only too happy to share this information, and often treat you with greater respect for having asked.

In the example provided earlier about Celeste's experience with the healthcare system, if she or someone accompanying her had asked before she was discharged from the hospital about the specific procedures for acquiring home care over the weekend, she might have been alerted to the fact that this might not occur. In that case, she might have chosen to contradict the physician's recommendation to return home, and instead she might have chosen to remain in the hospital until the Monday. Another possibility is that, by asking specific questions, she might have sparked the discharge planner or the home care agency to overlook some of their own policies to ensure that home care was provided over the weekend.

This is not to suggest that such organizations as hospitals and community agencies do not have a responsibility for making their own policies work. They do. But organizations do not always work perfectly, and individuals or those advocating on their behalf can do a great deal to keep them 'honest' even if that means they have to revise some of their own policies.

STEP 2: TAKE ACTION WHEN POLICIES DO NOT SUPPORT AN INTERVENTION

Policies are designed to make things work for large groups of people, but sometimes they do not work well at the individual level. They may not be helping an individual and they may actually be working against the success of an intervention. School policies of zero tolerance for bad behaviour support the orderliness of a school system, but they are likely to do little or nothing to help the child who is having behavioural problems. Prison terms for convicted criminals remove some of the danger from society in general, but being forcibly housed with other criminals is probably not a very effective way to rehabilitate individuals who have problems abiding by the law. Using the example of Celeste again, the rule of the agency providing home care services but not accepting referrals after 3pm may be generally useful, because the agency closes at 5pm for the weekend and it needs two hours to make arrangements for the referrals it receives up to 3pm. However, in Celeste's specific case, this rule worked against her.

Most organizations will bend their policies slightly if notified of a problem. Flexibility is a basic requirement of a quality of life approach. A telephone call or a brief visit explaining how a policy is adversely affecting a needed intervention can often result in a quick resolution to the problem. Sometimes, it is necessary to make a stronger case, which might involve going to a higher authority. Practitioners should not hesitate to take this action when policies have negative impacts on their planned interventions. Policies are made to provide the rules for those interventions, and when they do not work in a positive way, those who are in positions to amend the policies need to be made aware of the difficulties.

Policies change over time, but they usually only change if those who administer them are aware of and appreciate any negative impact they are having on individuals and groups of individuals. For this reason, it is crucial to inform organizations and to insist on the problem being redressed or 'fixed' when policies do not support an intervention. Frontline personnel, in particular, should never consider that policy changes are impossible, and this should not be a rationale for preventing a needed intervention or procedure from occurring.

For their part, policy makers and managers need to respond effectively to needs that are reported by the frontline professional or by individuals with disabilities. There are generally several ways to solve problems, and changing or adapting policy and management procedures has a strong role to play in such problem-solving.

STEP 3: BECOME INVOLVED IN SYSTEMIC ADVOCACY

Systemic advocacy means speaking up to try to influence a change for the better with the way a system works. Individuals can do this, but groups are usually more effective at systemic advocacy. Groups of parents who have children in school can be very effective in advocating for positive changes in school systems, and groups of family members who have children with disabilities can influence improvements in the services their sons and daughters receive. Systemic advocacy is occasionally successful with little effort, especially if the timing is 'just right'. More typically, though, it is slow, time-consuming, energy absorbing, sometimes costly, and a process that often ends in only partial success. Still, professionals and others who support interventions based on a quality of life approach should find it helpful to allot some of their time to involving themselves in systemic changes that are most meaningful to their work. It is important here that the practitioner recognizes this potential conflict between advocacy and recognition of actual needs and choices, and also between advocacy and ethical practice.

STEP 4: DEVELOP A BALANCED AND REALISTIC OUTLOOK

When taking steps towards integrating policy, management and practice, energy is required. In addition, not all actions are successful, and failure can be disheartening. It is helpful to develop a balanced and realistic outlook in order to reduce the stress when activities are unsuccessful.

An agency stated that it believed it should have a person with an intellectual disability on its board of directors. Management then took steps to do just that by inviting Chandy to sit on the board. But it turned out that the chairperson and several board members allowed Chandy to be involved primarily because they thought it was required by policy. She was not permitted to vote on every matter, and sometimes the chair voted for her thinking that she did not understand the matters involved. This led other board members and Chandy herself to feel disappointed with the situation, and to consider it something of a failure.

A quality of life approach suggests support for a person with intellectual disabilities being a member of a board of directors. But it also would require that board members learn how to include Chandy and how to conduct their business in such a way that she is able to understand the procedures and take a full part in the decision-making. It might also be helpful for the board members to re-examine their underlying values about disability (see Bullitis, 2001).

A quality of life approach does not suggest easy solutions to integrating policy, management and practice. This is an ongoing task. But effective service is more likely to occur when such integration occurs in an ongoing way using the main principles and ideas of the quality of life approach. A balanced and realistic outlook can go a long way to helping practitioners take the necessary steps required to carry out this work.

For thought and discussion

Bearing in mind the concepts and examples of what you have read so far:

1.   Think of an example from your own work or personal life where policies conflicted with what you wanted to do. How did you handle the situation?

2. Sheena is a 22-year-old woman with an intellectual disability who lives in a community residence with three other young women. They are not allowed to have overnight guests. Sheena wants her boyfriend to sleep over occasionally. If you were the manager of the residence, what would you do?

3. Imagine you have the opportunity to set up a new service that uses community volunteers to provide transportation for people with disabilities. List a set of policy and management procedures for a service that is closely tied to a quality of life approach.

Selected bibliography

Bickenbach, J.E. (1993) *Physical Disability and Social Policy*. Toronto: University of Toronto Press.

Bloemers, W. and Wisch, F-H. (eds) (2000) *Handicap – Disability: Learning and Living Difficulties: Policy and Practice in Different European Settings*. Frankfurt: am Main/New York: P. Lang.

Bullitis, E.A. (2001) *Individuals with Intellectual Disability as Board Members: Issues, Challenges and Strategies*. Unpublished PhD Thesis. Adelaide: Flunders University.

Chambers, D.E., Wedel, K.R. and Rodwell, M.K. (1992) *Evaluating Social Programs*. London: Allyn and Bacon.

Cummins, R.A. (in press) 'Normative life satisfaction: Measurement issues and a homeostatic model.' *Social Indicators Research*.

Mandelstam, M. (1997) *Community Care Practice and the Law, 2nd edition*. London: Jessica Kingsley Publishers.

Martin, E.D. (ed) (2001) *Significant Disability: Issues Affecting People with Significant Disabilities from a Historical, Policy, Leadership, and Systems Perspective*. Springfield, IL: Charles C. Thomas.

Priestly, M. (1998) *Disability Politics and Community Care*. London: Jessica Kingsley Publishers.

Stone, D.A. (1984) *The Disabled State*. Philadelphia: Temple University Press.

CHAPTER 12

Quality of Life, Disability and the Future

Where we are now

Disability is a challenge of considerable magnitude throughout the world. The data in Figure 12.1 give some idea of the size of the challenge in one country, Australia, with a present population of about 20 million people. Such data probably already underestimate the actual number of people with disability and impairments because of difficulties collecting full information. Furthermore, in the future we may face increasing numbers of challenges. Genetic, medical and social advances are resulting in the detection of new disabilities. New health and social conditions, such as HIV, are emerging that bring new disabilities. People are increasingly living longer, and with a scale of incapacity unknown in past generations.

A quality of life approach works to ensure that the level of well-being of people remains high despite the possibility of increasing numbers of people with disabilities or declining abilities. The main focus here is to maintain adequate levels of functioning and high enjoyment of life in areas that the individual thinks are important for as long as possible. This is, after all, the primary goal of quality of life for the population as a whole.

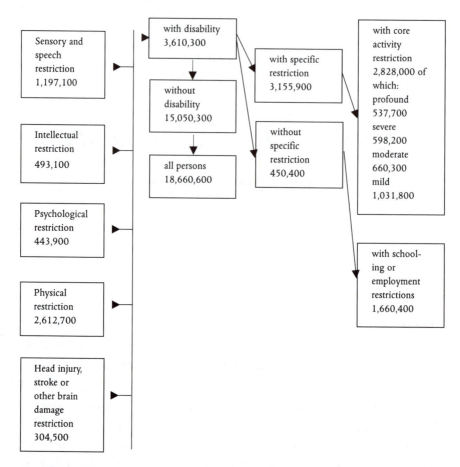

Reproduced with permission from Australian Bureau of Statistics (1993) Disability, Aging and Carers, Australia: Summary of Findings. *Canberra: Australian Bureau of Statistics*

Notes: (a) Total may be less than the sum of the components as persons may have a care activity restriction and a schooling/employment restriction. (b) Total may be less than the sum of the components as persons may have more than one restriction.

Figure 12.1 Number of people in Australia with disability and restricting impairments, 1993/8

Advantages of the quality of life approach

The quality of life approach appears to open new ways at looking at disabilities, and organizing our ideas about assessment and intervention in more organized and practical ways. At the same time, it helps us to ask questions about whether we are working in the best interests of the person with a disability. This is critical for our future development of services for individuals. It enables us to see the whole person more clearly and identify assets as well as challenges. It opens up new ways of looking at professional education, ethics, service design and evaluation.

It is not that all the ideas are new. They are not. But there is a sensitizing focus that leads to an integration of ideas.

Throughout the book, we have advocated some of the specific advantages of a quality of life approach, but three aspects are particularly relevant to future development:

- The quality of life approach, by focusing on principles rather than on specific strategies, encourages us to adapt proven methods and develop new methods of intervention. Some of these will be relevant to new technologies that will develop in future years.

- The quality of life approach has the potential to redefine professional education and training. This will necessitate the development of new service professional and academic partnerships so that the student or client can learn how to use theory and knowledge to apply a quality of life approach consistently to practice.

- The quality of life approach, when seriously considered, leads to a critical appraisal of disability. Here, we will need to respond to the individual needs of people with disabilities in creative and new ways, rather than addressing them only through current structures. There will have to be new policies to guide such changes, and many practices, such as assessment methods and interventions, will have to be modified to match. In the UK, as an example, young adults at university level who are perceived to be very able, but have educational challenges in writing, can receive grants to help them with the purchase of such items as computer aids. We know of individuals who proudly note their challenges and are delighted with the technical support they have received. The disability takes a secondary position – the emphasis is on the solution and its application. The individuals may not even regard themselves as disabled, although the services may still use diagnostic criteria. This is an approach that is too rare. Quality of life leads to knowing ways to see how people can be enabled, rather than be seen and kept disabled.

Looking to the future

Challenges for the quality of life approach

Quality of life is a relatively new approach to practice in the field of disability. It offers some exciting ideas that have been embraced enthusiastically in many quarters. As we stated from the outset, though, it is an overarching concept that is still evolving. Those who are promoting new quality of life ideas will face the ongoing challenge of making clear what their new ideas are and how they can be applied.

We need to continue to learn more about the overall effectiveness of a quality of life approach in practice. We have put forward in this book some ideas, principles and strategies that arise from a philosophical perspective. But they have not yet been tested fully in practice, and their overall effect on people's lives or on the way organizations and professional practice work has yet to be documented and reported. Such evaluation is an essential part of the development of any set of ideas, and future leaders of the quality of life approach will need to ensure that this is addressed. When it is addressed, the result will no doubt be a reshaping of some of the concepts and strategies.

A challenge for the quality of life approach, at a practice level, comes from a misuse of the concepts involved. There are many possible misuses in practice. One is the way professionals and others determine whether an individual has a satisfactory quality of life when the person is quite capable of perceiving and stating this. Sometimes, others determine quality of life on behalf of people who cannot speak. This is also a misuse. There are many examples: euthanasia for a person who is very elderly and infirm; encouraging abortion, if a pregnancy involves a disabled embryo; or preventing pregnancy, or preventing fostering and adopting children, if other people decide that a young adult with intellectual disability cannot raise a child with adequate quality of life. All of these situations already exist in our society quite independently of quality of life, and it is possible that the principles raised in this book might be quoted to support such purposes. If so, that would be a serious misuse of quality of life, for there must be a sensitivity to recognizing and taking into account the perceptions of the individual. We are not saying that adoption or euthanasia should not occur, rather we are arguing that we must re-evaluate our stance by evolving the type of quality of life principles cited in this book.

Another challenge relates to improving the level of functioning for each individual through applying quality of life principles. Of course, the ideas can be used negatively in a different context, just as our knowledge of radiation can be put to healing or harm by inventing and using specific tools and equipment. The ethical and professional requirements of quality of life are that the ideas and practices should be used to promote life in ways that the individual finds satisfying and supporting, and, further, that there is not one standard for quality of life, but as many standards as necessary to meet individuals' perceived needs.

There are also challenges relating to interpretation and application. In all applied approaches, judgements regarding use have to be made. It is possible to expend too much energy and time on assessment, and it is possible to apply insufficient structure when responding to an individual's choices. We have known service agencies that promote choices and allow clients to do just what they wish. But this is to misinterpret the approach we have put forward. A quality of life approach requires considerable thought, resources and encouraging of clients. When this is the case, we come to understand and accept that choices may lead to failure as well as success, that individuals change their minds, and that reinforcing choice can lead to perceptions of dissatisfaction. Learning that clients can make choices and exert control over their environments is not always easy for practitioners to accept, but is critical to the individual. Indeed, there is some evidence that individuals who are perceived as resistive or want to 'go their own way' sometimes recover better or live more successfully. Or, to put this another way, individuals who have an internal locus of control often do better than those who have an external locus of control.

Many of the challenges relating to quality of life concern issues of definition and interpretation:

- The approach we have focused on in this book looks at individuals' whole lives. This is one of three general approaches described in Chapter 1, each with somewhat separate concepts and strategies. When using quality of life, it is important to use the approach best suited to the reason for using it, and to be clear which of these three approaches is being taken.

- In assessment or measurement, we will need to avoid what David Goode has referred to as the 'tyranny' of a quality of life approach. Instead, we need to be vigilant that quality of life ideas help us to improve other people's lives and carry out a practitioner's work in ways that are beneficial to all.

- In developing required supports and interventions, we need to look at ways of ensuring we carry out necessary assessment with adequate attention to quality of life issues.

- In intervention, it is important to ensure we provide adequate structure around choice. Much research remains to be done in this area, especially regarding the amount and types of structure that promote helpful choice.

- There is a range of areas where little evaluation and measurement has been carried out. Emerson and Hatton (1994) indicated that quality of life or lifestyle indicators were just beginning to be incorporated into services in the early 1990s. They noted that very little attention had been paid to indicators of an individual's material quality of life, aspects of personal or intimate relations, opportunities for choice and control over their own lives and user-expressed satisfaction with services. As we have seen, work is being carried out in these areas, although it is through longitudinal studies that the full effects of a quality of life approach are probably best understood.

Research and practice

If practice is to improve, effective research is necessary. Because of the idiosyncratic nature of people's perceptions, choices, personal satisfaction, and similar concepts, it is likely that researchers will need to make use of qualitative methods in quality of life research to a much greater degree than is currently the case. It is also likely that researchers will need to take into consideration ideas that are central to a quality of life approach and use them as independent and dependent variables. For example, if we examine the effectiveness of an intervention to deal with reading problems, we will need to take into account whether this is an interest area of the students involved (i.e. choice and value on being able to read will need to be controlled for or manipulated within the experimental paradigm).

The emphasis on these concepts also means that research needs to remain focused on the desired outcomes of using a quality of life approach with people with disabilities and for the services that support them. These outcomes are that people with disabilities develop and lead lives that are in accordance with their own values, abilities and wishes, and that services and society as a whole are organized in ways that support them. Research needs to demonstrate effective ways to move towards these outcomes.

In quality of life research, we also need to be mindful of the fact that some aspects of life are difficult to assess and measure. However, this does not mean that they do not exist, or that they are not important. It certainly does not mean that they should be dismissed. For example, a man with disabilities complained of pain, but since health personnel could not determine the reasons for his perceived pain, it was dismissed. Yet he still claimed to feel pain. The ways such perceptions, both negative and positive, fit into a person's overall quality of life need to be explored.

One aspect of research that particularly needs to be developed is our understanding of individual thinking, including both cognitive and emotional behaviours. Understanding and obtaining valid measures of individual thinking is also needed. These are essential because so much of quality of life work is based on individual thinking. By way of an example, to help us understand the importance of researching individual thinking, Brown, Bayer and Brown (1992) explored choice and decision-making and noted individuals who appeared to show poor or no mental imagery. They appeared unable to experience or use imagery in social situations, and therefore seemed unable to forecast the effects of inappropriate behaviour. In more recent work, it has been noted that there is an absence of mental imagery in a number of instances associated with intellectual disability and also brain injury. The specific ways such people perceive the world, experience satisfaction and express personal choice are areas that require exploration through research that might move us to develop new assessment techniques and strategies for education, training and rehabilitation.

A quality of life approach is likely to move us further and further towards individualization, as we recognize the wide array of individual variability. This is likely to challenge our notions of inclusion, and our ability to offer satisfactory group programmes unless they are combined with individualized programmes. The involvement of people in their own rehabilitation through their agreement and input into design and content of programmes will be critical. However, the best ways to accomplish this, especially within service and educational systems, need to be carefully studied.

Redefining services

Holism and individual variability require of us much greater ability to recognize personal characteristics, abilities, values and wishes, particularly if we are to capitalize on individuals' strengths. The interests and abilities of individuals in the fine arts, recreation or spiritual activities, for example, all represent ways we can assist individuals to heighten their quality of life and improve their rate of rehabilitation. But it does mean that disability services will need to work in tandem with generic organizations, for individuals will need to be able to access their own areas of interest. This will require the use of disability dollars to promote well-being that is not now seen as directly relevant to rehabilitation. For example, to enable a place of worship to provide respite will allow a family to attend services and may well also provide the support and resources necessary to enable other individuals to remain in their home environment, and to help maintain the strength of their family environments. The ability to access the Winter Olympics may be what turns a depressed individual into someone with hope and fulfilment. It is what is relevant to the individual that is really important for services to address.

Disability in the future

Disability is generally considered to be made up of conditions recognized by society and, to some large degree, defined by society. We need to recognize that this limits the nature of recognized disability, including who is seen as disabled and who is not. It will be more helpful if services can recognize and respond to individuals' stated concerns. It is, for example, unacceptable that parents need to seek professionals who are willing to give a pseudo-diagnosis of intellectual disability or dyslexia before parents or the individual can access funding or programmes to get assistance. If behaviour and presentation indicate a need for intervention, this should be sufficient. If we are interested in individual well-being and quality of life, it is to these ends that we should direct our attention.

Further challenges for the future

The issues that we have raised in this book are increasingly being debated and considered. We are beginning to see service personnel search for the choices of individuals and explore ways of supporting these choices. This now seems possible regardless of the complexity or level of disability. We now need to develop more systematized procedures and assess how effective they are. It will be important to assess their impact within clearly defined programmes. It is likely that some of the concepts will have wider impact than others. It is also likely that the concepts will be applied by some individuals more effectively than others.

Schalock in 1997 examined some of the likely effects of quality of life concepts on development in the 21st century in the field of intellectual disability. Much, as he indicates, remains to be done, although he described such developments as proceeding. We suggest that many of the ideas and practices described in this book are part of the proceeding process, and could be explored and applied in a wide range of disability fields and practice.

Like Schalock, we see a further coming together of our practices across a wide range of disabilities. Although it is apparent that basic medical diagnosis will, and has to, continue, the next steps towards life development will need to be increasingly set within a holistic community paradigm where issues such as the ones discussed in this book are dealt with. How they are dealt with depends on individuals' characteristics and life experiences as well as their circumstances, but, overall, we will be primarily concerned with how their individuality and enjoyment of life is most effectively addressed.

Many people with physical disabilities may require minimal long-term support except for two aspects. The first aspect relates to attitudes, rights and discrimination. It is imperative that generic services ensure that society does not discriminate against anyone, whether that relates to access or to the protection of persons from indiscriminate practice or procedure. A second aspect is the provision of needed physical aids, including electronic aids. A challenge here will be to ensure that individuals receive physical aids that are adapted to their living conditions, and that they receive them in a timely and supportive manner. In some countries, this is a challenging concern and can give rise to particular difficulties in rural areas. One of the solutions is to involve generic local services, which as a rule have little to do with disabilities. We provide just one example. The batteries of wheelchairs can break down and leave individuals stranded. Why would they have to be serviced by the nearest but distant disability service when automobile associations have resources to deal with the problem? Certainly, in some areas such service links have been made, but in others they have not.

It is also going to become increasingly important to recognize that support and intervention provided in a timely manner, even if required for a long duration, is more effective than placing individuals on waiting lists. Time lags caused by waiting lists are seen too frequently in our services, and these result not only in declining quality of life for the individuals concerned, but in many instances in a permanently lowered sense of well-being.

To bring about greater effectiveness in these areas requires the evaluation of services, and such evaluations should contain strong components relating to individuals' quality of life. This requirement also applies to the professionals involved, since their well-being is fundamental to effective and timely delivery of services.

It is also necessary to heighten our sense of the ethical implications of not providing timely and adequate support and intervention services (particularly when we remember that most of these are low cost). It is unethical to employ personnel to carry out effective assessment and intervention if they are not given the wherewithal to carry out these needs. Policy makers and administrators are often so far from the front line that they can frequently be unaware of the daily issues that often put great stress on practitioners, and can too often leave individuals with less than desirable services. It becomes stressful to clients and families, as well as for enthusiastic personnel, when, for example, individuals with major mental heath needs cannot get the basic and required ongoing support, or aging parents find that the services that were to support their children, now middle aged, have disappeared or are very difficult to access. These issues are ones that require solutions by a civilized society.

There are also issues of multi-cultural and international concern. Quality of life is a generic concept with principles and concepts that, we suggest, can be applied universally. The weighting and interpretation given to these principles and concepts need to be examined within the structure of culture.

Finally, the increasing complexity of our civilization requires that we recognize that we are placing more and more demands on our populations, which means we shall probably heighten the number of kinds of disability and the number of people associated with each. The real value of a quality of life approach is that it encourages us to concentrate the development of services around people's challenges and their well-being. It encourages us to recognize that disabilities are not the experience of a small minority, but the daily life experience of a wide range of people who do not need to be seen as disabled but require support to live effectively in a society that we have all developed.

Selected bibliography

Australian Bureau of Statistics (1993/8) *Disability, Aging and Carers, Australia: Summary of Findings.* Canberra: Australian Bureau of Statistics.

Bradley, V.J., Ashbaugh, J.W. and Blaney, B.C. (1994) *Creating Individual Supports for People with Developmental Disabilities: A Mandate for Change at Many Levels.* Baltimore, MD: Paul H. Brookes.

Brown, R.I., Bayer, M.B. and Brown, P.M. (1992) *Empowerment and Developmental Handicaps: Choices and Quality of Life.* Toronto: Captus Press.

Brown, R.I., Bayer, M.B. and MacFarlane, C. (1989) *Rehabilitation Programmes: Performance and Quality of Life of Adults with Developmental Handicaps.* Toronto: Lugus.

Emerson, E. and Hatton, C. (1994) *Moving Out: Relocation from Hospital to Community.* London: HMSO.

Graham. H. (1995) *Mental Imagery in Health Care: An Introduction to Therapeutic Practice.* London: Chapman & Hall.

Keith, K.D. and Schalock, R.L. (eds) (2000) *Cross-cultural Perspectives on Quality of Life.* Washington, DC: American Association on Mental Retardation.

Romney, D.M., Brown, R.I. and Fry, P.S. (1994) *Improving the Quality of Life: Recommendations for People With and Without Disabilities.* Dordrecht, The Netherlands: Kluwer.

Schalock, R.L. (1997) 'The concept of quality of life in 21st century disability programmes.' In R.I. Brown (ed) *Quality of Life for People with Disabilities: Models, Research and Practice, 2nd edition.* Cheltenham, UK: Stanley Thornes.

Schalock, R.L., Brown, I., Brown, R.I., Cummins, R., Felce, D., Matikka, L., Keith, K. and Parmenter, T. (2000) *Quality of Life: Its Conceptualization, Measurement and Application: A Consensus Document.* Document for the WHO-IASSID Work Plan. The Special Interest Research Group on Quality of Life. The International Association for the Scientific Study of Intellectual Disabilities.

Selected journals in disability

All of the following journals are reasonably easy to access, and all contain articles on quality of life conceptualization, assessment, intervention and evaluation. A variety of other journals also contain articles on quality of life.

American Journal on Mental Retardation

Archives of General Psychiatry

Australian Journal of Rehabilitation Counselling

Disability & Society

Down Syndrome: Research and Practice

Exceptionality Education Canada

Experimental Aging Research

Health Promotion International

Hospital and Community Psychiatry

Human Relations

International Journal of Practical Approaches to Disability

Journal of Applied Gerontology

Journal of Applied Rehabilitation Counselling

Journal of Applied Research in Intellectual Disability

Journal of Community Psychology

Journal of Health and Social Behaviour

Journal of Intellectual & Developmental Disability

Journal of Intellectual Disability Research

Journal of Medical Ethics

Journal on Developmental Disabilities

Mental Retardation

New England Journal of Medicine

Social Indicators Research

Special Education and Rehabilitation

About the Authors

IVAN BROWN has worked and contributed to the field of disabilities for the past 20 years. He began his work life as an elementary school teacher for eight years before taking a position with the Toronto Association for Community Living, where he worked as a vocational counsellor and community living support worker for nine years while he completed his graduate studies in Counselling Psychology and Special Education.

In 1991, he took a position as a Senior Research Associate with the Centre for Health Promotion, Department of Public Health Sciences, University of Toronto, where he managed a number of large research projects. Several of these addressed quality of life of children with disabilities, adults with developmental disabilities, seniors and adolescents. He has appointments as an Assistant Professor in the Departments of Occupational Therapy, and Public Health Sciences, both at the University of Toronto. During the 1990s, he also taught for six years in the School of Early Childhood Education at Ryerson University in Toronto, which has a special focus on young children with special needs, and in the graduate programme in health promotion in the Department of Public Health Sciences. Currently, Ivan is manager of the Centre of Excellence for Child Welfare, a national body for research and policy development in child abuse and neglect, to which he brings an important disability focus. This Centre is housed within the Faculty of Social Work at the University of Toronto. Research in disability has been, and continues to be, a critical part of his ongoing work.

Ivan has a strong history of community involvement in disability, serving on numerous government and community agency committees and boards, participating in research projects, and acting in leadership roles with several professional organizations. In particular, he was a longstanding member of the Board of Directors of the Ontario Association on Developmental Disabilities, and served as its Chair for a two-year period. In 2001, he was awarded this Association's highest honour, the Directors' Award of Excellence.

Over the past ten years, Ivan has contributed substantially to the Canadian and international literature, particularly in the areas of quality of life and intellectual disabilities. He has more than one hundred publications to his credit, in the form of books, manuals, book chapters, peer-reviewed articles, and others, and has made more than 90 conference presentations in the past ten years. He is an editor of the comprehensive text *Developmental Disabilities in Ontario.* He was the founding editor of the *Journal on Developmental Disabilities,* and still oversees the journal as a member of its three-person Chief Editorial Board.

Ivan continues to be personally involved in disability issues, through sharing the lives of many friends with disabilities and through sharing his household with a man who has visual and cognitive impairments. He holds a strong belief that including disability as part of our daily life activities is an enriching experience for us all.

ROY I. BROWN has been involved in the field of disabilities, and particularly intellectual disabilities, for many years. As a psychologist, he started as a clinical and educational practitioner in the UK, finally setting up programmes in educational intervention for children and adults with special needs at the Institute of Education, University of Bristol, where he was Research Fellow. This followed a period as a clinical psychologist, working in hospital settings involved with vocational and social rehabilitation to the community.

In Canada, where he was appointed to the Department of Educational Psychology, University of Calgary, he also worked as Executive Director of the Vocational Rehabilitation Research Institute. There, with colleagues, he set up a wide range of programmes and devoted time to research, including the six-year study into quality of life with Max Bayer, Christine MacFarlane and Patricia M. Brown, which was funded by Health and Welfare Canada. He also devoted time to setting up the Community Rehabilitation Programme at the University of Calgary with its bachelor's, master's and doctoral degrees directed to a wide range of disability studies. At the same time, he worked on setting up educational programmes in disability studies in the Middle East, funded by the Canadian International Development Agency. He continued to pursue this interest while in Australia, funded there through the Australian Red Cross.

As a later life change, he became Foundation Professor and Dean of the School of Special Education and Disability Studies at Flinders University, Adelaide, Australia.

Roy has published extensively, largely in the field of research to practice, increasingly with colleagues whose collaboration is much appreciated. He became involved in quality of life research early in its development, and has published many articles, chapters and books in this area. He keeps involved in some practical work. He advises families on immigration issues for persons with disabilities, consults widely and has chaired various government committees in both Canada and Australia.

He has received several awards for his contributions to the field of disabilities, including the Order of the University of Calgary and an honorary doctorate from the University of Ghent. Currently, he is Professor Emeritus at both the University of Calgary, Canada, and Flinders University, Australia. Retiring to Canada has involved adjunct professorships at the University of Victoria and Simon Fraser University. He is also a research director at the Down Syndrome Research Foundation. He hopes to keep his hand in with some writing, research and occasional teaching. He regards the sensitive education of professionals supporting people with needs and challenges as a contribution to a very necessary role in any civilized society. He also sees this not unconnected to the art of parenting and the pleasures of grandparenting – the latter being an increasing delight to him at a personal level.

Subject Index

Author Index